Dear
Old Blighty

Dear
Old Blighty

E. S. TURNER

LONDON
Michael Joseph

First published in Great Britain by Michael Joseph Ltd
44 Bedford Square, London WC1
1980

ISBN 0 7181 1879 0

Photoset by D. P. Media Limited, Hitchin, Hertfordshire
and printed and bound by Billing & Sons Ltd, Guildford,
London and Worcester

Contents

Take me back to Dear Old Blighty

Soldiers' song of World War One

List of Illustrations

Acknowledgements

I am indebted to a wide range of newspapers and magazines of the period. Of especial value was *The Times*; and it is impossible, in passing, not to praise the high standard and composition of that newspaper even in the blackest days of the war. I have also drawn on a large number of biographies, autobiographies, local war histories and Government sources, which are credited at the end of the book.

The staffs of the Imperial War Museum and the British Library were, as always, most helpful and resourceful.

For permission to quote copyright material I express thanks as follows: extract from 'What Can A Little Chap Do?' by John Oxenham in *Princess Mary's Gift Book*: Anthony Sheil Associates Ltd; extract from *Fighting Lines* by Harold Begbie: Constable and Co Ltd; extract from 'Woman' by Hall Caine, in *The Queen's Gift Book*: Kneale and Co, advocates, Douglas, I.O.M.; extract from *Fanfare For A Tin Hat* by Eric Linklater: Macmillan Ltd; extract from *How Dear is Life* by Henry Williamson: Macdonald and Janes Ltd.

All the photographs and reproductions of posters are the copyright of the Imperial War Museum. The war film advertisement is reproduced by permission of the *Daily Mail*; the drawings of the scene at Victoria Station and of the street shrine are by permission of Illustrated Newspapers Ltd; and the two cartoons are by permission of *Punch*.

Author's Note

The first chapter of this book sets the scene on the outbreak of World War One and covers events until the end of 1914. Each of the other chapters deals with a selected aspect of life on the home front.

The reader unfamiliar with the sequence of events may wish to consult the summary of the war which follows.

THE COMBATANTS

The Allies: Great Britain and her Empire, France, Russia, Belgium, Italy, United States of America, Serbia, Montenegro, Rumania, Greece, Portugal, Japan.
The Central Powers: Germany, Austria-Hungary, Bulgaria, Turkey.

THE FOUR PHASES

The war falls conveniently into four parts:

First, the period from August to December 1914, when a quick victory by Germany in the West was frustrated and the opposing armies ended up embedded in trenches running from the Alps to the English Channel.
Second, the period of deadlock and attrition from December 1914 to December 1916, ending with a dubious German peace offer.
Third, the year 1917, with the deadlock still unbroken but with the balance of forces altered through the collapse of Russia and the entry of America on the side of the Allies.
Fourth, the touch-and-go year, when the German spring offensive in the West all but succeeded, followed by an Allied breakthrough and the collapse of the Central Powers.

HOW IT BEGAN

1914   June 28: the Archduke Francis Ferdinand, heir to the Austrian throne, is assassinated in Serbia.

July 28: Austria-Hungary declares war on Serbia.

July 30: Russia, as 'protector of the Slavs', mobilises.

August 1: Germany, supporting Austria-Hungary, mobilises and declares war on Russia. France, bound by treaty to Russia, mobilises.

August 2: Germany, in order to strike at France, invades Luxembourg and presents ultimatum to Belgium, whose neutrality she is pledged to defend.

August 3: Germany declares war on France and invades Belgium.

August 4: Germany ignores British ultimatum to withdraw from Belgium. At midnight Britain declares war on Germany.

August 12: Britain declares war on Austria-Hungary.

IMPORTANT DATES

1914   August 20: British Expeditionary Force fights Battle of Mons.

September 5–9: Battle of the Marne. German advance held.

October 12–November 11: First Battle of Ypres.

November 5: Britain declares war on Turkey.

December 16: German cruisers shell Scarborough.

1915   February 1: Kaiser authorises Zeppelin raids on London.

March 1: Britain declares blockade of Germany.

March 10–13: Battle of Neuve Chapelle. Shell shortages blamed.

April 22–May 25: Second Battle of Ypres.

April 25: Gallipoli landings by British and Empire troops.

May 7: *Lusitania* sunk.

May 21: Lloyd George becomes Minister of Munitions.

May 22: Italy declares war on Austria.

May 26: Liberal-Conservative Coalition formed. Asquith still Prime Minister.

1916   January 8: Evacuation of Gallipoli completed.

February 21: French begin Battle of Verdun.

March 2: First conscription Act effective.
April 24: Easter Rebellion in Dublin.
May 25: Second conscription Act effective.
May 31: Battle of Jutland.
June 5: Kitchener drowned at sea.
July 1–November 13: Battle of the Somme.
August 27: Rumania declares war on Central Powers.
September 3: First Zeppelin brought down in Britain.
September 23–October 1: Three more Zeppelins destroyed in Britain.
December 6: Asquith resigns. Lloyd George becomes Prime Minister, forms War Cabinet.
December 30: German peace proposals rejected.

1917 February 1: Germany declares unrestricted U-boat warfare.
March 12: First revolution in Russia.
April 6: America declares war on Germany.
July 31: Third Battle of Ypres (Passchendaele) begins.
November 7: Bolshevik revolution in Russia.
December 15: Russia signs Armistice with Germany.

1918 February 25: First experiments in rationing in Britain.
March 21: Germans open offensive on Somme, Paris in danger.
April 11: Haig's 'Backs to the wall' order.
April 14: Foch appointed Commander-in-Chief, Allied armies.
May 7: Rumania signs peace treaty with Central Powers.
July: General issue of ration books in Britain.
July 15: Last German offensive in West.
August 8: 'Black day' of German Army.
September 26: Allies start big advance in West.
September 29: Bulgaria signs Armistice with Allies.
October 23: Germans accept President Wilson's 14 Points.
October 30: Turkey surrenders.
November 3: Austria-Hungary surrenders.
November 9: Kaiser abdicates and flees to Holland.
November 11: Germany signs Armistice.

Introduction

The literature of World War One is prodigious in range and depth. There is an unstoppable flow of books about the great battles, about day-to-day life in and behind the Line. There are innumerable books about the causes of the war and its effects, its higher direction, its secret intrigues; there have been endless debates about whether it should have been fought at all and whether it should, or could, have been aborted. But present generations know very little about what went on in Britain in 1914–18. Those who can remember the Great War, as it was once called, are a much-shrunken company, so this book does not pretend to be an exercise in nostalgia. The time is perhaps far enough away to be treated like any other period.

The war which extinguished nearly nine million combatants out of 65 million mobilised and piled up 37 million casualties was the first major struggle in Europe since the days of Napoleon. It embroiled almost all the advanced nations. There were no serious attempts to call it off and the warring powers remained *acharné* – to use a fashionable word of the day – until the end. Britain and France, starting as democracies, became totalitarian states under pressure of war. Russia, starting as an autocracy, ended in Bolshevism. Germany, starting as a democracy under a Hohenzollern, passed through the totalitarian phase and became a revolutionary shambles. The Austro-Hungarian Empire disintegrated and Habsburgs followed Hohenzollerns into oblivion. The Ottoman Empire ended up under an Allied puppet.

In 1914–18 Britain lost three times as many combatants' lives as in 1939–45. Her dead numbered roughly three-quarters of a million; but when the Empire dead are included the total nears a million. On the Western Front alone the total British casualties (dead, wounded, missing, captured) came to over two and a half millions. What the British tend to forget is that in 1914–18 France lost twice as many men as Britain and Germany three times as many.

In 1914 there were citizens whose fathers remembered Waterloo and there were old soldiers who had served in the Crimea; there were also thousands of men, still of fighting age, who had been blooded in the South African War. That conflict had caused great bitterness at home between imperialists and 'Little Englanders' (of whom Lloyd George had been one). The bitterness lingered on. Radical Liberals (a more polite name for 'Little Englanders') were determined to keep clear of imperialist and militarist adventures. They refused to be panicked by the increasingly ominous sabre-rattlings from Berlin and regarded the anti-German policy of the Right newspapers as more likely to bring about war than prevent it.

The Liberals had been in power since 1906, and it was a very sorely buffeted government under Asquith which had to face the challenge of August 1914. Many looked on it as a government which would in no circumstances go to war. It had brought in social security measures like Lloyd George's National Insurance Act. In the industrial sphere it had passed the notorious Act of 1906 granting trade unions protection from the consequences of their actions, with the result that strife between workers and employers had been unusually splenetic. No less splenetic was the running fight waged by the suffragists against the Establishment. However, the real fount of anxiety in these last years of peace was Ireland. In 1912 the Liberals made an offer of Home Rule, only to provoke fury in Ulster, which began to arm illegally. In March 1914 Army officers at the Curragh 'mutinied' at the prospect of fighting their kith and kin in Ulster. Right until the last week of July Ireland had seemed set for an explosion. Any suggestion that a hecatomb was imminent in Europe would have invited the succinct comment popularised that summer in Shaw's *Pygmalion*: 'not bloody likely'.

Asquith's Liberals lacked the drive and the talent to conduct all-out war. Fatally high-minded, zealous to preserve human liberties, they found themselves forced to truncate one liberty after another. They introduced censorship of the press and speech, internment of aliens, direction of labour, direction of employers, seizure of profits and eventually conscription and rationing. In May 1915 they formed a Coalition with the Conservatives, who also lacked a talent for total war. Lloyd George, the 'counterjumper' from Criccieth, who became a furiously energetic Minister of Munitions, was the only popular politician of any real capacity. Asquith, skilful in debate, had a detachment and an inertness which dismayed even his friends; characteristic of his outlook was his comment, after two days of war, that it would be 'amusing' to see how Kitchener got on with the Cabinet. To many he seemed less like a war leader than the chairman of a company which is going through a bad patch, more concerned to hold the board together than to do battle with its rivals. Winston Churchill,. who began the war as First Lord of the Admiralty, was deeply distrusted by all parties, including his own, for his incorrigible zeal and 'pushiness'. The small Parliamentary Labour Party lacked any figure of mark.

On the domestic front conscription was the great watershed of the war. In retrospect nothing is more extraordinary than the Liberals' opposition to compulsion, the overdue spreading of the load which had been borne by three million volunteers. By their delays they wasted the country's natural leaders and fomented an absurd strife between bachelors and married men. By the time conscription came in Asquith had been ousted by Lloyd George. If the Welshman was not the man who won the war, he was the man who built up a mighty munitions empire and introduced the convoy system when sinkings by U-boat threatened starvation. Rationing was not introduced until the spring of 1918, though some belt-tightening preceded it. Britain never starved; there were undoubtedly more hungry people in 1914, before the war began, than at any time during it. The loss of white bread harmed nobody. Air raids, though a powerful irritant, were never a serious menace; they were something the Sunday papers were prepared to offer free insurance against, up to £50,000.

Britain was accustomed to the idea of her soldiers dying in far parts of the earth. It was a brutal shock to see them being shipped home mangled in the first month of war: armless men, halves of men, groups of three men with three legs between them. Emergency hospitals were brought into commission with astonishing speed – in schools, mansions, stately homes, even judges' lodgings and bishops' palaces. Lady Diana Cooper says that when she resolved to become a nurse she went to her kitchen and saw a hare's insides taken out to prepare her for operations. In time gently nurtured women were able, like Nurse Agatha Christie, to accept severed legs from the operating table and throw them into furnaces without too much of a *frisson*. The sight of men in hospital blue, with bright red ties, became as familiar as that of route-marching men in khaki. But there were some spectacles which not even stoics could take in their stride: for example, the sight of Westminster Abbey slowly filling with blinded soldiers shuffling up the nave, each man with his hand on the shoulder of the man in front.

Gradually the people of Britain came to realise how many Allies they had. Belgians colonised Richmond-on-Thames, where they had rushed up their own arsenal; Russian princesses nursed the wounded at Highgate; Australian soldiers coo-eed to each other down Piccadilly; Canadian soldiers helped the Australians to beat up strikers and pacifists; wounded Indian soldiers recuperated in the Pavilion at Brighton; and American servicemen played baseball in Arsenal's football ground. As for those who were not on Britain's side – well, there was a vast camp in the Isle of Man full of German waiters, barbers and seamen, and a valley in Wales where Sinn Feiners were interned after the Easter Rising.

The wartime traveller in Britain found scores of towns where none had previously existed, like the great munitions complex at Gretna (war workers were married from time to time by the local blacksmiths). He came upon enormous encampments of 50,000 or so servicemen, with hucksters and women clamouring at the gates. Everywhere parks and public places were overrun by wooden huts, most of them serving as canteens. There were aerodromes which, not long before, had been farms and racecourses. In the quads of ancient universities the traveller found no academic peace, only military inspections and pay parades. In the fields he noted two new kinds of labourer: those who had fought for Germany and those who refused to fight for Britain. On the moors he might meet parties of middle-aged women gathering sphagnum moss for bandages, or plucking wool from barbed wire; on the commons he would see women reservists at signal drill, semaphoring with their arms like a well-upholstered *corps de ballet.*

There were novelties everywhere, if one knew when and where to look. In Richmond Park at one time was a mile-long telpherage system, or aerial ropeway, dreamed up by H. G. Wells, designed to carry supplies to the forward trenches at no cost in men or horses – an idea which failed to enthuse the Army Staff, those 'fine, handsome, well-groomed, neighing gentlemen' with their supposed dislike of novelty. Anyone with a valid excuse for hanging about Hatfield Park, early in February 1916, would have seen the first tanks demonstrated. At Shoreham, late in the war, spectacular towers were being built for sinking in the Channel as supports for a twenty-mile submarine net. (The Nab Tower later installed at the entrance to Spithead is one of them.)

Public and private services suffered surprisingly little and some of them were almost scandalously efficient. In November 1916, with manpower supposedly at a premium, ten houses in a row at Hitchin were supplied with bread daily by eight different bakers. As Roy Jenkins has revealed, Asquith was able to post letters to his daughter's friend, Venetia Stanley, with all the day's secrets at six pm in Whitehall, and they would be delivered the same evening to the Whitechapel hospital where she nursed. Newspapers were published in uncommon profusion and new ones were started, like the *Sunday Pictorial* and *Sunday Herald,* in 1915. The only ones which failed to prosper were Labour sheets; the *Daily Herald* became a weekly and the *Daily Citizen* foundered. At the start of the war editors found they were liable to court-martial if they offended under Defence Regulations, but this salutary innovation was scrapped.

The *Globe* was briefly suspended for publishing a false rumour about Kitchener. Reports of sensational trials still occupied much space, notably the 'Brides in the Bath' trial in 1915. Photographs could still be taken in court, as of a judge putting on his black cap. For most of the war the courts continued to waste the time of their busiest and ablest citizens by calling them to serve on pre-trial grand juries. Although new laws brought much new litigation there was always time to settle such arguments as: *Is a winkle a fish?* Punishment in those days was graded; for hardened offenders there was penal servitude or

imprisonment with hard labour, and for the gently reared, like
Bertrand Russell, there was comfortable lodging in the First
Division. In the Guildhall Police Court in December 1915 a
father was invited to flog his thieving son with 'our birch rod',
which was kept in pickle. He did so, returning 'more upset than
the boy'.

The days of domestic service were numbered, but the death
was a slow one. Footmen of military age were called up; if
discharged wounded they often became footmen again, suitably
badged. Although tens of thousands of housemaids left for the
war factories, more than a million women remained in service,
washing money for old ladies, lighting fires for intellectuals who
would rather shiver than carry their own coals. The Bloomsbury
women tried to break down the traditional mistress-maid
relationship, but as Quentin Bell has related, it did not work out.
Although the fabric of society might be fissuring in all directions,
the Law of Subordination had not yet been repealed.

By modern standards there was much that was bizarre. The
author of *The Little Victims Play*, Vera Ryder, who became a
Land Girl and mucked out byres, was invited, late in the war, to
attend a ball for Empire soldiers. 'Of course my maid travelled
with me,' she writes. 'It would have been unthinkable for me to
go by myself and she was most useful in getting me unpacked,
my dress ironed and myself eventually attired in all my glory.'

A writer in the *Sporting Times* (the *Pink 'Un*) in February
1917 mentions a friend's daughter who is being sent up to
London to do her bit as a kitchen maid in a war hospital, and
who is taking her maid with her. 'Which is, I suppose, about the
first time a kitchen maid has kept another maid to do her hair
and button her boots.'

The war brought dismaying problems of etiquette. Ursula
Bloom, married to a captain, employed a between-maid who
was being courted by a major, and her husband was expected to
call him 'Sir'. There were difficult moments, too, when male
servants returned home commissioned, like the Baden-Powells'
chauffeur, or the footman from Cliveden who was kind enough
to say that he owed his advancement to the good manners he had
learned at the Astors' table.

Whatever else it did, wasting the nation's youth cured unemployment and brought prosperity to millions who had never

enjoyed it. It was not only the 'hard-faced men' who did well out of the war; so did quite a few hard-faced young women. The pretence by engineers that women were incapable of performing 'highly skilled tasks' was exposed as nonsense; it turned out that anyone, man or woman, could learn most of the precious skills in a week or two, even a day or two. This calling of male bluff was behind much of the industrial unrest of the war years. The reader will find some disconcerting parallels between events on the industrial scene then and now, notably in the way in which shop stewards made the running and defied their union leaders. In 1917 there were bruising quarrels between the same two railway unions which fight each other relentlessly today.

Financial comparisons with modern times are difficult, but a few figures will tell their own story. In 1914 income tax was 9d in the pound on earned incomes; by the end of the war it had reached 6s. At the start the average wage was not much more than £1 a week, with skilled shipyard workers receiving about £2 or upwards. An old age pensioner was paid from 5s to 1s a week, depending on circumstances. After two months of war the Cabinet took a vote on how much pension to pay a private soldier's widow. Churchill suggested 7s 6d a week, others 6s 6d, and Lloyd George and eight others voted for 5s; so 5s it was. The King was not alone in thinking this ungenerous (by 1918, with the cost of living rising, the pension had tripled). *Whitaker's* for 1914 shows that the Permanent Under-Secretary for the Foreign Office, with fifteen letters after his name, was paid £2,500; junior clerks, first class, in that department received from £200 to £500. A judge's salary was £5,000. For writing articles in the *Sunday Pictorial* on how to win the war, Winston Churchill, Arnold Bennett and Horatio Bottomley received never less than £100 a time and often much more. The Duke of Westminster's revenue in 1914 was put at £1,000 a day, a sum which would have bought five Morris-Oxfords ('190 guineas – complete and ready for the road').

CHAPTER 1

THE GREAT ANGER

On the night of August 4, 1914, a single cable remained open between Britain and Germany: the line to Berlin. The British Government awaited a reply to its demand that the Kaiser should withdraw his troops from Belgium or face the consequences. At midnight – according to Sir Evelyn Murray, then Secretary to the Post Office – the Whitehall operator sent the signing-off signal *GN*, meaning *Good Night*. The line stayed dead for more than four years.

In the morning the Post Office finished the job. Engineers severed the Anglo-German cables below low-water mark. A cable ship which had been standing by at Dover put to sea to cut the German cables to Brest, Vigo, Tenerife and New York. For overseas communications the Germans were now forced to use the new-fangled 'wireless'.

Meanwhile, as the London crowds whooped for joy, soldiers commandeered horses from the shafts of carriages. Railway managers, newly transformed into colonels, cleared the lines so that troop trains could speed to Newhaven and Southampton. Scotland Yard rounded up the most dangerous of the known German agents. To prevent a run on savings and investments, the August Bank Holiday was extended for two days and a moratorium was declared on the settlement of debts. The country was warned to prepare for paper money, instead of gold sovereigns. It was also warned, bluntly, in the first recruiting advertisements, that this was to be 'the greatest war in the history of the world'.

In this unprecedented hour quite a few people knew exactly
what to do and were doing it. Among them were the Army's
armourers who, in accordance with the rules of mobilisation,
were sharpening officers' swords for battle.

If Germany had not invaded Belgium, the Liberal Government
under Asquith might well have chosen neutrality. Austria's
threat to Serbia (then usually called Servia) had raised few
pangs in the breasts of 'Little Englanders'. The Liberal *Daily
News* said (July 29): 'Not a British life shall be sacrificed for the
sake of a Russian hegemony of the Slav world.' And (July 30):
'We must not have our Western civilisation submerged in a sea
of blood in order to wash out a Servian conspiracy.' The
Manchester Guardian was saying the same sort of thing, bluntly
denying that it was Britain's business to keep the peace of
Europe. The *John Bull* posters on the buses said TO HELL WITH
SERVIA! On August 1, Asquith noted, Lloyd George was 'all for
peace ... sensible and statesmanlike', although Winston
Churchill was 'very bellicose'.

What good Liberals could not swallow was the idea of fighting
on the same side as the Czar, fugitives from whose rule had for
long been crowding into the East End of London. By supporting
Russia, the argument ran, would not Britain be supporting the
knout and the torture chamber? France posed a more delicate
problem. Britain was not bound by treaty to support her, any
more than she was bound to support Russia, but there had been
an Entente Cordiale since 1904. The Entente apart, could
Britain look calmly on a German occupation of the French
Channel ports, or a bombardment of the French coastline, or the
destruction of France as a Great Power? There was a standing, if
unadvertised, agreement that if the French Navy maintained a
presence in the Mediterranean the British Navy would guard
French interests in the Channel and North Sea. Not all the
Cabinet seemed aware of this arrangement. While the heart-
searchings went on, the British Fleet, which was already on
manoeuvres, was kept ready for instant action.

From their exquisite and half-comprehended dilemmas the
Liberals were delivered by the Germans' contemptuous invasion of Belgium, in defiance of the 'scrap of paper' in which they
had guaranteed her integrity. With unimportant exceptions,

those who, like Lloyd George, had been 'all for peace' were now all for war. The Conservatives, while by no means baying for blood, had no doubt where the path of honour and duty lay and were ready to observe a party truce. As for the press, no editor, not even Horatio Bottomley, dared cry TO HELL WITH BELGIUM! On August 4 the reluctant *Daily News* braced itself to say: 'Let us fight, if it must be, without bitterness and without malice, so that when the tragedy is over we may make an honourable peace.' But who could not be bitter about Belgium?

Ireland, a week earlier, had seemed on the edge of civil war. After the invasion of Belgium, John Redmond, Parliamentary leader of the Irish Nationalists, rashly pledged his country's support in the struggle against Germany. The Government, he said, was free to withdraw all its troops from Ireland; but this was one invitation the Government did not see its way to accept.

No card house could have collapsed faster than the edifice of International Socialism. On August 2 resolutions were passed in Brussels urging workers to refuse to fight workers everywhere, but already the brothers were arming to exterminate each other. Vainly Keir Hardie harangued a 'Red Flag' meeting in Trafalgar Square. Beatrice Webb summed up the dilemma facing British workers: 'If we are not to defend Belgium, why defend our-selves? There is no morality in watching a child being murdered, refusing to interfere until you yourself are attacked. . . .' From now on anti-war orators were liable to manhandling and ducking.

Ramsay MacDonald, Member for Leicester, soon to be the most loathed man in Britain, resigned the leadership of the Labour Party, which backed the war. He blamed everyone for what had happened. He was convinced Britain should have stayed neutral. Yet even he banged the drum, saying 'those who can enlist ought to enlist and those who are working in munition factories should do so wholeheartedly'. But soon enough the MacDonald line began to be muddied as he increasingly found his friends in the pacifist-Marxist Independent Labour Party and various bodies which gave the impression of fighting for liberties rather than liberty. Like Bernard Shaw and Bertrand Russell, he had a fatal talent for playing into the hands of German propagandists.

So there it was: an unwanted but now well-supported crusade,

with even that once-execrated pacifist, Lloyd George, putting his
heart and soul and oratory into it; a man destined to be hailed,
by his friends at least, as the greatest war minister since
Chatham. He would tell the nation, in his first big speech, to set
its eyes on the forgotten peaks of 'Honour, Duty, Patriotism
and, clad in glittering white, the great pinnacle of Sacrifice
pointing like a rugged finger to Heaven'. In one sentence he
deployed the four abstractions which, over the years, were to
suffer a near mortal devaluation.

The men who would tackle these forgotten peaks were of
necessity imperfect, but they were nobler on the whole than the
reservists described by Sylvia Pankhurst struggling aboard the
ship at Dublin: '. . . incognisant as oxen; or wildly uproarious
. . . glassy-eyed, purple of face, foul-mouthed, with bibulous lips
slobbering . . . a writhing agglomeration of human folly, of
shuddering horrified reluctance . . . untouched by the cleansing
fires of enthusiasm, going like cattle to the slaughter.'

Sylvia Pankhurst remained splendidly untouched by the
cleansing fires of enthusiasm for war, other than the war against
capitalism.

Eric Linklater, in *Fanfare for a Tin Hat*, had a theory that the
derision which is nowadays inspired by the patriotism of 1914
might be silenced if it were given another name. Suppose, for
example, it were called 'protest'.

'Protest is regarded as a contemporary phenomenon. But in
1914 protest was louder, more general and much angrier than it
is today. It was, however, all directed against the insufferable
pretensions of the German Empire and the brutal behaviour of
its marching armies. Indignation was fierce and popular, and
everyone was delighted when [Rupert] Brooke, raising it to a
higher plane, identified it with patriotism, and simultaneously
made patriotism righteous.'

Sir Alan Herbert, who was caught up in that surge of anger,
strongly resented the implications in the musical play, *Oh What
A Lovely War!*, that he and his generation were 'duped into the
Forces by damsels singing patriotic songs or bullied in by
peremptory posters'. He calmly believed that Britain had gone
to war for a just cause and that he ought to be in it.

It is fashionable now to pretend that the German atrocities

were invented. But what happened? The Belgians, by refusing to surrender their forts on demand, dared to upset the Schlieffen Plan to invade France; they objected, as they were entitled to object, to their flags being hauled down, their cities occupied, their cathedrals burned and their hostages massacred. Six hundred citizens were shot in the market square at Dinant before the town was sacked – see any guide-book, or see Barbara Tuchman's *August 1914*. If some atrocity tales were false, were these not atrocities enough?

Any notion that the war was a bankers' ramp, or a plot by industrialists to wipe out their rivals, was scotched long ago by Lloyd George. 'Money was a frightened and trembling thing,' he says of the days when, as Chancellor, he had to steady the City's nerves; the last thing the bankers wanted was Armageddon. There are many comical stories about what financiers said on the eve of war. Lord Clark, then aged eleven, recalls hearing the Governor of the Bank of England, Walter Cunliffe, a guest on the family yacht at Inverewe, saying there would be no war because 'the Germans haven't got the credits'. He adds: 'I was much impressed.' A few weeks later Cunliffe was raised to the peerage.

If the Kaiser had been beaten by Christmas, as the more innocent hoped and believed, the war would have been hailed as the most salutary triumph of Right over rampaging Might for a millennium. Even Bertrand Russell, instead of jeering at the eagerness of parents to sacrifice their children, might have been tempted to accept it as a not wholly despicable crusade of youth. As it was, the German plan for a quick knock-out blow was frustrated, thanks in no small part to the Belgians. (*Belgium put the kibosh on the Kaiser*, said the song, with some truth.) The great deadlock set in and eventually not only the young men but the younger grandfathers had to be called up.

What would greatly have surprised the passionate young was that on the first day of war, August 5, Lord Northcliffe, the greatest Hun-hater in the land, was busy writing an article for his *Daily Mail* entitled NOT ONE BRITISH SOLDIER TO LEAVE ENGLAND'S SHORES. In his view, and indeed in that of some members of the Cabinet, the Royal Navy could do all that was needed. The editor of the *Daily Mail*, Thomas Marlowe, boldly opposed Northcliffe's argument and had another article, expressing a contrary view, set up. After a spirited dispute the noble proprietor allowed his article to be thrown away. He spent the rest of the war urging young men into the trenches.

Perhaps Northcliffe had been over-alarmed by the *Britain Invaded* serials which his newspapers and magazines had been publishing for a decade. To be sure, there *was* an invasion scare, possibly helped along by the defensive preparations of those who knew exactly what to do and were doing it. Along the East coast boats were hauled in from the sea, even carried inland on carts, to prevent their use by the enemy as pontoons. Many buildings were destroyed by Sappers, either because they were thought to offer an irresistible target to warships or in order to extend the defenders' arcs of fire. Pleasure piers were blown up or bisected to deny their use to landing troops. At Bridlington old ornamental cannon in the sea-front gardens were removed lest they be used as a pretext for firing on the town. Everywhere barbed wire was being uncoiled on the beaches. A new phenomenon, the motorcycle dispatch rider, raced about the country with passwords and was much barked at by dogs.

Invasion posters had already been secretly printed, though the secret was widely shared. In Hove the *Instructions to Inhabitants* urged people to stay quietly in their houses unless the military ordered them to move. If that order came, and roads and railways were blocked, the order was: '*Direction*: Proceed north-west over the Downs. Special constables at crossroads will direct you. Obey their instructions. Take to fields when necessary. What to take: money, food and blanket.'

Everywhere the rule was that the enemy should be denied the use of cars, carts, cycles, livestock, food, forage, petrol and even tools. In Folkestone special constables were assigned to look after the evacuation of hospitals, and motorcyclists were given handbells to ring as a signal to assemble. If animals could not be evacuated and if the Army did not want them, they were to be 'rendered useless to the enemy'. Owners of cars were instructed how best to destroy them and petrol not required by the military was to be 'run to waste'. (Luckily, petrol existed only in modest quantities.)

The Army on mobilisation had only eighty motor vehicles and 25,000 horses, but it had wide powers to commandeer. On the first day magistrates sat early, signing warrants authorising the seizure of horses, vans and cars. Farmers learned that the Army's long-standing interest in their beasts had not been an idle one; parties of soldiers descended and led away their stock to the mustering grounds, sometimes illegally and to the detriment of the harvest. In the village of Manaton in Devon a policeman lost no time in informing John Galsworthy that the Army needed his favourite horse Peggy; to his great relief she was rejected as unfit.

Most of the horses were required for transport, but the Yeomanry were paying up to £75 for an officer's charger and £50 for a trooper's. Everywhere parks and village greens were the scene of haggling and branding. At the Tower of London a long line of horses filled the moat. The mixture of equine temperaments and the excitement in the air sometimes led to fatal stampedes.

Many motorists who had been touring Europe (a rugged recreation in those days, even without the hazards of mobilisation) had their cars seized on the dash back to the Channel; Lord Lonsdale lost his new Napier at Boulogne as he was trying to book a passage. The risks were almost as high in London. Broad Walk, Kensington, was lined with cars for War Office inspection; Army buyers denuded Bond Street showrooms of their Sunbeams and snapped up new cars at the factories; even private petrol supplies were seized. While many London buses were hurriedly repainted and driven off to the war, commercial vans were turned into troop transports and mobile larders. In spite of requisitioning, car firms were able to advertise offering vehicles to those whose horses had been taken.

In the heroic hour not all were heroic. There was a run on the food shops, an exercise in which those with cars and carriages were not ashamed to use their advantage; however, some of them had to fight to retain their haul when others saw what was going on. A few laid in such stocks that four years later, when hoarding was banned, they had to disgorge their first fruits. Arnold Bennett, who served on an anti-invasion committee in Essex, met a farmer who was laying in ammunition 'against the time when the population will raid the countryside demanding provisions . . . he is determined to give out his stores evenly and not to the strongest'.

Attacks of 'breeze up' were few and soon the unbelievable became routine. Elderly countrywomen grew used to the sight of a couple of billeted soldiers dossing down in their parlours and it was some consolation that the folk in the big house had the figures '20' or '30' chalked on their gateposts. The papers ceased to publish Sunday editions and people showed less interest in the war telegrams displayed in town halls and post offices. Cinema pianists were no longer badgered to play all the Allied anthems, though *God Save The King*, hitherto much neglected, now became obligatory at entertainments and Will Crooks, a Labour Member, even persuaded the Commons to sing it at the prorogation in September.

Eighty thousand American tourists had gone home, some of them in a vessel, the *Viking*, which they had clubbed together to buy. Sir Owen Seaman, having doubted whether *Punch* should publish at such a time, had been persuaded to stay at the helm. Advertisers began to show their products being acclaimed by jolly, rubicund Tommies in an idyllic Flanders, and soon enough the world would know: 'How English Army Officer's Widow Killed Her Superfluous Hair'. A group of society ladies, among them the Duchess of Devonshire, tried to discourage any display of mourning, save for a white armlet to express grief and pride; but Courtaulds had other ideas, their advertisement for water-proof crape being boldly headed, 'For Fashionable Mourning'. Derry and Toms put out patriotic handkerchieves to enable people to blow their noses into the Union Jack. Those with venom to spare after abusing Ramsay MacDonald (soon to be excommunicated by Moray Golf Club) found another target in Bernard Shaw, whose stream of ill-judged witticisms about the war caused H. G. Wells to liken him to 'an idiot child screaming in a hospital'. The jest which was to haunt him was his assertion that the British officer caste and the Prussian junkers were indistinguishable and that if soldiers had any sense they would shoot their officers and go home.

The general state of morale could be judged by the incidence of attacks on aliens, who were persecuted in times of bad news. If a historian of Piccadilly is right, the numerous German street walkers became Belgians overnight and thereby attained a gratifying popularity. The circulation of false atrocity stories received a check when a seventeen-year-old Dumfries girl was arrested for uttering forged letters, purporting to come from Belgium, saying that her sister, a nurse, had had her breasts cut off by German soldiers before being put to death; the girl was a hysterical adolescent at odds with her father and stepmother and her 'literary creation' (as her counsel called it) cost her three months in custody. Not all literary creations of the war were exposed so resolutely.

The universal solvent for female hysteria was war work: usually dull, exhausting labour in hospitals, canteens and refugee centres. After a week of war the imprisoned suffragists had been amnestied; and though some of them were in bad shape they began putting their terrifying energies into the new crusade, abandoning the old one. Even the thousands of old ladies who had never made a pot of tea in their lives began to look for ways to make themselves useful.

There was such an outbreak of sock-knitting that the Government intervened, asserting that the War Office had enough socks and that there were better things people could do. When this caused an outcry, a Parliamentary spokesman said the authorities would try to regulate and co-ordinate production. It was also the day of 'Sister Susie's Sewing Shirts For Soldiers', but the standard of Britain's needlework was not always of the highest and many garments were almost unwearable. ('The soldiers in epistles say they'd rather sit on thistles'.) Some ladies with social graces, accustomed to singing to guests after dinner, now sang to captive audiences in hospitals.

Boys were doing men's jobs as perhaps never before. For Scouts there were hundreds of tunnels and bridges and reservoirs to guard, hundreds of miles of coastline to patrol daily. The pick of the Sea Scouts were given coastguard cottages where they cooked and cleaned for themselves, then went out to look for suspicious ships, suspicious aircraft, suspicious persons. Hospitals by the score needed orderlies; there were crashed aircraft to be guarded and (as a test of manhood) propellers to be swung. Not wholly welcome was the lady scoutmaster, but patrol leaders paid suitable courtesies until it was their time to lead platoons in France. There had been a scattering of Wolf Cubs early in 1914, and the war now gave the movement a big impetus. However, the first *Wolf-Cub Handbook*, which took its ideas from Kipling's *Jungle Book*, was not published until 1916.

Britain lacked an army remotely comparable in size with those of her allies and enemies. Kitchener, the new War Minister, scorning to build on the Territorial structure established by Haldane, asked for 100,000 volunteers as a first instalment of an army of seventy divisions, as against the existing six. He was thinking of a war lasting at least three years.

Winston Churchill is credited with saying that Britain was fortunate in having a large number of truculent young men used to giving orders, a category in which he probably included himself. She certainly had a large number of public schoolboys reared in the tradition of Newbolt's 'the voice of a schoolboy rallies the ranks', and who never doubted their right, as products of the Officers' Training Corps, to lead men old enough to be their fathers into battle. Britain also had a swarm of deceptively precious young men known as 'knuts' or 'nuts', for whom everything was 'absolutely too much bally fag, what?' Young men in spats were not what drill sergeants were looking for, but the 'knuts' saw themselves as officers; and having wangled commissions, they set about acquiring monocles, exotic firearms, swords, wide breeches, gleaming jackboots and fashionably squashed caps. The Prussians had monocled wasp-waisted officers too, but there the resemblance probably ends. Pavement artists loved the 'knuts' as they loved Admiral Beatty (of the rakish cap), but by the autumn of 1915 most of the breed had been wiped out, including Basil Hallam, who as 'Gilbert the Filbert' had caricatured the type on the stage.

There is a passage in Ernest Raymond's *Tell England* in which two young would-be officers inform a War Office colonel that they are eighteen years of age. 'Eighteen, by Jove!' exclaims the colonel. 'You've timed your lives wonderfully, my boys. To be eighteen in 1914 is the best thing in England. England's wealth used to consist in other things. Nowadays you boys are the richest thing she's got. She's solvent with you and bankrupt without you.' This has drawn many jeers, but the sentiments expressed are only a variation on the theme, more elegantly phrased, of Rupert Brooke's sonnets. Those who were eighteen, or even in their middle teens, shamelessly pulled every string to get into 'the show'.

Harold Macmillan, serving in a Kitchener battalion, wanted

to join the Grenadier Guards in action and urged his mother to use her influence. 'It was privilege of the worst kind,' he says, 'it was truly shocking. But, after all, was it so very reprehensible? The only privilege I, and many others like me, sought was that of getting ourselves killed or wounded as soon as possible.' When Macmillan crossed to France with the Grenadiers the officers sat down to a two-hour luncheon served by Charles of the Ritz, with a posse of Ritz waiters – a gesture by the wealthy officer commanding No. 1 Company.

For those with no strings to pull there were advertisements in the Personal columns, by officers who performed the function of the hostess prepared to coach debutantes: 'An officer commanding an infantry unit for Imperial Service is prepared to recommend suitable applicants for FIRST COMMISSION. Preference will be given to public school men of good appearance and address.' Some, of course, scorned to pull strings and entered the ranks, which had an unexpected social handicap, for all over the country hotels and restaurants were proclaiming 'Officers only', if not in so many words then by pretending to other ranks that they were fully booked.

Men who volunteered did so for the usual mixture of reasons: patriotism, love of adventure, an urge to escape domesticity, boredom in a dull job and a desire to be with one's friends. For the last category the Pals Battalions opened up some specialised opportunities; there were units for public school men and university men, sportsmen, footballers, bankers, 'commercials', artists and others. A press advertisement in September 1914 was directed at 'West End men', otherwise employees of West End stores, shops, outfitters and drapers who might wish to serve side by side in a regiment of the Line. All that 'West End men' had to do was to call at the enrolling office of Knight, Frank and Rutley, the estate agents in Hanover Square.

The psychological pressures which were applied to those slow to enlist will be discussed later. But even in these early days employers were dropping heavy hints. An advertisement in August 1914 by Aquascutum, the sporting tailors, said the firm had issued a notice to their employees saying: 'We think it is absolutely necessary for every single man between nineteen and thirty to answer his country's call. We shall be pleased to pay half his present salary to any of our present employees while serving and will keep his situation open for him on his return. In the event of a parent or parents being dependent on the volunteer, full salary will be paid him during his service.' This was a fair hint that it was time to join one's West End pals.

Not all employers by any means offered to make up salaries to this degree. Edward Thomas, who carried out a sort of Mass Observation survey into the state of England for the *English Review*, was told that 'the best firms' were dismissing their younger men in order to induce them to enlist – 'not exactly to drive them, but to encourage'. Few complained, since it was assumed the Government had put the employers up to it. One old man at Sheffield remarked, 'It used to be "Oh, you are too old for a job", now it's "You're too young".' At Birmingham a workman expressed the hope that not too many well-to-do men would go to the Front, as they were needed to give employment and control it; a rare spirit, this. In Guildford the local Member of Parliament, Edgar Horne, had his own idea for helping recruiting: he booked whole pages of the local paper and filled them with names of Guildford men who had joined the Colours.

In the rush to enlist – during one September day 35,000 men signed on – it was inevitable that some sprats should slip into the Army's net. Victor Sylvester, the dance band leader, enlisted at fourteen and was later discharged when his age was discovered. Late in 1915, Sir Arthur Markham in the House of Commons badgered the Government with accounts of lads as young as thirteen in the ranks. In Westminster Hospital, within 200 yards of Parliament, lay a fifteen-year-old who had lost a leg in the Dardanelles; he had gone out there after one month's training.

Markham's first ventilation of this subject brought him 300 letters from parents of under-age soldiers, some of whom were being rounded up as deserters. In the *Daily Mirror* on September 18, 1916, appeared a picture of Private S. Lewis, newly discharged, who joined the East Surreys in August 1915 when he was twelve and served for six weeks on the Somme. The Navy made no bones about enlisting boys. When the Fleet was mobilised Winston Churchill was asked privately to intercede to extract two fourteen-year-old midshipmen from one of the capital ships, but the Admiralty was in no mood to waive tradition. In the eighteenth century boys often served aboard men-of-war in battle and at least one stumped back to school with a wooden leg.

The raising of the new armies might have proceeded more smoothly if Britain's favourite soldier had not been so distrustful of Celts. When Lloyd George in September 1914 lent his support to a clamour for a Welsh regiment of Guards, if not a Welsh division or a Welsh corps, Kitchener vigorously opposed him. He was happy for Welshmen to volunteer for English regiments and for Wales to remain as a recruiting area for the Grenadier Guards, but the idea of a major military formation speaking its own language and going its own Welsh way seemed to him asking for trouble. In short, the Welsh were suspect and peculiar; it was no secret that when the Territorials were founded, Welsh congregations had been warned against mixing with them and girls walking out with them were held as having broken with their religion. Lloyd George conceded that the Welsh were not a martial race, 'but neither were the men who composed Cromwell's Ironsides'.

He thought that if they allowed themselves to be treated as inferiors, if they gave way to timidity, ignorance and indolence they would be unable to live down their shame for generations. The dispute between soldier and politician became uncommonly bitter and to Asquith it looked as though either or both might resign: 'The whole thing could have been settled in ten minutes by the exercise of a modicum of common sense and imagination.' (The Prime Minister had earlier said it might be 'amusing' to see how Kitchener got on with the Cabinet and now he was finding out.) Suddenly Kitchener gave in handsomely and agreed that there should be a Welsh division, and on St David's Day, 1915, Welsh Guardsmen performed sentry duty outside Buckingham Palace. (Compton Mackenzie had already invented the Welsh Guards in his *Sinister Street*.) With some misgivings, Kitchener also agreed to the formation of a Northern Ireland Division with the emblem of the Red Hand of Ulster, but baulked at the raising of a Southern Ireland Division displaying the Irish Harp. The Irish were very welcome to fight, but only in their existing, or in English regiments.

*   *   *

In December 1914, when the land war had reached stalemate and the trenches ran from the Swiss border to the sea, the home front suffered the sort of outrage from which it had been led to believe that, thanks to the Royal Navy, it was immune: bombardment from the sea of Scarborough, Whitby and the Hartlepools. This was a forty-minute breakfast-time onslaught by four German cruisers, causing the deaths of about forty, including women and children, and casualties of some 400. Among buildings hit were the Grand Hotel, Scarborough, and Whitby's ruined abbey. According to Wells's Mr Britling, it was 'the same kind of experience that our ships have inflicted scores of times in the past upon innocent people in the villages of Africa and Polynesia'. However, the inhabitants of Scarborough hardly thought of their spa as a corsairs' nest or a stronghold of slavers. Grimly, King George commented, 'This is German *kultur.*'

The raiders achieved the notable impertinence of hurling a piece of shell through the front door of Sir George Sitwell, who was dressing at the time. According to his son, Sir Osbert, he was convinced the Germans would return and claim him as a hostage, so to frustrate their plans he proposed, when that day arrived, to commandeer his doctor's car and get away to York. In the meantime he planned to establish a second-line retreat in a nearby lake hut, where he could live as a species of hermit.

The people of the bombarded towns drew what satisfaction they could from Winston Churchill's denunciation of the 'baby-killers'. The Germans, he said, had risked many large and valuable ships, largely irreplaceable, for 'the passing pleasure of killing as many English people as possible, irrespective of sex, age or condition, in the limited time available. To this act of military and political folly they were impelled by the violence of feelings which could find no other vent. This is very satisfactory and should confirm us in all our courses. Their hate is the measure of their fear.'

This act of 'hate' came shortly after the publication in the British press of a translation of Ernst Lissauer's *Hymn of Hate* which earned him an Iron Cross. The spirited English version was produced for the American press by Barbara Henderson and its best-known lines ran:

French and Russian they matter not,
A blow for a blow, a shot for a shot;
We love them not, we hate them not.
We hold the Weichsel and Vosges-gate,
We have but one and only hate,
We love as one, we hate as one,
We have one foe and one alone –
England!

He is known to you all, he is known to you all,
He crouches behind the dark grey flood,
Full of envy, of rage, of craft, of gall,
Cut off by waves that are thicker than blood . . .
We will never forego our hate,
We all have but a single hate,
We love as one, we hate as one,
We have one foe and one alone –
England!

There was a verse describing how the German officer corps, feasting together, rose as one man to drink the toast: 'To the Day!' Then came further assurances of enmity:

We fight the battle with bronze and steel,
And the time that is coming Peace will seal.
You will we hate with a lasting hate,
We will never forego our hate,
Hate by water and hate by land,
Hate of the head and hate of the hand . . .

and so on, much as before. Occasionally British military bands played the *Hymn* for a joke, but the tune was an indifferent one.

CHAPTER 2

NOBLESSE OBLIGE

The war shattered the nomadic life of high society, the leisured seasonal migrations on the *château* and *Schloss* circuit. It was now time to atone for one's wealth and set an example of public spirit. Summoned by drums, the young heirs went straight to their regiments and straight to their deaths.

No one guessed what a squandering of blue blood was now to take place. In the first year of war forty-seven eldest sons of peers died of battle wounds. By the end more aristocrats had been killed than in the Wars of the Roses. The roll, as kept by *Debrett*, was: twenty-three peers, thirty-eight baronets, fourteen knights, 913 companions, 151 sons of peers, 157 sons of baronets and 277 sons of knights. The succession of 217 hereditary honours was either accelerated or diverted. Some lines were extinguished, others were threatened with extinction. Thanks to the law of primogeniture, childless wives lost not only their men but their homes, as entailed estates passed to aged non-combatants or infants.

The war that was to have been over by Christmas was indeed over by Christmas for nearly 150 old Etonians, the vanguard of 1,157 who were to become names on the school memorial. Since wars were thought to be won on the playing fields of Eton, the newspapers carried tragi-comical photographs of squads of Eton boys performing rifle drill in top hats and tails. In 1915 there were alarming doubts as to the resolution of Eton's Headmaster, Dr Edward Lyttelton, who preached a much-abused sermon looking to the day when war might be abolished and suggesting that if Britain wanted the Kiel Canal internationalised she might have to think about internationalising Gibraltar. On learning how the Germans were acclaiming his sermon, Lyttelton formally denounced German aggression, but the governing body of Eton were happy to let him resign.

Much was written about the 'blood tax' willingly paid at the outset by leading families. Colonel Repington, the war commentator and intriguer, thought the fact that the public held steady was due to the example set by the upper ranks of society, though he did not overlook the stoicism of 'many humble homes'. The editor of the *Daily Express*, R. D. Blumenfeld, believed that peers' sons and labourers' sons together set the great example; the middle classes might be the backbone of society in trade, but they were not so in war, for while they could fight bravely their contribution was less spontaneous. These assessments need not be taken too seriously; the point is that such views were widely held.

Not the least problem for a nobleman was what to do with the family seat. For the wealthier grandees – a Rosebery or a Buccleuch – this could be a problem in quadruplicate or quintuplicate. The smart thing was to have one's principal mansion taken over by the military as a divisional or corps headquarters; this not only reflected glory but had the advantage that the building could be maintained in civilised fashion, provided not too many young officers swung on the chandeliers. However, the commonest use for a great house was as a hospital or convalescent home. An appeal by the Duke of Sutherland to his fellow aristocrats to lend their homes for this purpose resulted in the immediate offer of 250 country seats, including the most famous castles in the land. Some owners alloyed their generosity by trying to stipulate 'officers only'.

As it turned out, there was one great snag, revealed by 'Eve' in the *Tatler*: 'some of the finest of our old country seats are lamentably lacking in that very first essential not only of a hospital but of the most ordinary residence, proper drains. . . .' It was true that the people who lived in such houses were the

fittest class of all, possibly because they never occupied them for
very long, but it was another matter to expect sick soldiers to
recover amid smells and damp. So the War Office whittled
through the list of insalubrious citadels and declined a great
many of them. The best propositions tended to be the town
houses of the *nouveaux riches*, since they were efficiently heated
and fitted with lifts. There was talk of using Buckingham Palace
as a hospital but this too was declined, not on account of drains
but of old-fashioned layout. The King suggested that the Royal
Pavilion at Brighton would make an ideal hospital for Indian
troops. According to Clifford Musgrave, historian of Brighton,
stories have persisted of wounded Indian soldiers being brought
into the Pavilion unconscious, waking amid fantastic Oriental
splendours and assuming they had died and been transported to
Paradise. Those who did die were cremated on a burning ghat on
the Downs.

In the stately homes which passed muster the noble
châtelaines looked proud and fulfilled as they posed in crisp
hospital white in ancestral halls filled with heavily bandaged
men, or sat reading to officer patients or even turning the handle
of a sewing machine. Depending on the luck of the draw, a
wounded officer shipped home to Blighty might find himself
tended by a French empress, a Russian grand duchess, a
Rumanian princess, an English duchess, a Scots marchioness or
the wife of a naturalised profiteer. The octogenarian Empress
Eugénie, widow of Napoleon III, gave a wing of Farnborough
Hill as a convalescent home and engaged Lady Haig as commandant. The atmosphere tended to be that of a house party,
but each 'guest' was required to dine alone on one occasion with
his hostess. In the early days patients were regaled with extracts
from Haig's diary, copied out by his wife, a privilege to which the
medical superintendent eventually took exception, on security
grounds. The Empress kept the home going for five years from
her own resources.

For those who had no objection to being nursed by Russian
autocrats there were three hospitals at Highgate superintended
by the Grand Duchess George of Russia, wife of the Grand
Duke George Mikhailovich, assisted by her daughters, the
Princesses Xenia and Nina. However, the best hospital at Highgate and perhaps in London, according to Robert Graves who

was a patient there, was Queen Alexandra's, in the big town house of Sir Alfred Mond, the chemicals magnate.

Duchesses, grand or otherwise, were not expected to have medical knowledge, but the wife of the Duke of Bedford, later famous as the 'Flying Duchess', had already trained in a London hospital to fit her to run the model hospital she founded at Woburn. This became a military hospital and she supervised it in conjunction with the base hospital at the Abbey, rising each day at dawn. At the same time she trained in the duties of a surgeon's assistant and radiologist. Among her staff were the crew of the ducal yacht *Sapphire*.

Cliveden's hospital was built over the tennis court and bowling alley, leaving Nancy Astor to entertain undisturbed on a scale which was to shock Sylvia Pankhurst, who was easily shocked. The patients were mostly Canadians. The lives of Lady Astor contain alarming stories of how the handmaiden of Christian Science adopted a policy of taunting those patients who seemed to be losing the will to live. 'Yes, Saunders, you're going to die. You're going to die because you have no guts. If you were a Cockney, or a Scot, or a Yank, you'd live. But you are just a Canadian, so you'll lie down and die.' To two sailors wounded at Jutland she said, 'Where are you from? Yorkshire? No wonder you don't want to live.' The therapy of insult apparently worked wonders; but how many patients failed to respond to baiting we shall never know. Forty Canadian soldiers are buried in the grounds at Cliveden.

As well as giving up their homes for hospitals, the wealthier classes also handed over their yachts, which the Government would have commandeered anyway. Many of these spacious vessels became hospitals. Among them was Lady Beatty's *Sheila*, aboard which officer patients could call for meals at any time of day or night. Characteristically, Sir Thomas Lipton contrived the maximum publicity for the new role of his *Erin*, in which he had entertained the Kaiser. Painted white, and with Red Cross markings, she sailed twice to Serbia and Montenegro with hospital staff and equipment, calling en route at all the best ports. Later, as a patrol vessel, she was torpedoed and sunk.

One vessel declined by the Admiralty was Sir Ernest Shackleton's *Endurance*, which was all set to sail for the South Pole in the week war was declared. Officers and crew volunteered for a warlike role, but the signal from their Lordships said 'Proceed' and, amid some criticism, the *Endurance* sailed. Two years later almost all the survivors joined up.

While noble ladies were running hospitals, noble lords were raising regiments. There was a feudal touch to this operation which did not wholly escape criticism. Lord Derby, 'King of Lancashire', dubbed by Lloyd George 'the most efficient recruiting sergeant in England', raised a storm in Labour circles when he announced that, after the war, he would employ only those who had done their duty at the Front and would award farms to applicants on the same basis. He said that if he had twenty sons he would expect them all to go to the war; but his critics wanted to know whether he would sacrifice his ground rents as well as his sons. In very quick time he had his Territorial forces up to strength, but was always being pressed to raise new units (for his controversial Dockers Battalion see Chapter Thirteen). Five battalions of the King's Regiment camped on the Earl's estate at Knowsley. Each soldier received a solid silver cap badge and, by special permission, the regiment wore the Derby crest of eagle and child.

'The Yellow Earl' – Lord Lonsdale, owner of Windermere and Grasmere – was another of the many who had played host to the Kaiser. Unlike some, he refused to relegate souvenirs of the occasion to the basest room, and the bust of the Emperor retained its place of honour at Lowther Castle. Lonsdale threw himself into recruiting with vigour and indiscretion. He had to be restrained from devising his own grey uniforms for the battalion known as 'the Lonsdales', destined to be almost wiped out on the Somme; a reminder that noble lords could lose regiments as well as raise them. The Earl's own national service included taking over the National Stud – with a promise to pay the State one-third of his winnings – and keeping the Cottesmore Hunt at full strength. His economies included cutting out his private orchestra.

So many lords lieutenant were discharging their traditional roles that it becomes invidious to single out names. The Duke of Bedford, the aloof Herbrand, established at his own expense a Bedfordshire Training Depot in Ampthill Park, which later became a command depot with the Duke as commandant. He 'sent' 12,000 men to the battlefield and, as we have seen, his wife tended the returning wounded. In Yorkshire Lord Nunburnholme raised several battalions, including one of 'Commercials' and one of Bantams (men of short stature, deriving their inspiration from the diminutive Lord Roberts). He also raised and equipped a Hull Volunteer Battalion, drawn largely from older men of Hull Golf Club. Forming regiments was not just a matter of haranguing men from platforms; some who essayed the task bought, as did Nunburnholme, equipment, uniforms and weapons on the open market. To show that a woman could compete in this field Mrs Cunliffe-Owen obtained permission to raise a Sportsman's Battalion of the Royal Fusiliers. Advertisements issued on her behalf specified persons 'used to shooting, hunting and outdoor sport' drawn from 'upper and middle classes only'. (Footballers had their own battalion.) Among the sportsmen who arrived at Hornchurch on embodiment were 'the first Englishman to have killed a bull in Spain in modern times', a colonel who had shot five lions in a day, heroes of the Jameson Raid, assorted scullers, golfers and – stretching the definition a little – actors and raconteurs.

One nobleman who made an unusual sacrifice for his country was the elderly Lieutenant-General Lord Dundonald. All his life he had jealously guarded the secret of his illustrious grand-father, Admiral Cochrane, inventor of a mysterious weapon which in 1812 had been adjudged 'infallible, irresistible, in-human'. During the Crimean War its use had been considered, but again the Arcanum, or Secret Plan, had been turned down as too horrible. Now, however, General Dundonald felt the time had come to unleash it and he revealed the details to Kitchener. It was nothing more than a recipe for generating noxious fumes. Kitchener was not interested but Winston Churchill was, and limited experiments were conducted under the General's super-vision. In April 1915 the Germans used poison gas, which was more effective than the Arcanum.

Even before the war began the Marquess of Graham (later Duke of Montrose), who held a master mariner's certificate, had been trying to persuade the Government to build an aircraft carrier. Opposition was predictably heavy, but by 1916 the Beardmore yard was given orders to proceed. The *Argus*, the first naval aircraft carrier in the world, was ready for action just after the war ended. By then her designer owned most of Ben

Lomond, but the *Argus* was his chief pride. An Irish peer who made his name in an equally unlikely field was the unconventional Earl of Chetwynd, who ran the biggest explosives factory in Britain, at Chilwell, without which the Somme barrages might well have faltered. Lloyd George, who has paid him high tribute, says that when the Earl heard reports of spies in his factory he caused three 'graves' to be dug on a hillside, each with a black post at its head, to encourage a rumour of summary executions.

The richest man in the country, the Duke of Westminster, famous for his fast cars and hydroplanes, divested himself of his seats and yachts and presently was seen at the wheel of a splendid Rolls-Royce fitted with a Hotchkiss machine-gun; thus mounted, he joined General French's staff in France. He was not easy to employ and later ran the equivalent of a private army. In 1916 his force of armoured cars tore 250 miles across the North African desert to rescue a party of torpedoed men from the hands of the Senussi.

The war gave an outlet for the energies of a band of hard-driving society dames, some of them former suffragists, who could be described as Organisation Women. They had a well-developed talent, already displayed in their counties, for charitable fund-raising and fête promotion. Now they turned to organising relief for refugees, administering the Red Cross, stimulating the flow of comforts, regulating the home needlework industry and – in due course – acting as commandants of the women's police forces and women's services. They worked by strength of character, by judicious social blackmail and by ruthless manipulation of their menfolk. Plainly they were fuelled by a desire to show what women could do, which did not mean competing with Mrs Pankhurst and marching 50,000 women through the streets as a gesture. At times they were too much for Whitehall. Dr Elsie Inglis, eager to form a women's ambulance unit for overseas, was told at the War Office: 'My good lady, go home and sit still.'

A good account of these formidable ladies is to be found in David Mitchell's *Women on the Warpath* (1966). Their debutante daughters kept busy with 'stunts' which ranged from displaying their figures in patriotic tableaux and selling programmes at charity matinees to driving wounded soldiers on sightseeing tours or singing to them in hospitals. 'Eve' of the *Tatler* did her best at the Tipperary Clubs where soldiers' wives, in her view, were on to a good thing: free fires, newspapers, books and a crêche, and ladies and gentlemen going dinnerless to sing, dance and play for them. Never before had they enjoyed a settled weekly income; they were even 'redeeming' household goods they had never thought to see again 'while there was a man about the house . . . wanting meat three times a day'. Still, as 'Eve' conceded, 'they deserve all we can give them, poor dears'.

The rich were soon under pressure to 'liberate' their able-bodied servants, but houses void of labour-saving devices needed staffs of some sort to run them. Most readily dispensable were young footmen. Lady Randolph Churchill replaced them with 'footgirls' arrayed in footmen's livery re-cut for women: black jacket with shiny buttons, black tie, long black skirt and large apron. An advertisement by a livery firm showed a uniform consisting of narrow black skirt and a jacket buttoned across a striped waistcoat surmounted by a stand-up collar with a black necktie; the effect, half-woman, half-man, was highly disconcerting. A number of variations on the theme were attempted by other hostesses, but gradually more traditional maids' uniforms won the day.

The all-knowing 'Eve' kept her readers informed of the domestic problems of the great. She reported that staffs in big establishments liked to have officers' servants billeted in the house, since the orderlies could then be given the dirty jobs to do. She noted also that landowners were having much trouble in disposing of game, which was not welcomed in hospitals, either in the kitchens or in the wards. In vain the Dukes of Devonshire and Portland urged the public at large to consume their savoury carrion. As the press was to point out, the patriotic duty of the upper classes in war was to consume those luxury foods for which the lower classes had no appetite.

CHAPTER 3

SOUND OF THE GUNS

Early in the war the game birds of Britain began to behave neurotically in their coverts, fussing and crowing for no discernible reason. It was not long before the trouble was diagnosed: the creatures were upset by the sound of the Flanders guns.

Human ears were less sensitive than those of pheasants, but as the great strafes were intensified, the sound of gunfire became a running accompaniment to life on the southern and eastern coasts. It was even heard on the Surrey hills, on Wimbledon Common and – on rarer occasions – on Hampstead Heath, a good 150 miles from the Ypres Salient. The incidence of this sound became the subject of learned papers by meteorologists and others; and historians testified that in 1815 the guns of Waterloo had been heard in Kent.

It was a pulsing, thudding sound, something which was not so much heard as felt. At nights the sinister rumble was sometimes oppressive enough to keep people from sleep. Few seem to have found the sound inspiriting. It did not require wild imagination in the listeners to realise that they might be hearing their kith and kin being blown to shreds. For the mutilated men in hospital blue on the front at Brighton, and for the German prisoners working in the fields, the sound had its especial poignancy; they at least knew what it was all about and that their comrades were at the receiving end.

William Plomer, a boy at Beechmont School, near Knole, heard 'on still days . . . when we were bent over Xenophon or quadratic equations, the windows . . . rattled by a sudden crescendo of the interminable thunder of the guns in Flanders, and a wandering breeze would stir the war map on the wall.' Horatio Bottomley heard the roar as he corrected proofs of his ghosted articles at the Dicker, near Eastbourne. Kipling listened to the far-off sound from Burwash, and Conrad from Orlestone, near Ashford. At his house at Elmwood, near Broadstairs, Lord Northcliffe could also listen to the war which, his enemies said, he had done so much to provoke. In 1915 he helped to expose the shell shortage and thereafter was well placed to judge whether the cannonade was worthy of the nation. In a sense he was in the front line, as was Asquith on his weekends at Walmer Castle, for in February 1917 shells from a German warship fell near Elmwood and he was convinced the Huns were out to get him. Kitchener, assailed by Northcliffe in the shells controversy, was also within earshot of the Front, at Broom Park, near Canterbury. Even the men who made the shells and the women who filled them were able to hear their products exploding, as they relaxed on the summer beaches.

One of the best remembered barrages was the seven-day softening up which preceded the Battle of the Somme. In that prodigal week Winston Churchill, out of office, sat painting in the grounds of Herstmonceux Castle, in Sussex, a guest of the eccentric Claude Lowther, who wore black knee breeches and allowed the regimental ram ('Lowther's Lambs') the freedom of the house. The rumble of the barrage caused Churchill to lay down his brushes and speak bitterly to Violet Bonham-Carter of the ostracism which had been his lot since Gallipoli.

The greatest explosion of the war, when British Sappers blew the top off the Messines Ridge, in June 1917, was said to have shaken the camps at Aldershot. The roar was likened to that of the eruption at Krakatoa; it was probably the loudest man-made explosion since the French blew open the rock of Alicante, in 1709, engulfing a British garrison. According to the Press Association, Lloyd George, then Prime Minister, gave orders that he was to be called at three am in his home at Walton Heath, Surrey, to hear the blast. The sound came through on schedule. The Prime Minister appears to have denied that he was roused especially for the occasion; the *New Statesman* thought such an arrangement would have been 'subversive of the national

dignity', though it agreed that millions of loyal subjects would
have sat up to hear the bang if they had known it was coming.

To hear Kentish cattle lowing against the *obbligato* of a war
raging in another land was bizarre enough, but there were a
privileged few who, from time to time, were able to view both
Britain and the battlefields simultaneously. An airman flying
high over Flanders could look down on the scored pattern of the
trenches below and, to the west, glimpse the peaceful green
fields of Kent. Zeppelin crews homing at night from raids on
London were able to see fires blazing in the capital on one hand
and the flicker of the Flanders barrage on the other. Not less
remarkable was the experience of Churchill when, belatedly
reappointed to the Government, he was able to work at his desk
in the Ministry of Munitions in the morning, catch an aircraft at
Hendon and 'follow the course of a great battle in the afternoon'. His justification for these sorties was that the Ministry
had large establishments in Paris. The Commander-in-Chief
raised no demur and provided him with a *château* at Verchocq.
On two successive flights Churchill's aircraft had engine trouble
over the Channel.

The Continent on which this audible war was going on was by no
means out of bounds to civilians. Elderly citizens, though cut off
from the Central European spas, could still make their way to
the Riviera, if they did not object to stringent body searches at
the Channel ports. The frivolity on the Côte d'Azur was muted,
but the great compensation was the absence of German tourists,
who had swamped Nice and Menton the previous season. Monte
Carlo allowed itself to slump for the first two or three months of
war, but finding that San Remo and other resorts were stealing a
march, it fought back. In the spring of 1915 A. E. Housman
decided to pay his first visit to the Riviera, 'when the worst
classes who infest it are away'. By midsummer the Touring Club
de France was advertising in the British press that all French
summer resorts were open as usual – 'the mountain air cure
resorts, the celebrated spas, the sea-bathing beaches'. In small
print was a caution: 'Do not travel in France without joining the
Touring Club de France.' Gradually, the Riviera became a huge
rest and recuperation centre for wounded officers, tended as
often as not by well-born ladies. Lord Clark recalls that his

parents travelled to their villa at Cap Martin where they turned the family's hotel, the Imperial, into a hospital for French officers. But the holiday appeal never died out. Even in the doom-struck winter of 1917–18 British newspapers carried advertisements headed, 'Where To Winter: Monte Carlo.'

Roger Fry went to France in 1915 to help fellow Quakers restore shattered areas of the Marne and Meuse. Having worked away at this chore he awarded himself a holiday in Menton, where he bathed and sketched. In 1916 he was in Paris meeting Matisse and Picasso. Even Sylvia Pankhurst, the country's leading firebrand, was allowed a visit to Paris, where she had a tense meeting with her 'Jingoistic' mother. However, not all restless intellectuals were free to go abroad (see Chapter Eight).

The first conducted tours of the battlefields were organised in the spring of 1915. They were operated from France, chiefly for the Americans, who saw little more than empty trenches on the Aisne. Rather better value was offered by British GHQ in France, which maintained a cluster of *châteaux* near St Omer, whence privileged sightseers were escorted on 'Cooks Tours' to the Front. Early on there were complaints about society ladies being entertained at Headquarters, a sensitive topic resurrected by Lord St Davids in November 1915. His observations stirred up so much club gossip – had ladies been riding around like Mrs Henry Duberly in the Crimea, looking for a good battle? – that he was driven to make a personal statement emphasising that the ladies in question had been beyond reproach, and all he had wished to convey was that it was not decent that the war should be used as a peepshow.

Visitors to GHQ were usually politicians and writers whose goodwill the Army was anxious to secure; among them were Arnold Bennett, H. G. Wells, Rudyard Kipling, Horatio Bottomley, Bernard Shaw, Conan Doyle, J. L. Garvin, J. M. Barrie and Mrs Humphry Ward. The tour by Shaw in January 1917, at the suggestion of Haig, appalled a Member of Parliament who remembered the playwright's advice to soldiers to shoot their officers and go home. But Shaw, as his friends complained, had become a Jingo – 'more like an old-fashioned admiral on a quarter-deck than anything else', thought Lytton Strachey – and he paid for his tour with warm praise for the military machine. 'I must confess without shame,' he said, 'that I enjoyed my week at the Front better than my week at the seaside.' The belief, shared by the Government and by British GHQ, that a visit to the trenches increased people's desire to help the Army resulted in invitations to parties of miners, trade unionists, Labour leaders and even – in August 1917 – some 'extreme pacifists . . . pleasant, nice fellows, hugely ignorant about anything outside their own little shows'. They were amazed that the men should praise their officers and impressed by 'the whole atmosphere of comradeship and goodwill and the determination to win' (to quote Brigadier-General John Charteris, Haig's Intelligence chief). Also on the peepshow tour came the lord provosts of Edinburgh and Glasgow, a duke or two, press lords, the Archbishop of York, the King of Montenegro ('a very picturesque old brigand' – Charteris), Gabriele d'Annunzio and flamboyant military attachés from neutral countries, all of whom expected to be entertained by the Commander-in-Chief and usually were.

Civilian visitors started off as a rule in the luxury Staff train from Victoria Station, the service which drew so much acid comment from the fighting men doomed to travel in discomfort. Frederick Oliver, the wealthy draper-author, who boarded this train in September, 1917, noted 'one Pullman feeding car containing some curious-looking individuals in bowler hats, black tail coats, fieldglasses and Piccadilly button boots. Some of them wore gaiters, others didn't. I took them to be American journalists setting off to the Front.'

It was not impossible to bluff one's way into the battle zone. One of the boldest intruders was a diplomat's wife, Lady Isabella St John, who had heard at a London tea party that her son was a casualty in France. Unable to obtain satisfaction at the Officers' Casualty Inquiry Office in Whitehall, she decided to visit his unit, despite severe warnings that no unauthorised persons were allowed in the battle area. Late in 1915 she set off with a French visa and a bag of seven sovereigns for Bethune. At Calais a booking clerk declined to issue a ticket to Hazebrouck, but imperious English ladies were hard to gainsay and at length the clerk gave in. On the train French officers suspected she might be a spy, but on learning of her mission they wished her luck. After Hazebrouck a reluctant carter gave her a lift, handing her over when the cart broke down to a British officer who drove her to the village where her son was stationed. He tried hard to look pleased. 'Well, mother, you had better come in now,' he said. 'We can talk things over, you can explain matters later.' The son was acquitted of complicity and his mother was allowed to stay on in the village for two days, during which she tried to make her way to the trenches and begged a general to let her join the Royal Army Medical Corps. Back in London, she wrote a piously padded book about her exploit, *A Journey in Wartime*.

If Lady St John's son had been seriously wounded, she might well have been allowed to visit him officially. Many well-connected women were able, by pulling strings, to see their wounded menfolk in France and even to arrange special transport home for them. Lady Diana Cooper tells how she accompanied Sir John and Lady Horner, travelling with a titled doctor and a special nursing sister, on a cross-Channel visit to the Horners' wounded son. She agrees that 'this privilege – worse, favouritism – was considered outrageous by the many'. In 1916 Naomi Mitchison, newly married, was able to go to Le Tréport to visit her wounded husband, for whom special hospital arrangements were later made in Britain. It was odd, she thinks, that such things were possible: 'One only asks oneself whether the treatment of wounded officers was very different from that given to ordinary private soldiers.' Many old soldiers know the answer.

Even a schoolboy could find himself in the Line. Air-Commodore Patrick Huskinson, who served in both wars, says that when he left Harrow in 1915 he made his way in cadet uniform to Etaples, where his father commanded Base Details. Angry at first, his father relented and then took him to visit his old battalion in the Ypres Salient. 'For three wonderful days,' he writes, 'I wandered round to my heart's content and saw all I could of that nightmare of a place.' Only a year later this Harrow boy, in the rank of captain, was leading a flight of six aircraft over the Somme.

CHAPTER 4

HALLUCINATIONS

Of the war's great hallucinations, the first and best and most innocent was the one which concerned, not an enemy in Britain's midst, but an ally: the phantom Russian expeditionary force with snow still on its boots. Unlike the tale of the phantom warriors of Mons, its source could not be traced; it was plucked from the air by a civilian population hyperexcited by the events across the Channel, a bold first exercise in imaginative power under censorship.

The Russians, it appeared, with a logistical enterprise matched only by the strength of their desire to help the western Allies, had rushed a number of divisions to the arctic port of Archangel whence, in an armada of transports, they had sailed for Aberdeen and Leith. At once hundreds of vehicles had been commandeered so that half the force could be transferred to the rail route down the west coast, the rest going by the eastern route. In Perthshire Lady Baden-Powell heard the Russians were coming and rushed to the railway station to see them pass; and in the same county a landowner boasted that 125,000 Cossacks had crossed his estates. The trains travelled with blinds down, but that did not stop people espying tall, rugged soldiers with fur caps. Exact statistics always help a lie on its way; a marine engineer interviewed by a Cardiff paper said he had travelled with the Russians from Archangel and had been in the 193rd trainload to pass through York. In Edinburgh and elsewhere porters were seen sweeping snow from railway carriages.

At Carlisle the Russians called for vodka, at Rugby they drank all the coffee, at Durham they jammed roubles in station slot-machines, in East London they threw their useless coins to children. Euston Station was said to have been closed for thirty-six hours while the Czar's myrmidons detrained. No town liked to be left out of the saga. A landlady at Crewe had four Russians billeted on her and was unable to satisfy their fierce Slav appetites.

'Like everybody else, I kept the ball rolling,' writes Michael MacDonagh, a reporter on *The Times*, 'and the only excuse that can be offered is that it was a case of the wish being father to the thought.'

Another who kept the ball rolling was the itinerant German spy, Karl Lody, who passed on the rumour in a message intended for his masters. (He has even been accused of starting the story.) Not everyone believed that the Russians were bound for the Western Front; some said they were going to seize the Kiel Canal. A more disagreeable rumour was that when they reached France they would throw in their lot with the Germans. The British press mostly withheld the story, though the *Daily Mail* on September 1 had a satirical article called 'The Great Rumour' and the London *Evening News* also published sceptical comment. On September 9 the *Daily News* said, 'so extraordinary has been the ubiquity of the rumours . . . that they are almost more amazing if they are false than if they are true.' This appeared under a headline RUSSIAN ARMY IN FRANCE? along with a report from the Rome newspaper *Tribuna* that 250,000 Russians had reached the Western Front. A *Daily News* correspondent in France claimed to have found a force of Russians co-operating with the Belgian Army, but exactly where 'it would be indiscreet for me to tell'. Until September 15 the Press Bureau allowed the rumour to flourish, possibly in the hope that the Germans would believe it; then, with the Battle of the Marne over, came an official denial that any Russian troops had passed through Britain. This did not convince everybody, since it was traditional for governments to lie in wartime.

Many attempts have been made to pin down the origins of the rumour, but all lack conviction. Lord Bertie, then Ambassador in Paris, says that a ship was due to leave Archangel for Britain with gold worth eight million pounds, and a number of heavy warships were detailed to protect her, a precaution which could have aroused speculation. According to MacDonagh, a wholesale provisions dealer in London received a telegram from Russia saying, 'Two hundred thousand Russians are being dispatched via Archangel,' the message referring to eggs. (This explanation apparently satisfied General Charteris.) Some said the Russians were Scotsmen trying to explain in their uncouth speech that they were from Ross-shire. A French officer was blamed for going about the Front asking, 'Where are ze rations?' There is a curious echo of the affair in Churchill's *The World Crisis*, from which it appears that on August 28 the ever-helpful First Lord wrote to Kitchener pointing out that if Russia's Siberian troops were to be moved south against the Central Powers they would, as he understood, derange the communications, whereas it 'would probably be easy' to ship them from Archangel to Ostend, where two army corps could make an effective intervention. He thought, however, that such a move might not commend itself to the Russians. 'Don't trouble to answer,' he ended.

The legend of the Angels of Mons, whose shining presence put the German cavalry to flight, did not gain wide circulation until some weeks after the Retreat. In a diary entry dated September 5 General Charteris says the angelic rumour was being repeated in 2nd Corps, but possibly this reference was incorporated later. It is almost certain that the origin of the legend was a short story, *The Bowmen*, by Arthur Machen in the London *Evening News* of September 29, 1914. The inspiration for the tale, Machen says, came to him in church 'as the blue incense floated above the Gospel Book on the desk between the tapers'. It was a composite of the many legends in which heavenly hosts have come to the aid of the righteous in battle; also in his mind was Kipling's story of a ghostly Indian regiment. In Machen's tale a British soldier invokes St George to help his hard-pressed comrades and the sky fills with the spirits of the Agincourt bowmen, who annihilate the Germans with ghostly arrows. Machen denied that he 'stole' rumours from the battlefield; and he also denied that the whole thing had been presented to him in typescript by a lady-in-waiting. However, many of the public were ready to believe that angelic hosts had prevented a German breakthrough. If miracles could happen in

Judaea, why not in Flanders? Occultists and clergymen knew a good thing when they saw it and the legend began to find its way into sermons, pamphlets and parish magazines. How was it, some wondered, that out of the thousands who had survived the battle none had found the divine intercession worth mentioning at the time? Now, however, a handful of soldiers began to remember seeing something unusual. A lance-corporal with fifteen years' service said he had stood watching the vision for three-quarters of an hour: 'We came over quiet and still – it took us that way.' One of his mates cried, 'God's with us' and that 'kind of loosened us'. Their captain, when they fell in to march, said, 'Well, men, we can cheer up now; we've got Someone with us.' The lance-corporal added: 'I should be very sorry to make a fool of myself by telling a story merely to please anyone.' Then the press discovered a lieutenant-colonel who said that, after Le Cateau, his column was accompanied by squadron upon squadron of ghostly horsemen.

Exactly how God had turned the tide was never established. Machen's 'long line of shapes, with a shining about them' became a row of shining beings, and then a company of angels. In some versions the heavenly visitants had interposed themselves between the warring hosts and the Germans were powerless to go forward. The *Church Times* was informed by a correspondent that there had been a discussion in Berlin as to why a certain German regiment had failed in battle, to which the men replied that their horses, shying at a supernatural vision, had turned sharply and fled like the wind. The English, they said, were 'up to some devilry or other and we could do nothing'. There was also a rumour that the British had been playing tricks with 'turpinite' (presumably gas) shells. Inevitably, a German soldier was found on the battlefield with 'arrow wounds'.

By Easter 1915 the legend was going well. Most accounts of the vision were at fourth or fifth hand and those who claimed to have seen it tended to be identified, if at all, by their initials. Harold Begbie wrote a pamphlet in defence of the angels and T. W. H. Crosland, in *Find The Angels*, lambasted Begbie. We needed, he said, not anonymous tale-tellers but a society of persons who had Seen Angels and Were Not Afraid to Say So. 'If ever you see an angel, and I hope you do, don't hesitate. Write at once to Mr Begbie, c/o his publishers, and tell him he may print your letter and give your name and address.' Pamphlets like these served to inspire more sermons, which were then issued as pamphlets. A notorious believer was the Rev A. A. Boddy, vicar of All Saints, Sunderland, who had served for two months at the Front. A Nonconformist pastor, Dr R. F. Horton, preaching at Manchester, said he had heard that all those who were in the Retreat from Mons were changed men and had felt a spiritual uplifting. He endorsed Tertullian's *Credo quia impossibile*, adding that if angels were to appear to us every day we should lose the sense of the spiritual world.

Machen could make no useful comment on what the soldiers said they saw, other than to point out that exhausted men espy things that are not there, especially in mist. He was accused of boasting that he had started it all. 'Some ass . . . wrote me a solemn letter charging me to walk humbly and to give thanks for having been made the vessel and channel of this new revelation. A clergyman declared that I "strutted" in a highly unbecoming manner. . . . I cannot conceive of anyone being foolish enough to take pride in begetting some of the silliest tales that have ever disgraced the English tongue.'

Rumours about German spies – and especially the shooting of spies – gave a powerful zest to the early weeks of the war. Writing to his brother in Canada in September 1914 Frederick Oliver, of Debenham and Freebody, told how a German who was caught at the Aldershot waterworks loaded with poison up his shirt 'was put up against a wall and shot forthwith'. He had been the chief hairdresser at Aldershot for twenty years. 'As far as I can make out,' wrote Oliver, 'some hundreds of spies have been shot at naval and military barracks since the opening of the war, though not a single one of the cases has been in the papers.' He was far from unique in believing such tales, which flourished in an atmosphere of hysteria and xenophobia without parallel.

Spy novels had taught the public what to expect. The Kaiser's agents, preparing for the Day, were assumed to have meticulously checked on all available stabling and to have logged the location of every water trough. In great houses overlooking the North Sea naturalised German financiers were sending messages by Morse lamp and wireless to U-boats. Mysterious grey ladies drove about in mysterious grey cars, pausing only to release pigeons and flash their headlamps at Zeppelins. So thick were spies in this coastal belt, said the *Tatler*, that there would have to be a big clear-out if ever the Royal Family were to revisit Sandringham. On the west coast life was a little more relaxed, but Lord Leith of Fyvie told his fellow peers that German ships were coaling off the west coast of Scotland and also in Ireland. Enough credence was given to reports of enemy hydroplanes operating in south-west Scotland for the military to warn landowners to alert their estate workers.

Elsewhere in Britain thuggish agents were storming into railway signal boxes and murdering the occupants, preparatory to derailing trains. Others were massing explosives in workshops housed in the arches of London viaducts. In garrisons German barbers sharpened their razors to cut the throats of recruits. German shopkeepers were putting slow poison into the food they sold to Britons. Maundy Gregory's paper *Mayfair* told of a spy who had been found with enough typhus bacilli to incapacitate an army corps. Another spy was racing round on a motor-cycle, disguised as a scoutmaster, giving poisoned sweets to sentries. Those agents who could think of nothing better to do were causing stampedes of military horses.

Alert citizens were constantly spotting Germans in disguise. Girls recognised former German boyfriends who either looked straight through them or forgetfully clicked their heels before vanishing. On the tram to Victoria a Brixton woman saw four young women in nurses' uniform, sitting two by two opposite each other. One of them tossed a book to her friend, who instead of separating her knees to catch it as a woman would, drew them together in the fashion of men. The alert observer informed the police and supposedly received a reward of £50. (In World War Two German paratroopers disguised as nuns had presumably been taught how to catch parcels.)

Governess stories were legion. Everyone knew someone who, suspicious of a *fräulein*, had gone up into her room, opened her trunk and found a cache of firearms. Everyone knew of alien waiters who, on being asked sudden questions like, 'Well, Fritz, where are you due to report when the invaders arrive?' would leap to attention and say, 'Portsmouth, sir.' The *Daily Mail*'s orders for diners-out ran: 'Refuse to be served by an Austrian or German waiter. If your waiter says he is Swiss ask to see his passport.' Even the *Spectator* said: 'We can very well understand the Home Office deciding that the work of a waiter, since it lends itself with such peculiar ease to the work of espionage, should not in wartime be practised by enemy aliens.' A rule against them would be 'one to which no sensible person could object'. In fact, hundreds of them were interned.

Some rumours owed their origins to the fighting in Belgium. The invading Germans, it was said, had found instructions from their agents written on the backs of enamelled iron adver- tisements for Maggi Soup. So, in London, hastily convened 'screwdriver parties' went about ensuring that no such tricks had been played in the capital. The urge to unscrew things, for many a deep-felt compulsion, for once found patriotic expression. Less easy to prove or disprove was the rumour that a number of tennis courts all over London, and especially on high ground, had been constructed of heavy concrete to serve as gun em- placements. If the Germans invaded, hidden howitzers would be wheeled out, or raised from underground, to assist in the de- struction of the city. Secret emplacements of this sort were said to have been used by the Germans in their attacks on Maubeuge. A few tennis courts in the London area were inspec- ted and probed, but none appears to have been dug up. Not only tennis courts were suspect. In October 1914 police descended in strength on a lithograph factory in Victoria Road, Willesden Junction. It was a one-storey concrete building with floor and foundations apparently built to an unusually robust specificat- ion. The premises were close to the railway and enjoyed an unbroken view over London to the Crystal Palace (where, some believed, more emplacements were awaiting the Day). Amid jeers from a crowd, some twenty aliens of military age were marched out of the factory. The firm, which had a branch in Leipzig, protested its innocence and the architect showed his designs to the press, pointing out that a solid foundation was necessary in case the building was made higher.

Excited speculations about a concrete-based lake in the Japanese garden of a house called Ewell Castle, near Epsom, led to libel actions against the London *Evening News* and the *People*. An article in the former, headlined SUSPICIONS IN A SURREY GARDEN, suggested that the concrete lake-bed, hidden under a thin layer of sand, was capable of mounting five heavy guns to command the railway to London. To disarm the suspicious, an innocent rose trellis had been erected. In the occupant's possession was an 80hp car with a 500 candle-power acetylene searchlight. A local Member of Parliament, Watson Rutherford, was induced to ask a question about Ewell Castle, with the object of allaying public anxiety, but he succeeded only in increasing it. Eventually the occupant of the house, Captain Clarence Wiener, Austrian-born but naturalised American, hired as counsel the great Marshall Hall to clear his name. Evidence showed that the concrete was laid down by the landscape gardener simply to prevent the water escaping from the lake. A local doctor said he never knew Wiener display any pro-German tendency, which gave Mr Justice Darling the chance to say, 'I don't suppose you examined him professionally for it.' Wiener, who refused to answer questions about his private life, was awarded the very modest sums of £50 and £25 against the newspapers; probably the jury felt that he should have known better, with a name like that, than to build a concrete-bottomed lake on the eve of a great war.

One specialised field of rumour had it that well-known people were not who they pretended to be. Sir Oswald Mosley mentions a belief that Field-Marshal Mackensen, the German commander, was really Sir Hector Macdonald, a Boer War general who had committed suicide in Paris to escape disgrace. Lord Haldane, the Lord Chancellor, who had once privately described Germany as his 'spiritual home', was said to be the Kaiser's illegitimate brother, with a German wife, and to be in secret touch with Berlin. His kitchen maid burned his abusive mail by the sackful. By his own account he was in danger of being assaulted in the street and shot at. In 1915 he was dropped without ceremony from the Government, but by the end of the year was still being abused so heartily that Colonel Repington said one might as well try to stop Niagara with a toothbrush as attempt to halt a dinner-table tirade against Haldane.

Newspapers which scoffed at spy stories were belaboured by those which preferred to believe them. Was it not a good thing to have the whole nation on the *qui vive*? However, spy fever could be an embarrassment to the authorities. Sir Basil Thomson, then of Scotland Yard, says that whenever a worker on a motorcycle set off to examine telegraph poles somebody else on another motorcycle would be sent to arrest him. A group of Marconi

operators detailed to intercept possible messages from the
North Sea left London at noon and were locked up in Essex by
three o'clock. They were freed, but by seven were again in
captivity. After this they refused to move without Territorial
escort, but next day the whole party was under arrest.

Some of the more far-fetched stories still linger on. Dennis
Wheatley in his autobiography says that in the first week of war
Admiral Hall, head of Naval Intelligence, was passing Aspreys
in Bond Street when he saw von Rintelen, the German spy, who
had nipped over to see how things were going. Hall politely told
him to get home at once because there was a war on. This is
supposed to illustrate, not treachery or idiocy in high places, but
the gentlemanly way in which wars were conducted in those
days. In fact, Hall was then commanding a cruiser and von
Rintelen was at a desk in Berlin. Wheatley claims to have had
the story from von Rintelen, who was a great romancer.

The spy fever inspired a popular play, *The Man Who Stayed
At Home*, the authors of which, Lechmere Worrall and Harold
Terry, simply drew on the headlines for their material. Its hero,
a monocled silly ass, accepted a white feather from his fiancée,
put it in his pipe and smoked it; he could afford to do so because
he was busy breaking up a spy ring. The scene was an East coast
boarding house kept by a woman whose first husband was
a German general and whose son was a spy at the
Admiralty. There was a naturalised German governess; there
was a Dutch waiter who kept pigeons, with all the appropriate
maps tied to their legs; there was a secret radio behind the
fireplace; there was an infernal machine ready to go off; and a
German U-boat lurked off-shore, waiting for a signal. *The Man
Who Stayed At Home* had many imitations. *In Time Of War* had
a German princess-spy who passed herself off as a nurse and
poisoned the hospital water-filters. As late as October 1918 *The
Female Hun*, a melodrama set on the East coast, ended with a
British general putting a bullet into his traitorous wife within
half an hour of his butler being shot as a spy.

Despite all the frenzied spy-spotting, arrests for espionage
were few. A Home Office statement on October 9, 1914, said
that twenty known agents had been arrested on the day war
broke out and two hundred persons were still under suspicion.
Nine thousand Germans and Austrians were in detention

camps. Not a single telegraph wire had been cut and no unlawful wireless sets, pigeon cotes or stores of effective arms or bombs had been discovered. In a debate in November the Home Secretary said 120,000 reported cases of suspicious activity had been investigated and 6,000 houses ransacked. What the country wanted to hear about was spies being shot; but when, on March 3, 1915, a Member asked for the total so far executed he was told, 'One, sir.' There were some who thought such a pathetic admission could only afford comfort to the enemy.

The executed spy, first of eleven to face the firing squad, was Karl Hans Lody, who had been arrested at Killarney masquerading as Charles A. Inglis, an American tourist. He was a German reserve naval lieutenant and had accepted the assignment because of ill-health; but for his two missing ribs and weak eyes he might have served at Jutland or survived to scuttle his ship at Scapa Flow. He had lived in America long enough to acquire an American accent and had been a Hamburg-Amerika tourist guide.

The court-martial, an event for which it was hard to find a precedent, was held in the Middlesex Guildhall, opposite the Houses of Parliament, with Major-General Lord Cheylesmore presiding over a board of eight officers. Evidence showed that Lody had travelled widely in Britain for six weeks, visiting the Firth of Forth, Liverpool and Dublin. In London, where he had stayed at the Ivanhoe Hotel, Bloomsbury, he had reported on the methods taken to protect buildings from Zeppelin bombs. He also noted the great fear of espionage everywhere – 'one smells a spy in every stranger'. His reports, one from Edinburgh and one from Dublin, were posted to Stockholm, but intercepted by the Post Office.

Lody declined to identify the officer who gave him his orders. His instructions were not to 'spy around' but to pass on such information as any ordinary traveller could come across. He was to wait if possible for the first big naval battle and report on British losses. No pressure had been placed on him to perform this task. 'I have never been a coward,' he said, 'and certainly I won't be a shirker.' The prosecutor, A. H. Bodkin, found it incredible that Lody should have paid his own expenses; if this was so, then 'the man who acted as a spy at his own expense was a man who really had his heart in what he was doing'. The defence contention was that Lody had only done what any of them might have done in similar circumstances. Lody refused to say anything on his own behalf, or plead for mercy; but he took the opportunity to praise the treatment he had received at Wellington Barracks. Before he was shot, with eyes unbandaged at his own request, he said to the Assistant Provost-Marshal, 'I suppose you will not shake hands with a spy?' The officer replied, 'I'll shake hands with a brave man.' Lody met his death, as did ten others, in the garrison rifle range in Mint Street at the Tower, where spies were also executed in World War Two.

Sir Basil Thomson, who describes Lody as 'a good example of the patriotic spy', has left an account of many others who were arrested. One, who spoke bad English and was incompetent, hanged himself in Brixton Gaol. The later spies tended to be from neutral lands, among them Peru, Uruguay, Sweden and Norway. The lesson to be drawn from their fate was that suspicious citizens, though quick to denounce the innocent for silly reasons, were sometimes right after all. A fellow boarder of the Norwegian, in Bloomsbury, thought that anyone so taciturn, with apparently so much on his mind, must be an enemy and reported him to the police. And while many alien bakers had bricks unreasonably hurled through their windows, there was a baker in High Street, Deptford, who fully merited such treatment, since he was operating an enemy postbox. So was a barber in Caledonian Road, London.

Three men of distinction learned with varying surprise that they had been shot in the Tower. Prince Louis of Battenberg, dislodged from the post of First Sea Lord because of his alien birth (Chapter Eight), used to make a joke of it: 'Didn't you know I was executed last week?' A Pittsburgh report said that Sir Robert Baden-Powell had faced the firing squad 'without a quiver' after being convicted of hawking documents to the enemy – 'England has put into his last sleep one of the bravest soldiers who ever headed her armies in foreign lands.' The Chief Scout felt it worth being shot to earn such an epitaph. Claude Grahame-White, the pioneer airman, was similarly the victim of a press muddle ('Airman Dies At Hand Of Executioner'), possibly caused by his efforts to clear the name of his friend Gustav Hamel, falsely accused of defecting to Germany before the war. The German agent von Rintelen was also reported to have been

shot in the Tower. At the time he was in the German officers'
camp at Donnington Hall, suspected by his comrades of having
been planted to report on escape plots. The news of his death
disarmed them and they played Chopin's *Funeral March* in his
honour.

CHAPTER 5

CALLING ALL SWEETHEARTS

The Earl of Lonsdale, who has already figured in these pages, sat down one night in Lowther Castle to compose a recruiting poster. The first line came easily and really said it all: ARE YOU A MAN OR ARE YOU A MOUSE? This was followed by: 'Are you a man who will for ever be handed down to posterity as a Gallant Patriot . . . or as a Rotter and Coward?' The appeal ended with the Earl's 'humble advice' to enlist at once and was printed in his racing colours.

The poster is not mentioned in the Earl's authorised biography but is reproduced in Douglas Sutherland's *The Yellow Earl*. According to Sutherland the Mayor of Whitehaven was sufficiently angered by the tone of this exhortation, which seemed to him to reflect on the patriotism of the region, that he drove to the Castle to protest.

When the first frenzy of volunteering died down, a breadwinner in Britain could not walk far without having his manhood impugned, if not by his ground landlord then certainly by the Liberal Government. As he left work he saw in his neighbours' windows, masking the aspidistra, cards which read:

THIS HOUSE HAS SENT A MAN TO
FIGHT FOR KING AND COUNTRY

Alternatively, there might be a disc which read:

NOT AT HOME
A MAN FROM THIS HOUSE NOW SERVING IN THE FORCES

Some homes might even boast of having sent two, three or more men to the Front. Perhaps the cards were merely an expression of legitimate pride; but to a man with an uneasy conscience it did not seem so.

Then came the posters. There was nothing ambiguous about their message; they were hortatory and hectoring at the same time and with every week that passed their language became less subtle, more vulgar. Lord Lonsdale would have been proud of them. The more fastidious Liberals in the Government probably deplored their tone, while regarding the idea of conscription as even more distasteful.

The first recruiting calls had been simple and old-fashioned, with phrases like 'Your King And Country Need You', 'A Call To Arms' and 'Rally Round The Flag', all ending up with 'God Save The King'. Nobody objected to these except H. G. Wells, who professed to have been incensed by a poster in which the King called on 'My People'. He said: 'This abrupt realisation that the King was placing himself at the head of the people was like a bomb bursting under my nose.' Equal if not greater offence should have been caused in this patriotic breast by the famous Kitchener poster, 'Your Country Needs YOU', in which the warlord seemed to be usurping the monarch's role.

The straight call to service was good enough while patriotic fervour remained high, but as the shine went off the great adventure men decided that, patriotic as they were, they would 'wait to be fetched'. After all, the Army was restoring to mines and factories thousands who should never have been allowed to join up, so it seemed reasonable to let the Army sort out its confusions. The Army, however, had its sights inexorably on seventy divisions, preferably all volunteers. So the recruiters, rolling up their sleeves, varied the appeal to pride, honour, manliness and vengeance with warnings to eschew shame, disgrace, betrayal, sloth and cowardice. From a poster showing the ruins of Belgium a woman asked, 'Will you go or must I?' Under a photograph of the dead Lord Roberts ran the message, 'He Did His Duty. Will You Do Yours?' The breadwinner was asked, 'Is Your Conscience Clear?', 'Is Anyone Proud Of You?', 'Are YOU Doing Your Bit?', 'Are You The Man To Be Pitied?', 'Have You A Reason Or Only An Excuse?' He was urged, 'Sing God Save The King With A Gun In Your Hands'.

He was told to 'Be A Man'. He was then informed that there were three kinds of men: '. . . those who Hear the Call and Obey; those who delay; and the Others.' He was warned, 'It Is More Blessed To Go Than Be Pushed'. And he was invited to ponder how, in years to come, he would answer the question, 'Daddy, What Did YOU Do In The Great War?' (Robert Smillie, the pacifist miners' leader, said his reply would be: 'I tried to stop the bloody thing, my child.')

The middle and upper classes were faced with 'Five Questions' for themselves: 'Have You a Butler, Groom, Chauffeur, Gardener or Gamekeeper serving *you* who at this moment should be serving your King and Country? Have you a man serving at your table who should be serving a gun? Have you a man digging your garden who should be digging trenches? Have you a man driving your car who should be driving a transport wagon? Have you a man preserving your game who should be helping to preserve your country?' These were good questions and there must have been ribald spirits who would have liked to see similar questions addressed to the lower orders: 'Have you a landlord shooting pheasants when he should be shooting Huns? Have you a mistress nursing a lapdog who should be nursing wounded soldiers?'

Irishmen, as always, presented a special problem. They were a quarrelsome lot, so why not appeal to their fighting spirit? 'Join the Army today and prove that through *your* veins flows the Irish blood that has made the Irish fighting tradition famous through the world.' They were great people for paying off scores, so they were invited to 'Avenge the *Lusitania*' (torpedoed off the Irish coast). They were ardent Papists, so why not excite them with news of 'what Germans have done to the Churches, Priests, Women and Children of Belgium'? One poster told how 'the sacred vessels which had not been put in safety did not escape profanation', and how a pigsty had been emptied of pigs and filled with thirteen insulted priests. 'Men of Ireland,' concluded this poster, 'the sanctity of your Churches, the safety of your Homes, the Honour of your Women can only be secured by Defeating the Germans in Belgium.'

Many citizens wondered where the Government recruited the recruiters, the men who, in the hour of peril, did not flinch from teaching mothers to despise their sons and to sow dissensions between sweethearts. Would they dare to emulate Sergeant Hammond of the 14th Light Dragoons who, in Napoleonic times, directed his appeal to 'all you with too much wife'? The recruiters did not blush wholly unseen, for in the *Tatler* appeared a photograph of Hedley le Bas, director of the Caxton Publishing Company, who was described as 'the moving spirit in the wonderful recruiting publicity campaign, the success of which has probably averted the need for conscription'. Le Bas, a former regular soldier and the first advertising man to be knighted, has said that Kitchener was 'a little suspicious about the popular appeals that departed so drastically from traditions he had respected all his life'. He and his fellow practitioners were accused of selling patriotism as if it were pills or soap. The *Bystander*, which had its serious moments, complained on December 9, 1914, that the nation had lost its dignity and that the enemy were interpreting the recruiting pressures as a sign that Britain's heart was not in the war: 'Men who put on uniform as a result of exhortation by squires, parsons, retired officers, employers, schoolmasters, leader-writers, politicans, cartoonists, poets, music-hall singers and old women of both sexes are not volunteers; they are conscripts, but conscripted by the wrong people in the wrong way. They have gone in because it would have been so infernally unpleasant to have stayed out.' The *New Statesman* on September 4, 1915, objected to the Government's use of the language of the music-halls, the cheapening of honest emotions. How, one wonders, would the Webbs have framed a call to arms?

An appeal to the 'Young Women of London' especially irked the *New Statesman*:

'Is your "Best Boy" wearing khaki? If not, DON'T YOU THINK he should be? If he does not think that you and your country are worth fighting for – do you think he is WORTHY of you? Don't pity the girl who is alone – her young man is probably a soldier – fighting for her and her country – and for YOU. If your young man neglects his duty to his King and Country, the time may come when he will NEGLECT YOU. Think it over – then ask him to JOIN THE ARMY TODAY.'

Another exhortation ran:

'SWEETHEARTS: If you cannot persuade him to answer his country's call and protect you now, DISCHARGE HIM as unfit!'

And another:

'When the war is over and your husband or your son is asked. "What did you do in the Great War?" is he to hang his head because *you* would not let him go?'

Some of the crudest psychological pressure on women was applied by women. Baroness Orczy, creator of the 'Scarlet Pimpernel', founded the Active Service League, which urged women to sign the following pledge:

'At this hour of England's grave peril and desperate need I do hereby pledge myself most solemnly in the name of my King and Country to persuade every man I know to offer his services to the country, and I also pledge myself never to be seen in public with any man who, being in every way fit and free for service, has refused to respond to his country's call.'

Today, the harping on England's peril might seem no way to win recruits from Scotland, Wales or Ireland; but England was unabashedly used for Britain in those days, not least by poets (even in World War Two the song went, *There'll Always Be An England*). In any event, the Baroness had the excuse that she was born in Hungary. It was now an enemy nation, but her readers obviously trusted her, for they signed her pledge in hundreds and some may even have honoured it. In her autobiography she omits to mention this episode in her life.

The Mothers' Union urged its members to say: 'My boy, I don't want you to go, but if I were you I should go.' On his return, hearts would beat high with thankfulness and pride. If, however, God had 'another plan for him' . . .

'. . . you will have a yet deeper cause for thankfulness that he is among the long roll of English heroes, ever to be held in highest honour while the English name lasts, and better – far better even than that – the welcome of the King of Kings will greet him – "Well done, good and faithful servant, enter thou into the joy of thy Lord." '

The notion of distributing white feathers to young men (a symbol of cowardice made familiar by A. E. W. Mason's *The Four Feathers*, 1902) is supposed to have come from an admiral at a recruiting rally in Folkestone. One of the earliest distributions, less than a month from the outbreak of war, was at Deal, where the Town Cryer was induced to shout:'Oyez! Oyez! The White Feather Brigade. Ladies wanted to present to young men of Deal and Walmer who have no one dependent on them the Order of the White Feather for shirking their duty in not offering their services to uphold the Union Jack of Old England. God Save The King!' Before the announcement was cried, a number of young men had been befeathered without realising the significance of the decoration. Handing out these insults was a healthy open-air game in which hoydens and old ladies could for once unite. The former delighted to embarrass young men of a higher social class and the latter gave them out indiscriminately to teach the lesson that it is the duty of youth to die for age. Compton Mackenzie had a theory that 'idiotic young women' were using white feathers to get rid of boyfriends of whom they were tired. In autobiographies one may read of receiving feathers but never of giving them. Lord Brockway claims to have had a collection which he spread out like a fan; others tell of receiving them when they were schoolboys. According to Daphne Fielding, the capricious Rosa Lewis, who ran the Cavendish Hotel, 'distributed white feathers indiscriminately, sometimes making terrible gaffes, and Kippy, her Aberdeen terrier, was trained to fly at the heels of any man not in uniform'. In Parliament, Cathcart Wason asked the Home Secretary if he was aware that State employees were subject to 'insolence and provocation at the hands of some advertising young women presenting them with white feathers', and whether he would authorise the arrest of such persons for conduct likely to disrupt the peace. Reginald McKenna agreed that the practice was unlikely to aid recruiting, but felt the danger of disorder was slight. However, it emerged that thousands of dock workers at Chatham were being issued with protective badges testifying that they were serving King and Country.

The author of *The Unspeakable Scot*, T. W. H. Crosland, wrote a song called *The White Feather Legion*:

> Yes, somehow and somewhere and always,
>   We're first when the shoutings begin,
> We put up a howl for Old England
>   The Kaiser can hear in Berlin,
>   Dear boys!
>   He hears it and quakes in Berlin.

> Yes, a health to ourselves as we scatter
>   In taxis to get the last train,
> Cheer oh, for the White Feather Legion
>   Goes back to its females again,
>   Regards!
>   Goes back to its slippers again,
>   Hurrah!
> The Bass and the lager again,
>   Here's how!

And so on.

For the man not in uniform, the hazards of the streets included women in mourning, with reproachful looks and some-times accusing words. He might run foul of noisy recruiting parties, with military bands, tots bearing placards saying 'My Dad's At The Front' and strong-armed recruiting sergeants doing their best to hustle him off to the enlisting office. Refuge could be hard to find. In Hyde Park, London, cantered Winifred and Ivy Mulroney, two Irish sisters in semi-military uniform, their saddle-cloths proclaiming 'Do Not Hesitate: To Arms: King And Country', who bore down on young men and urged them to join up. Nancy Astor had her own way of applying pressure. Driving with Sylvia Pankhurst to Cliveden from the local station she espied a young horseman, put her head through the window and shrieked, 'Charlie McCartney, pride of the knuts! Why aren't you in uniform?'

Feminine blackmail could find an outlet in the Personal Columns of newspapers. In *The Times* of July 8, 1915, appeared this warning: 'Jack F. G. If you are not in khaki by the 20th I shall cut you dead. Ethel M.' The Berlin correspondent of the *Cologne Gazette* telegraphed a translation of this item to his journal and made the threat read, 'I shall hack you to death' – '*hacke ich dich zu Tode*').

Since war is a vulgar business it was right that the leading unofficial recruiter should have been the greatest vulgarian of the day. Horatio Bottomley, editor of *John Bull*, was sufficiently moved by the spirit of 1914 to inform his friends that he was making a complete break with his 'sordid past'. His ambition was to be Director of Recruiting, preferably with a seat in the

Cabinet, but he was tactfully assured by Asquith that he would be more use to the country in an unofficial capacity. The public who cheered the patriotic speeches of the People's Tribune were unaware of the high fees he received for delivering them (between £50 and £100 a meeting, sometimes more). He would have defended himself by saying that the advertising men who turned out the poster slogans did not work for nothing. To the suggestion that he ought to be in the trenches he had his answer ready: he was suffering from the two complaints of Anno Domini and Embonpoint. The first meant that he had been born too soon (1860) and the second that his chest had got into the wrong place.

West End impresarios were not blind to the appeal of Bottomley. He 'starred' in Seymour Hicks's *England Expects* at the London Opera House in September 1914, alongside Phyllis Dare singing, 'We don't want to lose you, but we think you ought to go', and actors declaiming *The Charge of the Light Brigade*. Thousands failed to get in. At a Grand Patriotic Rally at the Albert Hall in January 1915, police precautions which had been adequate for Lloyd George, Asquith and Churchill were unequal to the occasion; Bottomley himself had to struggle for nearly two hours for admission. The organiser, C. B. Cochran, says: 'I had to keep the meeting going with speakers I found in the hall, selections by the orchestra and Charles Coborn singing *Two Lovely Black Eyes* in several languages.' On occasions like these, recruiting officers attended and young men rushed to dedicate their lives as at a revival meeting.

Among Bottomley's proposals in the *Sunday Pictorial* in 1915 was one for mobilising the Empire: 'A Million Coloured Troops: Act Of Madness Not To Launch Them Against The Huns.' Another was for fighting the Germans with their own 'frightfulness': 'The Soul of Satan: No Hague Rules In Dealing With The Enemies Of Mankind.' In July of that year he felt his reputation strong enough to insert a full page advertisement in the *Pictorial* headed: MR HORATIO BOTTOMLEY: HIS EARLY RETURN TO PARLIAMENT. In this he appealed for readers to take up 60,000 £1 shares in his *John Bull* company. This was 'to enable him to adjust his business affairs', in other words to win his discharge from bankruptcy, though that word was not mentioned. 'Representations have been made to him from important quarters', said the advertisement, 'as to placing his services at the disposal of the State and he has therefore decided upon the present plan of removing all obstacles to his return to St Stephen's.' The office he coveted was thought to be that of the Duchy of Lancaster.

Bottomley's exhortations from the music-hall stage were little different in style and content from those of the martial Bishop of London. When sufficiently moved, or as some say when sufficiently paid, he would invoke 'the patient figure of the Prince of Peace, pointing to the Star of Bethlehem that leads us back to God'. He went to the Front on a conducted tour and reported back to the *Sunday Pictorial*: 'I have been in Hell – and from its depths have seen the striking splendour of Heaven. In the scorching and blackened track of the Devil I have met with God.' He was even willing to act as spokesman for the Almighty. Among *The Great Thoughts of Horatio Bottomley* (a wartime collection) is a declaration which could have been inspired only at the highest level: 'Every hero of this war who has fallen in the field of battle has performed an Act of Greatest Love, so penetrating and intense in its purifying character that I do not hesitate to express my opinion that any and every past sin is automatically wiped out from the record of his life.'

To a government reluctant to abandon the idea of 'voluntaryism' the sight of young men urged into the cannon's mouth by the Prince of Bankrupts, in league with the Prince of Peace, seems to have caused no more distress than the vision of youths being recruited with a sticky kiss from a plump monocled actress strutting the boards pretending to be a subaltern.

The heroic verse which had flooded the newspapers in the first weeks of war was subsiding in 1915; young men were no longer enjoined to seek glory as the bridegroom seeks the bride. Henry Newbolt, William Watson, Alfred Noyes and Laurence Binyon had all done their stint in the newspapers; and Kipling's first war poem in *The Times*, *For All We Have And Are*, had firmly designated the enemy as the Hun. There were streaks of gold among the fustian. It is not easy (though many have tried) to rend Rupert Brooke for writing:

Honour has come back, as a king, to earth,
  And paid his subjects with a royal wage;
And Nobleness walks in our ways again;
  And we have come into our heritage.

The Poet Laureate, Robert Bridges, envisaged a nation clean-
sed by suffering, winning to 'beauty through blood'. To Sir
Edmund Gosse, however, the war meant clarification through
blood. In the *Edinburgh Review* of October 1914 he wrote:
'War is the great scavenger of thought. It is the sovereign disin-
fectant and its red stream of blood is the Condy's Fluid that
cleans out the stagnant pools and clotted channels of the intellect.' In this curious belief Gosse was on his own.

One of the best remembered poems of the war, John
McCrae's *In Flanders Fields the Poppies Grow*, appeared in
Punch in late 1915; it was given no display but is remembered
when all the polished war verse of that journal's editor, Sir
Owen Seaman, is forgotten. Strangely, the closing lines of the
poem have recently incurred severe displeasure from Professor
Paul Fussell, of Rutgers University, who condemns as
'recruiting poster rhetoric' the warning, 'If ye break faith with us
who die, We shall not sleep. . . .' Words like 'vicious' and
'stupid', he feels, would not seem too strong for this propaganda
against a negotiated peace.

The journalist Harold Begbie had the common touch, some
said a very common touch. His *Fall In* developed a popular
recruiting theme and was sung from many a platform:

How will you fare, sonny, how will you fare
  In the far-off winter night,
When you sit by the fire in an old man's chair
  And your neighbours talk of the fight?
Will you slink away, as it were from a blow,
  Your old head shamed and bent?
Or say, 'I was not with the first to go,
  But I went, thank God, I went'?

The very young did not escape poetic blandishment. Anthony
Powell in *Infants Of The Spring* remembers (as does the present
writer) a pervasive poem which asked:

What can a little chap do
For his country and for you?
  What CAN a little chap do?

  This poem, by John Oxenham, appeared in 1915 in *Princess
Mary's Gift Book*, one of the numerous handsome volumes,
royally sponsored, to which authors were expected to contribute
free. It was also reprinted as a child's copy-book. In reply to the
question, 'What can a little chap do?' were such suggestions as:

He can shun all that's mean,
He can keep himself clean,
Both without and within –
  That's another good thing he can do.

Though his years be but few
He can march in the queue
Of the Good and the Great,
Who battled with fate
And won through –
  That's a wonderful thing he can do.

His soul he can brace
Against everything base,
And the trace will be seen
All his life in his face –
  That's a very fine thing he can do.

  It was an easy poem to learn by heart, but what exactly the
little chap was meant to do, and not to do, to win the war never
really became clear.
  Nothing high-faluting appealed to the soldiers on their route
marches. As early as October 1914 they were reported to be
singing (to the incredulity of the Germans):

Send out the boys of the Old Brigade,
  Who made Old England free,
Send out my mother, my sister and my brother,
  But for Gawd's sake don't sent me.

An even better song for satiric moments on the road would have been America's hit song of 1915:

> I didn't raise my son to be a soldier,
>   I brought him up to be my pride and joy,
> Who dares to put a musket on his shoulder
>   To kill some other mother's darling boy?
> The nations ought to arbitrate their quarrels,
>   It's time to put the sword and gun away.
> There'd be no war today if the nations all would say,
>   'I didn't raise my son to be a soldier.'

CHAPTER 6

'DEAR BELGIANS!'

Asked why she had made her hero, Hercule Poirot, a Belgian, Dame Agatha Christie explained that he was created in World War One, when Belgians abounded in Britain. It was a gesture to a stricken ally. Perhaps it was also a shrewd move to gain goodwill for a character who might otherwise have been dismissed as just another funny Frenchman.

The vanguard of almost a quarter of a million Belgians fled to England as the Kaiser's armies broke through to Antwerp and Ostend. Their numbers exceeded those of the fugitives from the French Revolution; they were the biggest flood of flotsam since the Huguenots were expelled by Louis XIV. At the height of the influx there was excited talk of founding a New Flanders in Britain or in French-speaking Canada.

As a social and administrative problem the refugees were comparable to the evacuees of World War Two, and like the evacuees they became a source of friction; but one need only ask what sort of problems would have arisen if a quarter of a million Londoners or Clydesiders had found themselves unwilling guests of any European country for four years.

Before the war the liberal view of Belgium had been slightly clouded by the revelations of atrocities in the Belgian Congo, but the reports of German atrocities in Belgium cleaned the slate. From that moment 'plucky little Belgium' rode high in the public estimation; probably no other country was ever clutched so fervently to John Bull's bosom. The Belgian flag flew beside the Union Jack and in patriotic tableaux the maid personifying Belgium raised an even bigger cheer than Marianne. Much quoted were the words of King Albert: 'A country which defends itself commands the respect of all; that country does not perish.'

Folkestone was the closely-guarded gate through which most of the Belgians squeezed into Britain; other gates, like Lowestoft, were closed for fear that infiltrating spies might escape scrutiny. The first wave were the well-to-do, fresh from burying or bricking up their non-portable treasures. Then came the floods of the forcibly dispossessed, crammed aboard Channel steamers, colliers, dredgers, yachts and rowing boats. All ran the gauntlet of mines. There were seasick, shivering old women in slippers, with all their possessions tied up in a blanket; there were young women with new-born babies; there were terrified children cowering away from strange voices, shepherded by priests. According to one account there were also 'young girls with flushed cheeks and wild, terrified eyes, whose story others whispered under their breath. They were the victims of German lust. They shrank with horror from the thought that they might become the mothers of the enemy's children.' For the people of Britain it was a problem as unfamiliar as it was horrifying. There was always the unspeakable thought: how long before it happens to us?

For the Government, the problem was whether to segregate or assimilate. The Home Secretary, Reginald McKenna, abandoned his first idea of building huge camps, possibly in Southern Ireland. The alternative was to make initial use of all those potential repositories for displaced persons to be found in any civilised state: barns, exhibition halls, skating rinks, racecourses, palaces, pavilions, armouries, warehouses and workhouses, besides hotels and boarding houses. Once that was done, the refugees could be siphoned off into billets or hostels, or into domestic service. Fortunately a singularly efficient voluntary organisation, the War Refugees Committee, inspired by Lady Lugard, wife of the colonial administrator, Mrs Alfred Lyttelton and Viscount Gladstone, sprang into existence and was backed by similar bodies. With the approval of the Local Government Board, some 2,500 local reception committees were set up, charged with finding homes for the outcast.

In Folkestone, some refugees ate their first meals in the homes of local fishermen and beds were laid down in Scout huts and church halls; but with arrivals of thousands a day – 26,000 in one week – quick dispersal was essential. Here the human problems began to multiply. Families, often a dozen strong, were anxious not to be broken up; the classes were by no means eager to be mixed; Walloons and Flemings continued to detest each other, even in adversity; and priests and nuns had to be housed in establishments purged of the opposite sex. The problems of communication were daunting; not only Flemish peasants but Antwerp's Russian Jews and Moroccan carpet-sellers looked blank when English schoolboys interrogated them in fifth-form French. Among the refugees were those who could be given second-hand clothes and those who could only be given money to buy new clothes. Helpers assumed that the first thing any refugee would want was a cup of tea, but they were wrong. The women also spurned gifts of woollen combinations, regarding them as the essence of *anti-chic*.

Stories abounded of Belgian children whose hands had been cut off by the invader. Folkestone received many enquiries as to whether any *petits mutilés* had been sighted, but could not report any. One enquiry was from a surgeon wishing to experiment with an artificial hand. An offer of £1,000 from America for the discovery of such a victim was said to have been a German propaganda exercise.

At the beginning it was the correct thing to accept Belgians under one's roof. The Countess of Warwick, former paramour of Edward VII, was not too busy with her plot to extract money from the Royal Family* to welcome Belgians to her tithe barn at Easton Lodge. Among refugees accepted by Lady Ottoline Morrell in the wildly unsuitable atmosphere of Garsington Manor was sixteen-year-old Maria Nys, who later swallowed chloride to attract attention, was sent to Newnham College but ran away to London, and eventually became the first wife of Aldous Huxley. Henry James allowed his home at Rye to be used as a gathering place for Belgians. In London he befriended refugees in Crosby Hall, an ancient building recently removed from Bishopsgate and re-erected in Sir Thomas More's old

*She wanted to sell letters from Edward VII but was legally prevented from doing so in July 1915.

Chelsea garden; a transplanted home for a transplanted people and offering 'the finest club conditions conceivable'. James had not long to live and his efforts to exchange small talk with inarticulate exiles do him credit.

Lady Lugard set up a series of large houses, each for a separate social or professional group – academics, lawyers, businessmen and so on. Each house had its own servants and resident woman manager. It was no way to sit out four years of war and many of the occupants found employment of some kind; but some remained dazed, mourning their losses and bereft of initiative, accepting free relief and the continuing prospect of it as a natural right. The more resilient and volatile frequented cafés in the West End of London, talking loudly about what they would do when Germany had been defeated. Shopkeeper refugees were quick to open *pâtisseries* and waffle shops. Journalists lost no time in starting up newspapers. In 1915 there were even plays staged by the Belgians in the West End: *La Kommandatur*, which portrayed Brussels under occupation, and *Zonneslag et Cie*, a farce about a Brussels gentleman's adventures in an Ostend hotel.

Self-supporting Belgians moved in some strength into Bloomsbury. In *The Times* they found small advertisements in French, offering accommodation *comme chez soi, près British Museum*, or *près église et chapelle*, with *tables séparées* and *bonne table copieuse*, preferably for refugees *de bonne education*. In Finsbury Park *une dame écossaise* offered *tous les avantages du home*. Other lures were *compagnie toujours gaie* and *volaille de notre basse-cour et légumes de notre potager*. One or two offered *leçons d'anglais si l'on désire*, others requested *Rep. en anglais si pos*. As a public service *The Times* translated readers' advertisements free.

In London, to meet the first influx, both Alexandra Palace and Earl's Court were taken over, along with the Aldwych skating rink. Earl's Court remained a War Refugees Camp throughout the war, housing mostly Belgians but also Serbs, Poles, Italians and Russians. The compound covered some thirty-five acres and was intersected by three railway lines. The day before the first refugees arrived the turnstiles were still clicking for a *Sunny Spain* exhibition. There were relics of many earlier displays, including a Doge's Palace, a pagoda café, a ducal hall, a German beer garden, a water chute, an aerial railway and two menageries (which the Belgian children had no wish to see dispersed). The Empress Hall was the principal shelter, but beds were also erected under the arches and on the stairs of the aerial railway. Among the peasants in blue overalls and sabots, straight from their fields, was a circus performer who had lugged with him the cannon from which he propelled his wife. Others had been content to bring sewing machines, coffee grinders, dogs, poultry and parrots. One old woman sat on endlessly, surrounded by her luggage, saying she would stay there until the next boat home; another woman, with boxes of clothes, sallied out daily, ill-dressed, cadging more garments; and a male refugee called assiduously at every charity he could locate. Eventually the permanent residents of Earl's Court, which was administered with good sense by the Metropolitan Asylums Board, were whittled down to those who, for various reasons, found work hard to get and mothers of large families. To occupy idle hands, kitchen industries were started up, among them shirt-making and basket-making, and there were workshops for tinsmiths and carpenters. It may not have added up to 'the finest club conditions imaginable', but there were such necessities as a school, a concert room and a cinema. Among those who passed through this camp were fur-coated Belgian Canadians who had come over 'to kill twenty Boches each and then go home'; Serbs who had escaped from German prison camps; small parties of Montenegrins and Rumanians; Greek soldiers; gypsies from all over Europe; and finally Russians who had fled the Bolsheviks and escaped via Murmansk. In all nearly 100,000 foreigners found a temporary home in Earl's Court. German propaganda represented it as a prison camp full of starving wretches.

Belgian teachers found no great difficulty in finding employment as the call-up emptied Britain's staff rooms. There were also the refugee children to teach. The headmaster of Eton announced that Belgian boys of good family would be considered and twenty-one of them were in residence early in 1915; but to judge from a question in Parliament they were finding it difficult to worship in their own faith. Dora Russell has told how Girton took in three or four Belgian girls, who were too lively for that strict foundation and were packed off to study in London.

In contrast, some of the refugees were of an unearthly simplicity. A family was sent, on invitation, to the village of Kelly, near Tavistock, but 'whether it was the steepness of the hill, or because there are many trees in the vicinity, the fact remains that on arrival father, mother and child sat down and wept, declaring that they could not possibly stay, as there were wolves in the forest'. They were fisherfolk who had never seen a hill or wood and they had to be returned to the coast.

Most of the Belgians, as the newspapers kept saying, were by nature industrious and that was what worried the trade unions; the last thing they wanted was an inrush of hard-working foreigners. Miners in Yorkshire and Wales made it clear that refugees would be unwelcome. The Government was much exercised by this problem. A handbook issued to all Belgians urged them not to take British workers' jobs, or to work for wages below the accepted standard. They were steered away from the Kentish hop fields, traditionally reserved for the poor of London; and the Government decided not to use them in activities like land reclamation or afforestation which could be detrimental to the long-term interests of British labour. However, much goodwill and resourcefulness were shown in attempts to tap the available skills. Cloth-makers in Yorkshire remembered that their industry sprang from the Low Countries and found jobs for a few weavers. Selfridges were ready to recruit lace-makers and craftsmen who specialised in 'dainty gong frames'. *The Times* wondered whether some of the refugees could not usefully teach their hosts more efficient dairy methods. Many useful jobs had to be refused because they were in defence areas, prohibited even to friendly aliens. Thanks to local initiative, small workshops were set up in many towns where refugees could make furniture, leather goods or clothes; sometimes the raw materials were provided by the Belgian Government, which then accepted the finished products. Gradually the drain of Britain's manpower into the Services allowed the refugees to be absorbed into industry, even into the pits.

The refugee who put the British Government to shame was the industrialist Charles Pelabon. Only three weeks after closing his factories in Merxem, in the path of the Germans, he had acquired a hangar at Teddington, on the Thames, and was preparing to manufacture shells for the Belgian Army. The hangar was too small, so he took over an unfinished skating rink at Twickenham and began extending it, wing by wing, into a sizeable arsenal. Justin Wallon, in *Une Cité Belge Sur la Tamise*, claims that this was the first new shell factory to go into production. The site was not one where industry would normally have been welcomed, so Pelabon was at pains to preserve such amenities as he could. The local 'Town Advancement Association' welcomed the Belgian influx, as it had nearly 600 houses to let thanks to the war, including luxury villas and '*châteaux*'. In due course 6,000 Belgians, many of them Pelabon's own skilled workers, were employed at the Twickenham plant. The streets of nearby Richmond echoed the sounds of café life; some fifty shops underwent a change of nationality and the signs proclaimed *alimentation*, *charcuterie*, *pâtisserie*, *épicerie liégeoise*, *boucherie chevaline*, *moules*, *frites*, and *le kip-kap bruxellois*, to be followed by *bijouterie*, *horlogerie* and all the rest. At Richmond Bridge vendors waved *L'Indépendance*, *La Métropole* and *La Belgique Nouvelle*. Belgian Grenadiers played on the Green, Belgian Boy Scouts bugled. Only the Manikin Pis was lacking.

Wallon's account does not gloss over the strains caused by the clash of cultures in Richmond-on-Meuse. Some landlords said 'No Belgians'. The newcomers were noisy, over-gesticulatory, given to chewing quids of tobacco and spitting elsewhere than in their handkerchieves. In short, many were *médiocrement gentlemen* and their women went about hatless; but at least their ranks had been purged of work-shy martyrs. Readers familiar with the vagaries of the Bloomsbury Group will know that it was in the house of a Belgian landlady, on Richmond Green, that Virginia and Leonard Woolf took rooms in 1914, along with hearty refugees who demanded *une belle table copieuse*; one of them was a count who spat elsewhere than in his handkerchief, namely in the bath. In these insensitive surroundings Virginia lost her reason.

Another Belgian firm, that of Kryn et Lahy, converted 'an immense meadow of spring flowers' into a steelworks in little more than two months in 1915; and all this, according to Armand Varler in *Les Belges en Exil*, while British firms struggled impotently to expand. However, by this time, despite union hostility, nearly 1,000 Belgians were working for Vickers at Barrow, and eventually this firm had 3,000 on the payroll, in one works or another. In 1915 Lloyd George tried to shame the Trade Union Congress at Bristol by revealing that at Enfield, Woolwich and Coventry Belgian workers had been warned not to work so strenuously. Eventually, in the service of the war machine, 'Little Belgiums', with names like Albertville and Elizabethville, could be found sprinkled all over industrial Britain. At the end of the war 2,000 Belgians worked in the National Projectile Factory at Birtley, Durham. At various times the Germans tried to convince neutrals that the Belgians in Britain were exploited like coolies in Ceylon.

Sadly, many a book of reminiscences testifies to the gradual, sometimes sudden, cooling of relations with *les braves Belges*. Baroness Orczy was there to welcome the refugees who descended on Maidstone 'like locusts ... expecting everything, demanding everything, every attention, every comfort. Dear Belgians! How we loved them, how we pitied them, how we were all of us happy to do what we could for them . . . for a long time.' And how glad they were, in the end, when the authorities ordered all Belgians from the area for security reasons. Sir John Wheeler-Bennett has said that his mother knew better than to introduce Belgian guests into her house, for his father, while public-spirited, believed an Englishman's home to be his castle. She therefore installed refugees in a separate house where they quarrelled and then one night 'levanted in several directions and we never saw them again'. Hostesses compared notes about their troublemakers (as, in World War Two, about each other's evacuees) and it even became a joke to ask, 'How are your Belgian atrocities?'

That handbook issued to the refugees had warned about insensitive behaviour: 'Friendliness may easily become familiarity; unceremoniousness, disorder; and old habits, eccentricity.' One who did not read his handbook carefully, perhaps, was M. Van der Pant, the engineer from Antwerp who figures in H. G. Wells's semi-autobiographical novel, *Mr Britling Sees It Through*. (He was probably based on one of the Countess of Warwick's refugees at Easton Lodge, in the grounds of which Wells lived.) Though outwardly amiable enough, Van der Pant

became too critical of English inadequacies and inefficiencies:
the slow telegraph service, the lackadaisical labourers, the ways
of pig-keeping, the tortuousness of the lanes, the lack of cafés.
Fair criticism in its way, but not to be accepted from a foreigner,
so Mr Britling spent his time trying, in an unfamiliar tongue, to
defend 'the subtle estimableness of all that was indolent,
wasteful and evasive in English life'.

A few Belgians let it be known that they thought the British
intervention in Europe had been late and inadequate. A tempting riposte was to ask what able-bodied young Belgians were
doing in Britain, the sort of refugees towards whom Princess
Clementine of Belgium was 'cold and distant' when visiting a
colony near Guildford. To be fair, most of these young men
went back to fight under the Belgian colours. Since the refugees
were an urban cross-section, it was inevitable that misfits should
be found among them. Headlines like BELGIANS IN AFFRAY began
to appear in the press. The West London magistrate, fining
refugees for drunkenness, said, 'It looks as if we have the scum
of Belgium over here.' This caused deep offence and later the
magistrate joined those who praised the Belgians for their
industrious qualities.

In rural Wales there were also upsets. The Belgians found that
they were more hospitably received by Nonconformists than by
their fellow Roman Catholics. Some of them, billeted several
miles from the nearest priest, began looking in at the local
chapel, not realising, until informed so by their priest, that this
was a sin against the Holy Ghost. Dr J. Vyrnwy Morgan, shaking
his head over such matters, regretted that so many Belgians
were 'of low degree and low intelligence'. He noted that they
were becoming disillusioned with the Pope, Benedict XV, for
his apparent sympathy with the Germans.

A substantial number of Belgians, homesick, returned to their
country long before the end of the war, an exodus which caused
an anxious Member of Parliament to enquire whether this did
not constitute a security risk. Others were so happily integrated
that, a year after the war ended, the Belgian Government had to
appeal to the stragglers to return. For those exiles from the
fought-over areas it must have been a peculiarly dismal experience to read, year in, year out, of the battles which were blasting
their farms and villages to oblivion. If, sometimes, their morale

slumped, it was not surprising. Once again, it is necessary to do a mental reversal. If the population of Kent had been evacuated to Brabant, there to watch the Garden of England become the Cockpit of Europe, how long would they have kept that *flegme anglais*?

CHAPTER 7

THE KING'S ERROR

On March 14, 1916, the *Morning Post* carried this news item:

'At Southampton yesterday Robert Andrew Smith was fined £1 for treating his wife to a glass of wine in a local public-house. He said his wife gave him sixpence to pay for her drink. Mrs Smith was also fined £1 for consuming and Dorothy Brown, the barmaid, £5 for selling the intoxicant, contrary to the regulations of the Liquor Control Board.'

The lawless trio could not plead that they had been harshly dealt with, for the maximum penalty for defying the Government's 'No Treating' Order was six months' imprisonment. Of course, the Order had not been introduced to prevent husbands buying drinks for wives, but to counter the wasteful tyranny of 'Whose round is it?' among war workers and the standing of drinks to soldiers. If wives had been exempted from the order, publicans would have had to ask customers for their marriage lines. In fact, the 'No Treating' order did much to cut down heroic swilling by a nation whose foodstuffs were being squandered to produce drink.

When the war began, Russia had set Britain an example of austerity. The Czar, described in the *New Statesman* as 'the biggest dram-shop keeper in the world', had closed his 400 state distilleries and 28,000 spirit shops. In other words Russia was off the vodka and the peasants were even said to be putting their money into savings banks. These instant suppressions were possible in an autocracy, yet even France had prohibited the sale of absinthe. Britain, where war production was being hampered by drunkenness, made no attempt to curb the sale of spirits. By tradition, the first call of many a labourer, after leaving his home for work, was the public-house, which was open from dawn till midnight.

The teetotal lobbies were quick to hoist the flag of patriotism. By April 1915 King George was persuaded that a gesture in support of his cousin Nicholas would be well received. Under pressure from his over-excited Chancellor of the Exchequer, Lloyd George, he gave his famous pledge forswearing the consumption of liquor in his Household for the duration. He did so with reluctance and it was not long before he was complaining that he had been made a fool of (the German magazine *Simplicissimus* had a cartoon showing a whisky bottle being hurled from a turret of Windsor Castle, captioned 'Serious Times at Windsor'). Certainly it was one of the most fruitless acts of self-abnegation to be found in the pages of history. 'The failure of the Prime Minister to take the King's Pledge has naturally aroused comment,' said the *National Review*, but nobody seriously expected 'Squiff', as the hard-drinking Asquith was known, to make this supreme sacrifice. The far-from-teetotal F. E. Smith said to the Chancellor, 'My dear George, next time you see His Majesty I hope you will tell him with all respect that he isn't going to put a key on my wine cellar.' Kitchener, who had been urging the workers to abstain, followed the King's example, and so did Lord Haldane, while in ministerial office. The bars of the House of Commons remained as busy as ever; and if C. S. Forester's *The General* is any guide, society diners-out who suspected that their hostess had gone dry took their own liquor in flasks.

Early attempts were made to discourage people from pouring drink into soldiers. The Lord Mayor of Norwich put up a notice saying that Servicemen had been entertained 'beyond the bounds of prudence' and counselling restraint. One of the last acts of Lord Roberts was to issue an appeal on similar lines; the strain awaiting young men in France, he said, was one which 'only the strongest, physically and morally, can be trusted to endure'. Under early Defence Regulations commanding officers were allowed to shut down, or put out of bounds, public-houses in garrison and harbour areas; but military rule of this sort invited comparisons with the edicts of Cromwell's killjoy major-generals. Local authorities did what they could to shrink the span of permitted drinking hours. In London there was a much-criticised ban on selling drinks to women before 11.30 am. It was directed at soldiers' wives.

The main agitation against drunkenness was fed by revelations about conditions in arsenals and shipyards in early 1915. A few days before the shell-starved Battle of Neuve Chapelle Lloyd George had been maintaining, in a speech at Bangor, that drink was doing more damage to the war effort than all the U-boats. A month later he told the Shipbuilding Employers Federation: 'We are fighting Germans, Austrians and Drink, and so far as I can see the greatest of these deadly foes is Drink.' The shipbuilders, heads of war factories and Service leaders were quick to feed him with verbal ammunition. A battleship which put in for urgent repairs was ignored for twenty-four hours because the riveters refused to leave their public-houses; a transport needed for military service took twenty-two days to overhaul instead of the peacetime seven, and this because men could now earn in two or three days what would keep them in drink for a week. A Newcastle shipbuilder complained that double overtime on Sunday meant no atten-dance on Monday; he enunciated, and Lloyd George endorsed, what seemed to have become the first law of industry: the lower the wages, the better the time-keeping; the higher the wages, the worse the time-keeping. Out of the wilderness came the voice of Keir Hardie, attacking Lloyd George for representing the workers as 'drunken bullies'.

The Chancellor, a Blue Riband enthusiast in his youth, was mightily agitated by the problem. His difficulty was whether to press for total Prohibition or for a State-run restrictive mon-opoly of the drink trade; proposals which the Prime Minister dismissed as 'the twin poles of absurdity'. The first, thought Asquith, would lead to something like a universal strike; the second would merely waste a badly needed £250 million (the estimated cost of nationalisation) and introduce corruption. Lloyd George, in the Premier's view, had 'completely lost his head on drink'.

The anti-drink crusaders were losing their heads too. In response to an appeal to the public to tell him their views on

Prohibition, Lloyd George received more than 250,000 letters, which had to be sifted from the ordinary mail. Clamour for Prohibition inevitably led to the buying-up of liquor by those who could afford to do so. From A. J. Balfour came the suggestion that the consumption of drink should be prohibited except with meals. For their part, teetotallers found abhorrent the notion of the State trading in liquor and making a profit from it and were shocked that Lloyd George could contemplate such a thing. The Chancellor took the editors of the Liberal newspapers to lunch and asked what they thought of buying up the drink trade; only the *Daily Chronicle* objected. The more independent *Daily Express* took the popular line that pits and boiler rooms were thirstier places than throne rooms; surely the Government did not want to drive workers to methylated spirits?

Late in April 1915 Lloyd George mounted one of his famous Parliamentary performances to call for higher duties on liquor. He asked what was the use of commandeering factories and supplies when the power to use them fully was ruined by human weakness. The real pressure for action, he was careful to point out, was coming not from teetotallers but from industry, transport and the Services. He even read out shamefaced letters by drunkards employed in the shipyards, the sort of confessions normally reserved for temperance rallies. None of it impressed the Irish Members, who could think only of the hardship that would be caused by increased liquor duties to Irish distilleries and the threat of unemployment to the 8,000 heads of families who worked for Guinness. ('Could they not enlist?' an MP asked.) The Member for south-east Cork, Eugene Crean, did not mind what duties were imposed on wine, but his constituents badly needed their whisky, which was essential for women in the toils of childbirth. It was not less essential in the workhouses where 'gallons upon gallons' were administered 'to keep alive the poor creatures whose stomachs cannot bear food. . . .'

The Irish Members were laughed out of court, but the general feeling at the time was against heavy taxes on liquor, and Lloyd George found himself isolated. Instead the Government adopted a piecemeal policy of trimming the licensing hours still more, watering the product and forbidding such practices as treating, drinks 'on the slate' and 'the long pull'. By November 1915 London's permitted hours of drinking – formerly from 5 am until half an hour after midnight – were from noon to 2.30 pm and 6.30 to 9.30 pm. In some rural areas, however, the hours were little affected throughout the war. A. J. P. Taylor has said that, 'Anyone who feels thirsty in England during the afternoon is still paying a price for the Battle of Neuve Chapelle'; to which unions are entitled to retort that drunkenness had nothing to do with giving the Army the wrong kind of shells.

The 'No Treating' Order, effective in London and many other areas from October 1915, laid down that any drink ordered was to be paid for by the person supplied. Initially it was taken in good part, even by the bar staffs who had to make many separate journeys to the tills and pumps. The first husband to be convicted for buying his wife a drink was a Bristol man. His case was taken up by Members of Parliament but they received short shrift. So did union deputations who protested to the Central Control Board (the body charged with regulating the liquor traffic) that the ban on treating was undermining the spirit of brotherhood and manliness. What mattered was that, according to police reports, the Order quickly brought about a fall in consumption; though not, apparently, at Westminster, where the legislators continued to buy each other drinks. In Scotland a temerarious sheriff ruled that treating was no offence in common law and contravened no Act of Parliament, but he was trounced on appeal. In Newcastle police reported a licensee who, with his manager, had sought to evade punishment by causing a customer who had ordered eight drinks to consume all of them. As time passed the Order began to be flouted, to the relief of bar-room scroungers who had been having a thin time, but the police fought back. In Middlesbrough fines on inn-keepers went as high as £40. The licensing authorities had powers to close public-houses which allowed treating and occasionally exercised them.

It was the belief of the *Spectator* that the 'No Treating' Order had freed hundreds of thousands of men from 'an expensive and senseless social tyranny'. Gentlemen accustomed to paying for their own drinks in their clubs, the writer said, were perhaps unaware how widespread was the custom in other classes of buying drinks for chance-met acquaintances, each of whom then had to stand a drink to everyone else. It was a pernicious habit which, the *Spectator* hoped, would never be revived.

What caused much head-shaking as the war progressed was the way in which the women of Britain were taking to the bottle. The first outcry was directed at soldiers' wives, who were thought to be drinking away their over-generous allowances. Police and military began to show a close interest in their drinking habits and drinking friends. When these attentions drew feminist protests 'it was explained . . . that the police desired lists of the wives of soldiers in order to treat them leniently should they be charged with drunkenness'. Women arms workers were next to come under attack. 'We do not all realise the increase in drinking there has been among the mothers of the coming race, though we may yet find it a circumstance darkly menacing to our civilisation,' wrote a special correspondent of *The Times*. In Lancashire women workers had started paying half-crown subscriptions for a 'tea party', at which beer and whisky were drunk. In London afternoon drinking in the public-house had given way to drinking in the home. Census-takers reported that of the customers entering four licensed houses in North Paddington in one hour on a Saturday night 122 were Servicemen, 1,361 male civilians and 1,946 women. It was clear that munitions workers and soldiers' wives alike now had more spending money than ever before and that they saw no reason why their menfolk should have the exclusive right to drink their earnings.

The Government's first venture into the nationalisation of the drink trade – the 'Carlisle Experiment' – was launched in July 1916. An enormous cordite factory at Gretna, started in mid-1915, had attracted some 15,000 labourers, mostly Irish, into a rural area incapable of housing or amusing them. They overran the surrounding villages and jostled by the hundred into the public-houses of Carlisle. Mostly they were well-behaved, but the drunkenness convictions doubled and quadrupled; there were also complaints about goings-on behind the partitions of 'snugs'. Goaded into action, the Government bought up the local breweries and 320 licensed premises. (Two large hotels and a licensed restaurant in Carlisle were excluded.) The policy now was to reduce the number of public-houses, while building a few model taverns; to withdraw grocers' licences; to prohibit advertising of drink (many taverns bore only the name of the house); to bring in salaried civil servants as managers, with no inducement to push sales; to instal eating-rooms and encourage the sale of food; and to abolish 'snugs'.

By the time the 'Experiment' began many of the navvies had moved on and half the customers were women and girls from the munitions plant. In Carlisle 48 out of 119 public-houses were shut down. Although here and there the navvies resisted the spirit of improvement, the Gretna Tavern, converted from a redundant post office, was soon deriving three-quarters of its receipts from food. Soon a ban was put on the consumption of spirits on Saturdays. The 'pernicious system' of chasing down neat spirits with a draught of beer, known locally as 'a heater and a chaser', was discouraged by making it impossible to order spirits and beer together. Also, a rule was introduced several years before it became general law, prohibiting the serving of drink to persons under eighteen. At the Admiralty's request the 'Experiment' was extended to the Cromarty Firth, and public-houses were also nationalised in the Enfield munitions area. Astonishingly, the 'Carlisle Experiment' was to last until 1973, when the premises were sold back to the brewers. State-brewed Border Bitter was drinkable enough, but the taverns remained almost as austere as dispensaries and the State barmaids were never renowned for their voluptuary aspect or readiness to listen to maudlin confessions.

When U-boat warfare was intensified in 1917 the anti-drink crusaders returned to mount ferocious attacks on 'the Trade'. In two-and-a-half years of war, their advertisements said, the brewers and distillers had 'destroyed four million tons of food', mostly sugar and grain. Yet the Demon Drink was demonstrably on the run. Reeling soldiers were becoming a rarity in the street, thanks in no small measure to watered 'Government ale', or 'Lloyd George's beer'. In terms of absolute alcohol, Britain's consumption fell from 89 million gallons in 1914 to 37 million in 1918. London's convictions for drunkenness in 1917 were 16,567 as against 67,103 in 1914. In 1918 the price of a bottle of whisky, at £1, was five times what it had been when the war began.

Throughout the war the cellars at Buckingham Palace remained out of bounds, except when liquor was needed for medicinal purposes (as when the King was suffering from the effects of a severe fall from his horse). In 1917 the United States

Ambassador, Walter Haines Page, stayed overnight with the King and was offered 'only so much bread, one egg apiece and – lemonade'. Would the hard-working King have been the better for a drink, even when not in pain? According to Lloyd George, there was endless, but inconclusive, debate at ministerial and military tables over whether Kitchener's vision and efficiency had been increased by abstinence. Asquith thought that Haldane's abstention from liquor while in office reduced his energy and buoyancy. As for 'Squiff' himself, a biographer, Stephen Koss, has said: 'The trouble with Asquith was not that he imbibed too much, but that it failed to stiffen his backbone.'

CHAPTER 8

HUNWIVES AND OTHERS

When Prince Lichnowsky, the German Ambassador, and his Princess left London, with their retinue and dachshunds, by special train for Germany after war broke out, two English society ladies rode with them. They were married to German aristocrats and had been faced with the choice of forsaking their native country or forsaking their husbands. One of them was Daisy, Princess of Pless, formerly a Cornwallis-West, a familiar figure on the Edwardian social circuit and a sister-in-law of the Duke of Westminster. The other, formerly Evelyn Stapleton-Bretherton, was the Countess Blücher (Princess, as she became during exile) whose aged father-in-law had been living on the islet of Herm, in the Channel Isles, a refuge which he had converted into a reserve for wallabies. Ironically, he was descended from the Marshal Blücher who had come to Wellington's aid at Waterloo and it was the French who now objected to his off-shore presence. Shortly after her marriage the Princess-to-be had christened the cruiser *Blücher* for the Kaiser. The two English wives, with a few others in similar plight, sat out the war in Germany. Prince Blücher worked for the German Red Cross while four of the Princess's brothers fought for Britain, one being killed. The *Blücher* was sunk early in 1915.

The Lichnowskys had been a popular couple in society, not least in Downing Street, and the outbreak of war did not stop cordial adieux being said. At Liverpool Street when the German party of 250 left, there were tears and bared heads. 'It was as if a dead monarch was being borne away,' wrote Princess Blücher, in her book *An English Wife In Berlin*. Equally well liked had been Count Mensdorff, the Austro-Hungarian Ambassador. On the evening before he left he rang up the Duchess of Marlborough (the former Consuelo Vanderbilt) and asked, in French, whether he might call to say goodbye. A voice cut in saying, 'English, please.'

The German Acting-Consul-General, R. L. von Ranke, who took space in the Personal Column of *The Times* on August 3, 1914, to urge German reservists to return to the Fatherland 'without delay, as best they can', was an uncle of Robert Graves, who was christened Robert von Ranke Graves. Like the Sovereign whose commission he held, Graves (as he tells in *Good-Bye To All That*) found himself ranged against his relatives. 'I have three or four uncles somewhere opposite and a number of cousins too,' he told his messmates in France.

The King, as everyone knew, was the Kaiser's cousin; probably he had more relatives on the wrong side than any of his subjects, not excepting the much-attacked financiers 'of foreign extraction' in the City. However, the occupants of thrones are not faced with the embarrassment of actually sticking bayonets into each other, nor are international industrialists. From humbler homes, Englishmen who had married German women went off to the Front to kill Germans and so did their sons, leaving Mum/*Mutte* to like it or lump it. Was she not now a British subject? In some ways 'Hunwives' were luckier than those English women who had married Germans of low degree and had no opportunity of going into exile, even if they had wished to do so. Overnight the war turned them into second-class citizens. Their husbands, if of military age, were interned and because they themselves were aliens in the eyes of the law they were subject to travel restrictions; they also received lower allowances than German-born wives. In Acton Police Court the father of a weeping English-born woman told the bench that her husband, a German, had been ordered to leave his house after the *Lusitania* sinking. Her father protested, 'My daughter is English.' But the clerk retorted, 'She is German, not English.' The court ruled that the landlord was entitled to turn the couple out if he wished. There was little sympathy for such victims, the general feeling being that 'it serves them right for marrying

Huns'; but the Quakers who befriended persecuted aliens did what they could for these native outcasts.

Perhaps the most notorious 'Hunwife' was D. H. Lawrence's Frieda, a member of the von Richthofen family and a cousin of the 'Red Baron'. The Lawrences were married just before the war began. Numerous books about the Bloomsbury Group have told of the upsets which followed the ever-tactless pair, notably at Zennor on the Cornish coast. At first, as Frieda admitted, the cottagers were 'extra nice' to her for being a Hun, but tolerance faded when the Lawrences and their friends took to singing defiant German folk songs. Frieda not unnaturally took pride in the achievements of Manfred's Flying Circus and her sympathies were with the officers in Zeppelins and U-boats with whom she had danced in happier days. Lawrence, whose red beard alone was the mark of a suspect (as were the beards of Shaw and Augustus John), stopped his wife from capering on the beach, for fear she should be denounced for giving scarf signals to submarines. Coastguards harried the couple, policemen popped up from bushes, neighbours crouched under the windows listening. Eventually, after searches by police and military, the Lawrences were expelled from the coastal area and, like Bertrand Russell, found that one-third of Britain was out of bounds to them; they could go to Manchester but not Liverpool, Surrey but not Norfolk, and so on. As Compton Mackenzie has said, the furious, frustrated Lawrence regarded the war as a plot directed against himself. But for his bad health he would have been called up to fight the Richthofens.

The public had no great desire to distinguish enemy from friendly aliens. In October 1914 the golfers of London passed a resolution, affecting fifty clubs, that all members who were Germans or Austrians, naturalised or not, should cease to frequent their clubs for the duration of the war, and that those not naturalised should be expelled. For patriotic golfers it did not much matter that there were Prussian Poles, Austrian Italians, French-speaking Alsatians, Serbo-Croats, Armenians and Greeks who bitterly hated the Central Powers; if they looked and behaved like foreigners that was enough. Swiss governesses incurred all the odium visited on the German *Fräulein*, but gradually, with welfare help, the 'Swiss miss' was steered back to her homeland. A few families remained daringly loyal to their

Trinity Hall, Cambridge, goes to war: 'officer material' at mess.

A trade union leader on a 'Cook's Tour' of the battle line: Ben Tillett, who wanted to see the clergy conscripted into the trenches.

Left: 'Wholesome Pride' runs the caption to this propaganda picture showing a soldier home on leave.

The two worlds: officers and men on leave being welcomed by their relatives at Victoria Station, London.

Where the spies were shot: the rifle range in the Tower of London.

Play-time in the cloisters: Belgian schoolboys in a Cambridge college.

'We don't want to lose you, but . . .' A poster variation on the theme.

Left: In a munitions colony Belgian refugees buy meat – including horse flesh – in their own butcher's shop.

Below left: 'Somewhere in England' German prisoners water their horses.

Right: Roll-call at Donnington Hall, Leicestershire, the stately home which housed captured German officers.

Below: Wreckage of one of the Zeppelins brought down over Britain in September, 1916.

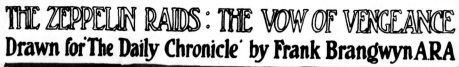

THE ZEPPELIN RAIDS : THE VOW OF VENGEANCE
Drawn for 'The Daily Chronicle' by Frank Brangwyn A R A

'DAILY CHRONICLE' READERS ARE COVERED AGAINST THE RISKS OF BOMBARDMENT BY ZEPPELIN OR AEROPLANE

The Vow of Vengeance . . . and the Solace of Insurance.

governesses. Asquith's refusal to eject 'The Woman of Downing Street', a naturalised German maid of a relative, only served to strengthen the rumour that the Prime Minister and his wife were pro-Germans who toasted the Kaiser at dinner every night. In schools German masters were not necessarily turned adrift, or interned. Sir Victor Pritchett has an entertaining account of how the Fourth Form at Alleyn's ragged Dr Ludwig Hirsch, who said they would never beat the 'Chermans' if they did not work as hard as the 'Cherman' boys did. This raised jeers, coupled with taunts that the Germans would never get to Paris. The Herr Doktor then called on the form captain to bring the class to order. It reads like something out of Frank Richards's Greyfriars.

Attempts to boycott musical works by Germans, alive or dead, had varying success. At the beginning it was decided that the London Promenade concerts should be purged of Beethoven, Strauss and Wagner, a decision widely applauded; however, concert-goers stayed away in droves and the alien composers were soon back. It was hard to hate Handel, but the Vicar of Netherton, Worcestershire, decided that the Dead March from *Saul* was unsuitable for a memorial service to Kitchener, the greatest Englishman who ever lived. Thomas Beecham seized the early opportunity to break the German tradition of the Hallé Orchestra and found that audiences were ready for works by Allied composers. In the later years of the war he conducted *Tannhäuser* and *The Valkyrie* in London. Their popularity irked an unnamed press baron, who threatened hostilities. Beecham offered to abandon Wagner if his critic would burn his valuable German paintings in Trafalgar Square. After a pause the publisher said, 'It is rather silly, isn't it?'

Some hasty name-changing went on in the early weeks of the war. Not all those who declared in the *London Gazette* that they had 'absolutely renounced, relinquished and abandoned' their German-sounding names were necessarily aliens; some were British-born or British-naturalised. In the *Gazette* one finds Rosenheim changed into Rose; Brueggemeyer into Bridges; Honig into Honey; Schwabacher into Shaw; Kaufman into Kay; Krailsheimer into Kerr; Schacht into Dent; and, even more impressively, Siegenberg into Curzon and Schutz into Sterling. After mid-October it was an offence for an enemy alien to change his name; a Jack Pepper was taken to court and reminded that his name was Jacob Pfeffer. Writers who changed their names included Ford Madox Hueffer, who became Ford Madox Ford; Arthur Schloss, who became Arthur Waley; and Arnold Bennett's collaborator on *Milestones*, Edward Knoblauch, who became Knoblock (under his original name he was billed as co-author of the patriotic show *England Expects*, but this was hardly what England expected, so in subsequent advertisements his name was dropped and he was called simply 'the Author of *Kismet* and *Milestones*'). Among buildings later renamed was the Coburg Hotel, Mayfair, which became the Connaught.

From time to time alien-baiters overstepped themselves. The *London Mail*, a weekly too smart for its own good, asked under 'Things We Want To Know' how long it was since Mark Hambourg had discovered he was a famous Russian pianist, having considered himself a German in the old days. Hambourg was Russian-born, naturalised British. After the paragraph appeared he was abused by crowds at Cromer, where he was due to play. The libel cost the magazine £500. Socially, a name like Muller or Meyer was a handicap, though financially it could be an asset; British-born owners of these names, accused of being Huns, obtained damages of £300 and £250.

The Royal Family's first major setback was the hounding from office of the First Sea Lord, Prince Louis of Battenberg, a cousin of the King, who had been a naturalised Briton for nearly half a century. It was he who, on the eve of war, gave the order for the Fleet to stand fast (Churchill, who was out of London, later endorsed it). The press-fomented outcry against an admiral of German birth at the head of the British Fleet was so intense that Asquith and Churchill, and even the King, felt they must bow to it; so Prince Louis was invited to submit a letter of resignation (with suggestions as to what he should say) and in reply Churchill, with a reference to 'ineradicable difficulties', assured the victim of the Admiralty's profound respect. The correspondence was published at the end of October 1914. One of the few to be openly revolted by Prince Louis's treatment was the union leader J. H. Thomas, who wrote an angry letter to *The Times*, which did him no good in the Labour movement.

The King had already been jogged into removing from the

Army List the names of the German Emperor and the Crown Prince, who enjoyed honorary command of British regiments. This deletion was managed quietly, but the next demand, for the removal from St George's Chapel, Windsor, of the Garter banners of the Hohenzollerns, was conducted in anything but quiet. The King's view, says Harold Nicolson, was that these banners were symbols of history and should stay until after the war. Public opposition was vociferous and the Prime Minister persuaded the King in May 1915 to have the offending articles, eight in number, taken down; they were not, however, trampled in the dust, in accordance with what some believed to be ancient precedent. Later the Kaiser's banner was replaced by that of Kitchener, as a royal mark of confidence in the Secretary for War and a rebuff to Northcliffe, who had been assailing him.

Meanwhile Swift MacNeill, Member for South Donegal, had started a move in the House of Commons against two princes of the United Kingdom who were reported to be commanding troops in Germany. One of them was a great-grandson of George III, the Duke of Cumberland and Teviotdale, whose paternal grandfather, the 'wicked' Duke of Cumberland, became King of Hanover while retaining his seat in the Lords. He was married to a daughter of the Kaiser and in Germany was Duke of Brunswick. The other was the Duke of Albany, Earl of Clarence and Baron Arklow, a grandson of Queen Victoria (like the Kaiser), who was born in Britain but was now Duke of Saxony and Duke of Saxe-Coburg-Gotha. Was it true, asked MacNeill, that these dukes had divested themselves of their British nationality, or were they guilty of high treason? Would they be deprived of their seats in the Lords? Asquith could find no reason for assisting MacNeill to promote what looked like being a one-man Bill of Attainder; the matter, he considered, could be left until after the war. The King thought that a pursuit of these dukes would be petty. However, Asquith set up a commission to consider the question and its recommendations led to the Titles Deprivation Act of 1917. In the House of Lords doubts were voiced as to whether these dukes constituted any real menace in the field; but Lord Curzon said Cumberland had had the impudence to congratulate the Kaiser on the outcome of the Battle of Jutland. Eventually, for adhering to the King's enemies, the Dukes of Cumberland and Albany were deprived of their titles, but by that time the war was over. Also struck off was an improbable warrior called Viscount Taafe of Corren and Baron of Ballymote, a Count of the Holy Roman Empire who had served as a lieutenant in an Austrian regiment of dragoons.

None of this nagging over titles was good for the Royal Family. Although the King was working indefatigably at his public duties there were mutterings against the Throne; some of them came, as always, from H. G. Wells who, in *Mr Britling Sees It Through*, had talked of 'an alien and uninspiring court', and who, in a letter to *The Times*, had called for the formation of Republican societies in Britain. The King, while ready to concede that he might be uninspiring, heatedly denied that he was an alien. However, there was much talk of an Unseen Hand (Chapter Twenty-One) and people were saying that even the head of the British Empire had a German name. It is hard to credit, though Harold Nicolson assures us it is so, that the King and the College of Heralds were uncertain what his family name was; but whether it was Guelph or Wipper or Wettin, the King decided that his dynasty must bear a new name. Lord Northcliffe would gladly have asked readers of the *Daily Mail* for suggestions, if the problem had been put to him; as it was, the King's Private Secretary, Lord Stamfordham, came up with an inspired suggestion: Windsor.

To pave the way for a proclamation of the new dynasty, and a renunciation of all styles and dignities of the dukedoms of Saxony and Saxe-Coburg-Gotha, the King announced that the families of Teck and Battenberg were to be renamed. His brothers-in-law, the Duke of Teck and Prince Alexander of Teck became Marquess of Cambridge and Earl of Athlone respectively, with the family name of Cambridge; and his cousins, Prince Louis of Battenberg and Prince Alexander of Battenberg, became Marquess of Milford Haven and Marquess of Carisbrooke, with the family name of Mountbatten (even though there was already a distinguished Dorset family called Mount Batten). The title of Serene Highness, it was announced, would disappear. Great satisfaction was expressed in the press at these changes; *Truth* wrote of 'a visible growth of opinion' that future kings should marry their subjects, or even look for some 'suitable damsel' from America.

Nowhere was the hunting of aliens pursued more bitterly than in the City of London. Thanks in part to Edward VII's advancement of financial favourites, German influence in banking and heavy industry had been growing fast; and the fact that the favourites were often Jews as well as Germans encouraged the anti-Semitism indigenous in the City. Sir Ernest Cassel, a naturalised Jew from Cologne, had founded an Anglo-American institute to help young businessmen who settled in each other's countries, but his record of good works did not disarm his enemies. Also attacked was Sir Alfred Mond, of the great Brunner-Mond chemical combine, the Lancashire-born son of a German Jew, who directed the *Westminster Gazette* and was a Privy Councillor. (Both Mond and Sir John Brunner received an apology and costs from a manufacturer who called them 'German swine'.)

However, the most inviting target for envy and calumny was Sir Edgar Speyer, the chairman of London's Underground services. The son of a Jewish banker in Frankfurt, he had been naturalised in 1892 and was a Privy Councillor as well as a personal friend of Asquith and the German Chancellor. He was hospitable and lavish, and for many years he had defrayed the £2,000-a-year losses on the Queen's Hall 'Proms'. By unhappy chance he lived in a large house at Cromer, overlooking the North Sea, so it was easy to spread the rumour that, like all wealthy men on that coast, he spent his time signalling to U-boats, if not entertaining their crews. The *National Review*, under Leo Maxse, was incensed at the thought of an alien controlling London's Underground; would Berlin be so foolish as to hand over its communications to a British businessman? Speyer, whose telegraphic address was 'Spy. London', had a brother in the New York office of the family firm, 'a rabid pro-German' who was a confidant and host of Count Bernstorff, Germany's propagandist in America and 'a nobleman with whom Ananias would with difficulty compete'. Because of a rule against maintaining indirect links with Germany, Sir Edgar severed his connection with the New York branch. But, asked the *National Review*, 'does not that give him a moral and even material interest in the transactions of the firm meanwhile?' What were the relations between Edgar in London, James in New York and Eduard in Frankfurt?

After some months of these attacks the Speyers' friends had

dwindled. In May 1915 Sir Edgar wrote to Asquith offering to resign his baronetcy and Privy Councillorship. 'I have known you long and well enough', the Prime Minister replied, 'to estimate at their true value these baseless and malignant imputations upon your loyalty to the British Crown. The King is not prepared to take any step such as you suggest in regard to the marks of distinction which you have received in recognition of public service and philanthropic munificence.' An attempt to oust Speyer and Cassel from the Privy Council failed in the courts. But Speyer had had enough. He packed up and, to the distress of his remaining friends, joined his brother in New York. There he engaged in activities which were construed as trading with the enemy and in 1919 his name was struck off the list of Privy Councillors and his naturalisation revoked.

Maxse and his pack had many other City targets. Why had Baron von Schroder, head of the biggest acceptance house in the City, been naturalised three days after war was declared? The Government's explanation was that if any other course had been taken the House of Schroder would have closed its doors and there would have been a great financial disaster; in any event the firm had been British for a hundred years and it was a pure accident that its head at the start of the war happened to be a German. Less easy to defend was the continued existence of the German banks, the Deutsche and the Dresdener. Failure to shut down these 'drain-pipes of British wealth', these supposed toe-holds for commercial spying, was a source of running recrimination against the Government right through the war.

It was left to the Duke of Connaught, Victoria's favourite son, to strike a blow at aliens in the humbler ranks of the City. In 1917, awarding prizes offered by London Chamber of Commerce, he said that twenty-five years earlier half the clerks in the City were foreigners, 'and in many cases, I imagine, Germans'. Now the proportion was five per cent and even that was too high. 'We do not want the foreigners here,' he said, 'England for the English!' These remarks came ill from one with a Prussian wife, daughter of the 'Red Prince' who had played a dashing role in the 1870–71 war. As it happened, the Duchess died a week later and was much praised for her loyalty to her adopted country by those who normally proclaimed 'once a Hun, always a Hun'. Why, asked the *Herald*, must it always be the humbler-born who were persecuted for their German birth?

In commercial fields, manufacturers had been quick to clear their names of any German taint; and some of them, regrettably, had been just as quick to smear their rivals. Sir Jesse Boot rushed out a British *eau de Cologne*. Schweppes emphasised that Jacob Schweppe had been a Swiss who came to London in 1794. Dr Jaeger was conceded to have been a German scientist, but the firm selling his sanitary woollens was a British one. Kruschen whooped with delight in an advertisement headed GERMAN SPAS CROSSED OFF THE MAP; the spa habit had given way to the Kruschen habit – and let no one say that Kruschen had any German links. Shell and Osram were among firms which threatened to prosecute anyone who impugned their origins. Royal Worcester Corsets attacked rivals who were under suspicion of importing German corsets from France. In the High Court Liptons were restrained from saying that Lyons or any of its directors were Germans or that buying Lyons products was helping the enemy. This decision was splashed by Lyons with the assurance: 'An All-British Company with All-British Directors, 14,000 British Shareholders and 160,000 All-British Shopkeepers selling Lyons Tea.'

Such trading with the enemy as went on was carried out as a rule through neutrals. The laws were full of loopholes and lawyers were kept busy in the courts. What, for instance, was a British company? What was meant by 'enemy'? What was meant by 'trading'? It was possible for firms to make honest mistakes. However, one in which it is hard to find excuses involved two partners in a Glasgow firm of metal merchants in which Bonar Law had once been an active partner. They were tried in Edinburgh High Court on charges of arranging for agents to forward 2,916 tons of iron ore already on the quay at Rotterdam to Krupps of Essen and to deliver a further 4,443 tons to the steel works at Ruhrort. An intercepted letter was found to contain the expression 'our friends, Messrs Krupps'. It said: 'We quite realise that they are very anxious to secure ore and if we had been allowed by the laws of this country to send further steamers to Rotterdam with ore for delivery to them we should have been only too glad to do this. . . .' It emerged that the firm were unwilling to allow any more ore to go to Germany unless they were paid cash for what had already been shipped, and one of the accused partners contended that the whole idea was 'to screw money out of the enemy'.

The Judge: 'You were perfectly willing to let them have the iron ore if they paid for the back cargoes?' – 'Yes.'

These transactions occurred in September 1914 and the jury recommended the utmost leniency, bearing in mind 'the violent derangement to ordinary commercial transactions'. For this exercise in 'business as usual' the two men were sentenced to six months' imprisonment and fined £2,000 each; a modest, and much criticised, punishment compared with the five years' penal servitude awarded, also in Edinburgh High Court, to another Scots businessman in November 1914 for trying to sell coal to Berlin with the help of a hotel porter in Gothenburg.

The strange saga of the tonic Sanatogen shows how in the midst of Armageddon British nerves continued to be calmed and fortified by a German product. In November 1914 Reginald McKenna, questioned in Parliament, said the proprietor of the tonic was a German living in Germany and he had applied to convert the business into an English limited company. Permission had been denied and steps were being taken to ensure that no profits reached Germany. Meanwhile the product was still manufactured, advertised and sold. In May 1916 an order was made by the Board of Trade for the business to be wound up and a few weeks later the Controller of Enemy Businesses decided to sell it by tender as a going concern. In November it went to Lord Rhondda, the coal owner, for £360,000. Disclosing that for years he had used Sanatogen as brain food, he complained of the Board of Trade's delay in handling this transaction and urged other businessmen to buy up German concerns. In the meantime a Battersea firm had begun to make Sanagen, which was 'richer in organic phosphates' and cheaper than Sanatogen. In the *Illustrated London News* Sanatogen fought back with a full-page advertisement showing Tommies in a trench holding up to the enemy a sign: 'A Sporting Offer: chuck us over ten tins of Sanatogen and we will stop strafing you for the rest of the day.' This was said to be based on a real-life incident. The authentic product, readers were told, was now being made at Penzance by the original German process, once described as 'a triumph of synthetic chemistry'. With such a tonic, how could Britain lose?

The Sanatogen sale was effected at the same time that the Bechstein piano-making firm in London was sold off to Debenhams, complete with the Bechstein Hall (renamed the Wigmore Hall). This meant that patriotic citizens had no further need to paste black strips over the name 'Bechstein' on their pianos.

CHAPTER 9

BEHIND WIRE

It is by now widely believed that Britain 'invented the concentration camp' in the South African War. However, in 1914 the term had not attracted any real measure of obloquy and it was often used to describe the numerous corrals for aliens and internees set up in wartime Britain.

The last unwilling visitors to the British Isles to be kept under armed guard were probably the French prisoners taken in the Napoleonic Wars, many of whom were housed in hulks off the coast. Some of them helped to build the military college at Sandhurst. In 1914 there were no obvious, traditional places to stow away large numbers of aliens, belligerent and otherwise; so, as with the Belgians, makeshift repositories had to be found. London's first batches of aliens were conveyed to Olympia, some of them in buses proclaiming 'Your King and Country Need You'. Alexandra Palace was then being used to sort out Belgians, but it became a permanent internment camp early in 1915, with a wired compound extending into the park. Another early internment camp in the capital consisted of a large warehouse at Edmonton, where Osbert Sitwell, a Guards subaltern, found himself glaring at inmates whose faces seemed familiar. One man asked him, 'Which table would you like tonight, sir?' It was after a hard day at this camp that Sitwell drew his sword in the street and commandeered a motor omnibus to take his party back to Chelsea Barracks. Driver and conductor, he says, took this in good part, but the passengers seemed less anxious to perform this simple sacrifice for the lads in khaki. Oddly enough, Robert Graves's first posting was also to an internment camp; it consisted of a dirty unused wagon works at Lancaster, choked with aliens who had been assured they would be safer inside than out.

One of the first outdoor camps for Germans provided a weekend spectacle for Londoners, eager to see the blond beasts for themselves. The Frith Hill Detention Camp covered forty acres of sandy common above Camberley and the road running through it divided the military prisoners from the civilians. Around the thick barbed wire defences, patrolled by armed Territorials, the cars of visitors were ranged in depth in a fashion reminiscent of Derby Day on the Downs. Through the wire were to be seen Imperial Guards, Uhlans, sailors in white caps, wounded men in field grey, all lolling in the sun or playing cards; the civilian section, full of waiters and 'spies' of all kinds, contained German bands playing *Die Wacht am Rhein* and other helpful melodies. Gerald Biss, motoring correspondent of the *Tatler*, said that a visit to Frith Hill was 'the very last word nowadays'. Among those behind the wire, he thought, were 'some we have broken bread and drunk with in good faith'; they were having quite a gay party and the authorities allowed them 'everything but pigeons and cars'. At one time there were 8,000 'enjoying the open-air cure' at Frith Hill, but by degrees they were dispersed, some to the Isle of Man, some to ships off Southend, and some by a fearful irony were sent on the long, long way to Tipperary.

Of the temporary camps one of the biggest was on Newbury racecourse, whose inmates waved cheerfully to travellers on the railway. The German press made much the same complaints about conditions at Newbury as the British press levelled at the camp for British internees at the Ruhleben trotting course; in both men were said to be lying on straw in horse-boxes. Reporters invited to Newbury decided that the lower classes of German had never been so well off. Later, when Asquith looked in, he was given a cheer, which had to be suppressed as contrary to regulations.

A permanent camp much in the news was Donnington Hall, a Tudor mansion in Leicestershire. Acquired from Frederick Gretton, it was converted at a cost of £13,000 into a home for

320 German officers with their servants. Cries of 'coddling the Hun' were met with a statement that 'the general scale was that of a sergeants' mess'. The inmates were allowed to order German wines from a London store, presumably because no patriotic Briton would wish to drink enemy vintages. Of the 400-acre park, the inmates enjoyed only twenty acres. Nevertheless, there were protests that they had been privileged to enjoy a lawn meet of the Quorn, whose pack had been brought close to the wire barrier for their benefit. According to the *Ladies' Field*, the master raised his cap to the officers, who bowed in return; but in Parliament it was denied that courtesies had been exchanged. Unusually, a German newspaper, the *Zeitung am Wittag*, of Berlin, published a flattering account of conditions at Donnington, where 'one can have everything, just as in a hotel' and 'the commandant is very charming ... and permits everything'. Margot Asquith, wife of the Prime Minister, was falsely accused of playing tennis with officers at Donnington and sending them regular parcels of dainties. These charges brought her such abusive mail that she sued the *Globe* and obtained £1,000 damages. She had an unlikely theory that a duchess looking over her shoulder in Fortnum's at the address on a parcel had mistaken 'Dardanelles' for 'Donnington'. After the war Donnington Park became the scene of motor racing and in World War Two it was again a camp for captured German officers.

The great internee camp at Knockaloe, near Douglas in the Isle of Man, housed well over 20,000 aliens for most of the war. Originally it had been a summer holiday camp for young men at £1 a week. By November 1914 it contained 3,300 'non-belligerents', but this proved to be a misnomer. There were grievances about wet tents and wireworm in the potatoes; then one day in the great dining hall the symbol of a blood-red hand was stuck on a window and the inmates began to smash everything in sight. A detachment of Manx soldiers under a sergeant-major rushed to the hall and were bombarded from all sides; so, as one witness said, 'it being impossible to use the bayonet, they loaded and fired'. Most of the shots went high but five men were killed and a sixth died later. The inquest jury decided that the military had taken justifiable measures. A United States inspector reported that Knockaloe was the best camp of its kind in Europe; he talked to wounded aliens who told him that a 'bad lot' from the East End of London had been responsible. Those who died had the distinction of being the first Germans (if one excepts Karl Lody) to be shot on British soil. Knockaloe gradually settled down. Probably few believed Sylvia Pankhurst's story, printed in her magazine, of how starving inmates were driven to kill and eat a cat.

The only major row over the treatment of German prisoners occurred when the Cabinet authorised punitive treatment for officers and crews of U-boats. The King was unhappy at this idea. To put a man in solitary confinement, he felt, was the same as shutting him in a prison cell. The U-boat crews were only obeying orders, even if they were brutal orders (an argument which carried little weight after World War Two). In the end it was the Germans who put a stop to this experiment in harshness; they shut thirty-nine British officers and men in solitary confinement until the British Government changed its mind. Admiral Fisher's early proposal to shoot batches of prisoners as a reprisal for air raids found no support.

The prisoner-of-war camps were not escape-proof. A good deal of tunnelling went on at Donnington Hall and the occasional officer turned up in a crate at the ports. Other escapers were found wandering in the Welsh mountains and a party of four were arrested in Birmingham trying to enter a theatre to see a pantomime. The most exciting escape story was, alas, only a rumour; a Zeppelin was said to have descended during a raid to the terrace of Alexandra Palace and snatched away a number of internees before the guards could intervene.

Permission to visit prisoners and internees was not too difficult to obtain. Thomas Hardy used to call in at the big camp at Dorchester, where a wounded Prussian died in his presence, 'to my great relief, and his own'. John Galsworthy journeyed to Wakefield to visit his resentful Bavarian brother-in-law, Georg Sauter, an artist of some standing interned despite all Galsworthy's eloquence; and also to Alexandra Palace to cheer his nephew Rudolf Sauter (one day Rudolf's friends smuggled him beyond the visitors' compound so that he could have a good look at the place). Sylvia Pankhurst would have liked to visit internees at Holloway but was barred because she had once been an inmate.

In 1916 the Government released Austro-Hungarian prisoners on parole to carry out agricultural work; however, there was heavy opposition from many farmers and the scheme made slow progress. In the spring of 1917, faced with severe labour shortage, the Government allowed Germans to be used on farms, but as Lord Bryce said in the Lords, 'No one would suggest that we should force an alien to work. That would be Prussian.' The newspapers began publishing pictures of 'Fritz on the land', and a cheery old soul he turned out to be. In the market gardens of Evesham prisoners with gleaming forks on their shoulders were escorted to work by soldiers with gleaming bayonets; it took eighty men and thirty guards to tend the early asparagus. A number of the internees from Knockaloe were moved to the mainland to work. Germans could also be employed in certain trades unconnected with warlike operations, as in food manufacture and distribution, but not as car-men, messengers, waiters or servants.

What to do on meeting Germans was something of a social problem. Should one look at them, through them or away from them? The guards did not like anyone to talk to them in German, though the Countess of Warwick did so. *John Bull* was for ever attacking girls who ogled and blew kisses at prisoners and a few were prosecuted for throwing them cigarettes. The mother of a sailor who fought at Jutland was fined £7 for giving sixpence to a German prisoner leading horses through Cheltenham.

In 1889 a Welsh whisky distillery was established at Frongoch, beside a clear stream near Bala. The product was advertised in Barnum terms – 'the most wonderful whisky that ever drove the skeleton from the feast or painted landscapes on the brain of man'. But Welsh whisky failed to capture the public and the distillery languished. Nothing more was heard of Frongoch until the summer of 1916, when the name was rarely absent from the tongues of Irish Members at Westminster. For Frongoch had become a detention camp for Sinn Feiners, rounded up after the Easter Rising in Dublin. Fifteen of their leaders had been court-martialled and shot, a protracted retribution which served as a powerful discouragement to voluntary enlistment by Irishmen in the British Army (some 100,000 had joined the Colours by then). The men selected, or as some said seized, for internment were put away without trial under Defence Regulations, but an appeals committee was soon freeing them in large numbers. One they did not free was Michael Collins, the militant 'Big Fellow', who stirred up much trouble in the camp and helped to reorganise the Irish Republican Brotherhood which had been behind the rising.

Frongoch had already housed German prisoners, who had been dispersed to make room for the Irish. Obviously, said the Irish Members of Parliament, Frongoch had been chosen because it was unfit for Germans, and month by month they strove to represent it as a living hell. To start with, it was six hours by train from London and Members were allowed only fifteen minutes to interview internees. They were told that Knockaloe Camp, in the Isle of Man, where two-thirds of Britain's internees were held, was even less accessible and that fifteen minutes was the legal time limit for visits. The camp, Members said, was overcrowded; in fact, its dormitories had held twice as many Germans. It was badly ventilated, the sanitation was dangerous, the dynamos were noisy, there was too much heat from the boilers and there was a vegetarian inmate who could not get cheese. Herbert Samuel, who answered much of the barrage, said a United States Embassy inspector had described the camp as ideal. The Member for North-East Cork, Tim Healy, then tried to rattle Samuel by calling him 'the father of the Sinn Fein movement', contending that at Frongoch he had started a Sinn Fein university where men from Ulster, Munster, Leinster and Connaught could meet to exchange ideas.

In November one of the Parliamentary snipers, Lawrence Ginnell, Nationalist Member for North Westmeath, was fined £100 (later reduced to £50) for signing himself as Lebras MagFingail in order to visit Irish internees at Knutsford. According to the prosecution his manner showed that he was visiting the camp to stir up discord. Already he had been 'chaired' by Irishmen at Wandsworth and had made a speech to other internees at Stafford saying, 'We are all proud of you.' Ginnell's defence was that he had merely 'Irished' his name. In November 1916 the Speaker told the House that Ginnell, having refused to pay his fine, had been taken to Pentonville to serve twenty-one days in the First Division. (In 1918 he was gaoled again for incitement to illegal cattle driving.)

Roll-call trouble broke out at Frongoch when the commandant was accused of trying to compel Irishmen to identify comrades who were wanted for military service. Collins was one of
those who forced his comrades to absent themselves from
parade in protest. In Parliament Samuel pointed out that those
liable to call-up had been resident in the United Kingdom and
taking up arms against the Crown did not exempt them from
military service. 'Probably,' he said, 'they would not be put in a
fighting unit.'

Next came allegations that the camp was rat-infested, that the
meat caused scabies and that prisoners fainted from weakness
on waking in the morning. A Dublin Member, Alfred Byrne,
who passed on these charges, wanted the commandant posted to
France, 'where he will not have unarmed men to deal with'; then
he said it was the men's belief that the commandant was trying to
goad them into revolt so that he could shoot them down; and in
no time he was alleging that the commandant was insane and
that 'our countrymen are being tortured to death'. Supporting
him, Ginnell said the prisoners were being 'almost driven mad'
by 'this Prussian god'. The allegations hardly seemed borne out
by a press report that a batch of released internees arriving in
Ireland said they had been shown great kindness by the camp
surgeon and the adjutant, who had shaken hands with them on
leaving. The Galway men among them were not too faint to
raise a cheer as they marched past the ruins of the Dublin Post
Office.

Herbert Samuel's judgement on Healy (who became the first
governor-general of the Irish Free State) as one who 'never or
rarely strayed from the realm of fancy into the realm of fact'
would have applied to most of the Irish Members. It was not all
good clean fun; for that December the medical officer at
Frongoch was found drowned near Bala, having been worried
over allegations against his staff and himself.

In June 1917, about a year after the Parliamentary harrying
started, Bonar Law announced that the Government had
decided to free all interned Irishmen, so that the approaching
Irish Convention might meet in an atmosphere of harmony. The
arrival in Ireland of the last of the deportees at Kingstown was
greeted with suitable frenzy, culminating in an uproarious
march on Dublin, led by Eamonn de Valera. Cork made the

occasion an excuse for a riot, and thirty ended up in hospital with bayonet and bullet wounds. Soon afterwards de Valera was elected as Sinn Fein Member for East Clare, with a majority of nearly 30,000. One who helped him at the hustings was the Countess Markievicz (formerly Constance Gore-Booth), who had commanded the detachment of rebels which attacked the Royal College of Surgeons in Dublin and who had been imprisoned at Aylesbury. On November 28, 1917, a full-page photograph of this dashing young woman, in Sinn Fein uniform with epaulettes and nursing a cuddly dog, appeared in the *Tatler* and must surely have pained those readers who regarded that magazine as the pantheon of the Red Cross ladies and generals' consorts. She was to go to gaol again before being elected Britain's first woman Member of Parliament in 1918.

CHAPTER 10

UNDER THE ZEPPELINS

In the summer of 1914 'looping the loop' was a society craze. The Royal Automobile Club staged a Looping the Loop Party, with all the furniture upside down, Charles Coborn singing a song while standing on his head and the courses of a long meal eaten in reverse order, from dessert to hors d'oeuvres. Nobody thought of this aerial stunt as a serious military manoeuvre.

For those who were children in 1914–18 the daily antics by the young men in their flying machines are still fresh in the deep-freeze of memory. That loop was a tingling joy to watch, however often repeated; but most sharply remembered (as this writer can testify) was the spin, in which the pilot stood the machine on one wing tip and spiralled all the way down like a falling leaf, pulling out at the last moment with a reassuring roar of the engine. These and other manoeuvres, judged necessary for survival in aerial combat, were not always successful; spectators shut their eyes as wings fell away in the air or spinning pilots corkscrewed into the fields. For some young men an aircraft engine was the first internal combustion engine they had ever controlled and there were those for whom it was the first and the last.

The happy-go-lucky fliers lived on intimate terms with the world below. They dived under suspension bridges, they swooped low over their parents' roofs, they beat up sleepy villages, they tossed bouquets to girlfriends, they dropped in at their old schools. Even that stronghold of conscientious objectors, Garsington Manor, was impressed when a flyer dropped a *billet doux* for a guest. In the big engineering strike of 1917 *The Times* reported how a young airman repeatedly dived on a meeting of strikers in a munitions town (unidentified for security reasons) harassing them until they dispersed. Sometimes when a pilot swooped low over a railway station he was merely trying to find where he was, assisted by the map in Bradshaw's *Guide*.

Forced landings could lead to some pleasing social adventures. The place to choose when in difficulties was the paddock of a big house, preferably not a lunatic asylum. With luck one would be dined well and spend the night in a peer's silk pyjamas. Not all landings of this type, it seems, were emergency ones. Ivor Montagu, whose family entertained a good-looking young pilot 'forced down' at Townhill, says he later learned it was quite the thing to choose soft-looking propositions for the weekend. The game was known as 'hunting Jew palaces'.

The first aircraft ever assigned to the support of Britain's armies in the field took off from Swingate Downs, near Dover, just over a week after the war started. Only a privileged few saw the flimsy war birds labouring out, one by one, across the Channel. On Swingate Downs the machines had lain in the open, for there was no aerodrome; aircraft came down where best they could, on farms and playing fields and racecourses. But soon, all over Britain, the landscape was being hacked about to meet the needs of the air age. The hangar joined the barn as a rural appurtenance. At the outset the Government took over London's best-known aerodrome, Hendon, from Claude Grahame-White, who had done so much to make Britain air-minded. (Here came Bernard Shaw for a war-time flip, at two guineas, in an 'Aerobus'.) Emergency landing grounds were laid out in London parks and even in the grounds of Buckingham Palace. By the later stages of the war aerodromes were being established in the unlikeliest places. At Loch Doon 3,000 men were busy for more than a year draining a bog, laying a railway and erecting hutments. It was then found that the site and the prevailing weather were alike unsuitable and the project was abandoned at a loss of £500,000.

Until Christmas Eve, 1914, no offensive object had ever been dropped by an airborne enemy on the soil of Britain, though British airmen based in France had already been hurling bombs on Zeppelin sheds and other installations in Germany. The Yuletide bomb was thrown from a German aircraft high over Dover Castle and blew a man from a tree where he had been gathering holly. Next day a German aircraft penetrated the Thames Estuary and later shed a bomb harmlessly at Cliffe, in Kent. These pleasantries caused little concern to a nation smarting from the naval bombardment of Scarborough. But intelligence reports insisted that Zeppelin raids were soon to be expected; and in February 1915 the Kaiser signed the necessary order. Against the great dirigibles there were no real defences, no networks of observers or searchlights or sound-location systems. Londoners gossiped to each other about the steel nets which had been draped over Buckingham Palace, the War Office, the National Gallery and a few distinguished homes, in the hope of deflecting bombs. Queen Mary, surveying the flimsy false roof over the private apartments, is said to have likened the precautions to those of a poultry run. Shaw was of the opinion that children's playgrounds should have been netted. The Duke of Westminster was observed to have heavily buttressed his picture gallery containing Gainsborough's *Blue Boy* at Grosvenor House. But the most startling anti-Zeppelin measure was the draining of the lake in St James's Park so that it should not serve as a bomb-marker for Whitehall. To complete the ruin of the finest view in London the lake-bed was covered with a hutted camp whose inmates were charged with the prevention of trading with the enemy.

The Zeppelin, first of the strategic bombers, combined terror with majesty. It was a glorious artefact, however much one chose to hate it. Small boys wished for nothing more than to see one of these silver maggots creep glistening from cloud cover, or wriggle on top of a cone of searchlights (later the under-bellies were painted black). Fascinated, the King watched his cousin's raiders from his palace windows. From a logistic point of view, the early Zeppelin was a nonsense: an apparatus nearly 700 feet long to carry bombs which, at first, weighed only a few pounds each. In military terms, it was the equivalent of a four-coach train carrying one old lady. But if the Zeppelin could spread an unwholesome terror, causing the British to dim their lights, draw their fires, and halt their trains and buses for hours on end, as well as diverting fighters from the Western Front, then it had a useful function. It could fly at 20,000 feet, a height which fighters took nearly half an hour to attain. To guide it to the moonlit capital were the railway tracks shining silver all the way from Colchester (and reinforced, as some believed, by the beckoning headlights of spies' motor cars). To the north-west of London was sited a bogus explosives factory containing only an electric plant which was switched on during raids to give the impression of a war factory working overtime, but it does not appear to have fooled any raiders. There was a widespread belief, partly deriving from interviews with the Zeppelin commander Heinrich Mathy in the American press, that the raiders were primarily out to bomb the Bank of England. (A *Bystander* cartoon, characteristic of the times, showed a Zeppelin lowering an excited, top-hatted Jew to spy out the City.) The Kaiser's orders, according to Mathy, were that St Paul's and Westminster Abbey should be spared; but accurate bombing was, of course, impossible.

An early inspiration in the war against Zeppelins was to recruit the blind, whose ability to hear the throb of distant engines was deemed to be greater than that of the sighted. In south-east England they manned a binaural listening service which fed information of range and altitude to the defences. Commander A. Rawlinson, who claims some credit for this innovation, has explained that the system was based on the natural instinct which urges a person, on hearing a distant sound, to turn his head towards it, so that it is heard equally in both ears. In the early experiments the blind man was fitted with a stethoscope to intensify his hearing and a pole was attached to his head, which would turn in the direction of the raider and indicate the bearing on a compass dial. For the blind, argued Rawlinson, what could be more gratifying than 'the feeling that their everlasting dependence had for the moment ceased, and work lay before them in which *they alone* could ever hope to excel, and that the best of all such work would be done in the defence of their country and in the hour of its greatest need'? How substantial was the contribution of the blind does not emerge from Rawlinson's account; certainly listening posts consisting of stethoscopes attached to wide-mouthed, rotatable 'trumpets' were eventually worked with some success by the sighted.

Commander Rawlinson directed the early anti-aircraft

defences, which remained an Admiralty responsibility, until early in 1916. He had a naval gun in Regents Park, another at Tower Bridge and a scratch lot of Hotchkiss six-pounders and pom-poms scattered about the city. One day, stung by criticism of London's defences, he drove off in his car to Paris and escorted back a 75 mm Auto-Canon on a 50 mph De Dion chassis. When the Bank of England, or any other major target, seemed to be threatened the Auto-Canon was rushed into action by a crew of solicitors, accountants and librarians, for whom saving the metropolis was a part-time duty. A headquarters for the force was provided by courtesy of the Grand Duke Michael of Russia in his palatial stables at Kenwood, leased from Lord Mansfield. 'Conditions at the Grand Duke's breakfast-table were exceptionally enjoyable,' reports the Colonel, who was privileged to mess there, and he paid tribute to the 'remarkable beauty and charm of the ladies'. This was all very civilised, but it was not bringing down any Zeppelins.

The fighter pilots encountered nothing but frustration. Night flying was a new and dangerous exercise, to be attempted only by the highly trained. When a pilot was able to attack an airship his bullets ripped through the fabric and did no perceptible damage. A dirigible could lose three or four of its gas bags without being seriously crippled, though if the collapsed containers were centrally placed the craft might break in two. It was the function of riggers to climb up among the girders and pitch the torn bags overboard, and also to apply sealant from a pot to those which were not too severely ripped – all this with frozen fingers in a savage wind. The public, knowing little about these Jules Verne-ish activities, began to criticise their young fliers when the Zeppelins sailed on apparently unscathed. They took unkindly to being bombed, even on a modest scale; the notion that this was a war between peoples, not just between the young men of those peoples, was slow to sink in.

The nation was in some need of a tonic and the *auto-da-fé* of the airship L 21 on September 3, 1916, provided it. She was an old-style craft, not a Zeppelin proper, largely wood-built and carrying a crew of sixteen. Picked up by searchlights over north London and attacked by both guns and fighters, she seemed as invulnerable as her predecessors, but at last one gondola caught fire and flames began to spread along her fabric. Then, like a great fireball, or 'an immense incandescent mantle of white heat', the L 21 dropped slowly down the sky and crashed into a field at Cuffley, near Enfield; the first Zeppelin to fall on English soil. The crowds which had rushed into the street watched the preliminary engagement in silence, but when the airship blew up there rose one of those great shouts, full of triumph, execration and gloating, which many of those who heard them were afterwards to recall with fit apologies.

A writer in the *Spectator* was awed by the dramatic aspect. 'Half London formed the proscenium for this tragedy of the air and saw on the aerial stage the triumph of right over might. . . . Never before in human history had men sat in such a theatre and seen such a curtain rung down from the starry heights above them.' As for the great cry, 'the lordliest city in the world shouted for a great deed gallantly accomplished, cheered as men cheer from pent-up feelings when a goal is nobly won in a football match', in the spirit of 'Well played, England!' And who had treated the lordliest city to this stunning entertainment? Why, 'a lad just out of his teens', a fighter pilot of the Royal Flying Corps.

The death of L 21 happened at three am on a Sunday morning and by nine pm purported souvenirs of the airship were on sale in north London. Tens of thousands made their way to Cuffley, choking the trains, blocking the roads for miles with cars and carriages, trudging over the fields with only the vaguest idea where the wreckage lay. The papers agreed that 'Derby Day was nothing like it'. In the hope of protecting their fields and hedges farmers put up decoy signs 'To the Zepp'. Some of the pilgrims were hoping to see a dead German, but police and military had forestalled them. One man who tried to peer at charred corpses under a tarpaulin was knocked flat in the mud. Mostly, the crowd contented themselves with hunting for souvenirs, a practice which – according to a belated warning by GHQ, Home Forces – was an offence under the Defence of the Realm Act. It turned out that the night's raid by a dozen airships had killed only one man and one woman; but in the issue of *The Times* which described the scenes at Cuffley were the names of 178 officers and 4,530 men killed or wounded on the Western Front.

An inquest on the crew was held in an old public-house, The Plough, near the scorched field where the wreckage lay. The bodies were in a corrugated iron church, guarded by soldiers. Some thought the corpses deserved to be thrown into a pit of quicklime, but the Royal Flying Corps had other ideas. Six of their officers carried the coffin of the L 21's commander to a grave in Potters Bar cemetery. On the coffin lid was a silver plate inscribed: 'An unknown German officer killed while commanding Zeppelin L 21, 3 September, 1916.' The bodies of the crew, carried on a motor lorry, were laid in a communal pit, their coffins uninscribed. An aircraft flew overhead and a bugler sounded the Last Post. Thus the Royal Flying Corps maintained the military decencies, which included preserving distinctions between officers and men.

The public showed an inferior sense of occasion. They lined the funeral route, climbing trees when they could, to savour the spectacle. Some reporters said they were well-behaved, others that they were not. A woman who threw eggs at the officer's coffin, shouting obscenely, had to be protected by police.

The destruction of L21 earned a Victoria Cross for Lieutenant William Leefe Robinson, who had been in the air for two hours that night and had also attacked another airship. It was the first VC to be won in Britain. More controversially, Leefe Robinson qualified for an award of £500 by a shipbuilder and another of £2,000 by the proprietor of the *Newcastle Daily Chronicle*, as well as other sums. However, it was not the spur of blood money which accounted for three more Zeppelins over Britain in a month. Two of these were shot down on the night of September 23, 1916, one at Wigborough near the Essex coast, the other at Billericay. The crew of the former, twenty-two in number, were unharmed and were escorted into custody by a special constable, who met the brawny band, minus their headgear, wandering down a lane; arguably, they were the first German 'invaders' to set foot on English soil. Their airship lay broken-backed across two fields, near a labourer's cottage. According to one report, the Zeppelin commander grudgingly accepted tea from a vicar's wife and then demanded a bedroom in the house for the rest of the night, as he objected to sharing quarters with his men. His demand was refused, though a bedroom was prepared for an injured member of the crew. The commander was finally left to sulk all night on a makeshift bed in the hall.

The Billericay airship came down in furious flame – 'like a bar of white-hot steel', said one witness – to the accompaniment not only of cheers but of sirens and factory whistles. It had been crippled shortly after one am, not too late for sightseers in evening dress to motor out from London. Next morning the scene was like Cuffley all over again: a procession of cars, traps, brakes, carriages and bicycles (with passengers on the rear step), vendors of drinks and all the rest. This time no inquest was held, but the funeral followed the Cuffley pattern; the vicar altered 'our dear, departed brethren' to 'these men here departed'.

The third Zeppelin, commanded by Mathy, followed the railway from the East coast on the night of October 1 and was destroyed over Potters Bar, filling the sky with a false sunset. Like the commander of the Billericay airship, Mathy jumped from the flames and was found still breathing in a man-shaped dent in the ground. This success also inspired one of London's great shouts, rising from all over the capital, variously likened to thunder from a rockbound shore and the baying of demons. As the crew frizzled to death strangers shook hands and embraced.

The exultation over the fate of Zeppelins is mentioned in many memoirs. Shaw, who motorcycled to view the wreckage at Potters Bar, told the Webbs that the joy in having seen the show was such that 'the destruction of a dozen people or so in hideous terror and torment does not count'. Bertrand Russell tells how his first night with Lady Constance Malleson was interrupted by 'a shout of bestial triumph in the street'; leaping from the sheets he saw a Zeppelin flaming. In this dreadful hour her love was a refuge to him. Edith Nesbit roundly rebuked her lady companion who applauded the fall of a Zeppelin as if it were an entertainment: 'Do you realise that there are people being *burned alive* over there?' Malcolm Muggeridge mingled with souvenir hunters at the scene of a Zeppelin crash: 'Somehow it recalled scenes I had read of in historical novels of massacres and martyrdom in which the spectators bathed their handkerchiefs in the blood of their victims.'

In response to demand, London mounted a display of Zeppelin trophies at Finsbury. Among the more remarkable items, recovered in East Anglia, was one of the 'spy baskets' which were lowered by cable through the clouds above which the airships lurked. The device was like a finned torpedo, about fourteen feet long, with two observation windows. Inside were a mattress and a telephone. Had there been a man in the basket? Had he regained the gondola and if so how? Was the basket jettisoned or shot away? The *Daily Mail* asked these questions but did not know the answers. Commander Rawlinson mentions the discovery of a spy basket containing 'a very nasty mess which shortly before had been a live German'. His judgement is that it was deliberately cut away to assist the Zeppelin in a sudden rise. Such observers, he says, often hung suspended for hours, aware that the lives of their comrades depended on them. Another source describes how the appendage on its 800-metre cable would trail behind the Zeppelin, 'resembling nothing so much as a little dog running after its master'. From one such observation post the elderly Lieutenant Baron von Gemmingen, a nephew of Count Zeppelin, is said to have directed an attack on Dover, earning an Iron Cross.

The Zeppelin danger largely subsided after the failure of a mission against the Midlands by eleven naval airships on October 19, 1917, when a rising gale from the north dispersed the invaders. What followed was a melodrama deserving the attention of a producer of film epics. Only one vessel was able to recross the North Sea to its base in Jutland; the rest rode in disarray before the freezing gale, their crews inert and half-paralysed by altitude sickness and with black ice caking on their boots. Two of the invaders regained the Fatherland by way of Holland and four more straggled perilously home across the Western Front. It was one of the hazards of Zeppelins that a man could be frozen alive one minute and burned alive the next. This fate overtook a crew whose craft was shot down by the French near Lunéville. Another was forced by fighters to land at Bourbon-les-Bains, another crashed in the Alps and was destroyed by its crew. One luckless fugitive, cut off by the Alps, drifting helplessly down the Rhône valley, landed briefly near Langres, left behind two officers and fourteen men, cut away an unwanted gondola and took off again, probably to perish with all hands in the Mediterranean. At the time it was believed that other Zeppelins had met the same fate. Rejoicing in Britain at the rout of this armada was tempered by the knowledge that her defences could claim none of the credit; the destruction was wrought by the French and the Almighty, in skilled partnership. In Britain it was also known as the 'silent raid', because the guns stayed quiet for fear of guiding the invaders to London and the craft themselves were too high to be audible.

In any event, what was now needed was an answer to the new 'baby-killing' Gotha, that heavy wide-spanned biplane which, in the summer of 1917, had virtually taken over from the Zeppelins the task of mutilating London. In a memorable raid on May 25, some twenty-four of these bombers heading for London were forced to disperse, but not before killing nearly 100 people in south-east England, a quarter of them children. This was by far the heaviest loss so far; the news of it was held up for two days, which caused wild rumours to circulate. On June 13 another flight of Gothas reached London, at the defiant hour of midday, and killed more than 150, as well as causing heavy damage to two railway stations. This was the pre-war Harmsworth serial come true at last, with a scuttling capital naked to her enemies. On July 7 came an even more daring daylight raid: some twenty aircraft in steady formation bombed from about 5,000 feet. By now Londoners had learned to dive for the nearest basement or crypt. To appease popular anger, two squadrons of fighters were pulled back that summer from France, a concession grudged by the military. Then a furious cry went up for reprisal raids against German civilians, but once again the Army's reply was that the place to win the war was in France. The two squadrons were recalled by Haig and at once the Gothas returned to London. From now on the capital had to take it, as it did on a vastly greater scale in a later war. The Gothas grew heavier and carried ever-larger bombs. Belatedly the Government introduced a proper warning system of maroons; one of the earlier methods had been to send out a fast open car with a bugler (sometimes a Boy Scout) standing in the back, or a policeman hard-pedalling a cycle with a 'Take Cover' notice. Engine drivers had their own way of sounding 'All clear'; they blew a cock-a-doodle-do on their whistles.

At times of bright moon there were 'funk' migrations from the capital to Brighton and other outlying towns. In his *War Memoirs* Lloyd George says: 'Every night the commons around London were black with refugees from the threatened metropolis.' In the Guildford area hotels and boarding-houses would be besieged and families would pay to sleep in garages, sheds and stables. For East Enders there was always Epping Forest – or the Underground. Lloyd George insists that 'the undoubted terror inspired by the death-dealing skies did not swell by a single murmur the demand for peace'. An inference that he himself suffered from air-raid funk might have been deduced from paragraphs in the *Star* and *Westminster Gazette* in September 1917, stating that he had left Downing Street for his home at Walton Heath on hearing that raiders were approaching London. In fact he was in the Dover train on his way to Paris and during the raid it was stationary on a Thames bridge. The Prime Minister had to sue to obtain an apology.

In the West End of London revelry was driven underground. A bomb fell in Green Park within thirty feet of Churchill when he was dining with Lord Wimborne. Everybody had a bomb story and soldiers on leave were told they did not know what real war was like. Sometimes one man's funk was another man's opportunity. Borys Conrad, son of the novelist, was riding on leave in a taxi when the alarm went, causing the driver to abandon his vehicle and bolt down into the Tube. Conrad climbed into the driving seat of the Napier and drove to his destination, later handing the car over to the police. Some who dived for shelter into the crypt of St Martin-in-the-Fields found themselves in the company of soldiers on leave, street girls, respectable old ladies and the odd tramp. Under the Rev. 'Dick' Sheppard, much accused of 'stunting', the church with its ambiguous red lamp was ever open to all, whether they came in piety or fear.

Raids did strangely little to deter opera-goers, who would make their way through deserted streets to hear the reprieved works of Wagner. Sir Thomas Beecham could be relied upon to keep conducting against an accompaniment of gunfire, merely shrugging when the police cleared the upper tiers of the house for safety. Travel on the Underground now posed class problems; superior voices condemned the way in which the workers' families, along with 'scented aliens', were allowed to camp overnight on the platforms. The Underground was sometimes a lethal magnet. Holding an inquest on eight out of fourteen persons killed in a rush for an East End Tube station, a coroner said the panic was caused almost entirely by persons of foreign extraction behaving less like men than animals. According to the police, property found on the dead included more than £500 in notes and Russian bank deposit receipts.

Shot-down Gotha crews, aware of their unpopularity with the public, were eager to be handed over without delay to the military. Cecil Lewis, author of *Sagittarius Rising*, has told how he helped to escort a Gotha crew from eastern England to London. At each station on the line an angry crowd had to be fended off by an officer with a revolver. One flyer tore off his badges for greater safety. The hatred for German aviators enters into Kipling's notorious story, *Mary Postgate*, in which a lady's companion refuses aid to a badly wounded German airman, watches the baby-killer die, then goes home and relaxes in a hot bath before tea. Her employer comments on how well she looks. The story has been well probed for hidden meanings.

At the end of the war the total killed in air raids, by both airships and aircraft, came to about 1,000, with some 3,000 injured. Though the totals seem small, the incidence of tragedy was often shocking enough: seven of a family wiped out here, another seven there. A bomb on Odhams, the periodical publishers, killed thirty-five. But the civilian dead for the whole war amounted to only about one-fifteenth of those slaughtered on the first day of the Somme.

CHAPTER 11

LIVING WITH TELEGRAMS

To turn the pages of *The Times* for the months which followed the Battle of the Somme is to experience something of that mixture of numbness and awe which afflicts the hardiest as they look on the great graveyards of the Western Front. Here, day by day, are the casualty lists, with sometimes more than 5,000 names in an issue, and rarely fewer than 1,000. Here is the running chronicle of Attrition, compiled and edited by the bureaucracy of Moloch. For thousands of victims it was the first time their names had been in the papers. The next-of-kin were informed before the lists were published; it was in these endless columns that people looked for the names of friends, lovers, colleagues, neighbours, former schoolmates.

By buying a popular newspaper, like the *Daily Mail* or *Daily Mirror*, it was possible to escape the casualty lists. Newspapers of record like the *Daily Telegraph* and *Morning Post* printed the names of the lost generation until the end of the Somme battle, then gave lists of officers' casualties only. *The Times* published the names of other ranks until the end of 1917, then it too concentrated on fallen officers. Thereafter, the roll of the uncommissioned ranks appeared only in the weekly lists published by the Stationery Office.

The newspapers made no attempt to dramatise the lists. Sometimes these began, unobtrusively, across the foot of a page of classified advertisements, before spreading to other pages. There were no editorial head-shakings over the monstrous totals. On the main news pages the dispatches from France were confident that the battle was being won and that the enemy's losses were gigantic.

In *The Times*, under the single-column headline ROLL OF HONOUR, the names of officers were printed alphabetically one to a line; and there was a feature headlined FALLEN OFFICERS which contained biographical details of those with especial claims to notice. Under the headlines ROLL OF HONOUR: LOSSES IN THE RANKS the names of the uncommissioned ('privates unless otherwise described') would be run together in an impacted mass of small print extending, regiment by regiment, for seven or eight wide columns; any attempt at typographical display would have left little enough room for anything else. As if to show that in the midst of death we are in life the slabs of type would be broken up by the bold headlines of advertisements: DANGER FROM WINGED HUNS – THE FLY PERIL or IN THE SHADOW OF GOUT or THE DAYFIELD BODY SHIELD – SAVES OFFICER WHO THREW HIMSELF ON EXPLODING BOMB. Sub-headlines in the lists included *Killed in Action, Died of Wounds, Wounded, Seriously Wounded, Missing, Missing Believed Killed, Missing Believed Wounded, Wounded and Missing, Suffering from Gas Poisoning, Accidentally Killed, Prisoners in Enemy Hands* and so on, through all the hazards of battle. There was also a category which did not appear in the officers' lists: *Wounded – Shell (Shock)*. From time to time the Admiralty and Merchant Marine contributed their lists, with classifications like *Drowned* and *Missing Feared Drowned* (which is how some died on the Flanders battlefield). There were even tolls to be recorded on the home front: one Spring day in 1915 a battalion of the Royal Scots lost 157 dead and 200 injured in a matter of seconds in a multiple train crash at Gretna.

The first casualty list appeared on September 3, 1914, with a roll of thirty-five officers killed, wounded or missing. 'At first,' says R. D. Blumenfeld, 'people discussed the deaths of second-lieutenants with bated breath. Gradually the familiarity of the thing became apparent. You received the news of the death of your friends as a matter of fact. You seemed somehow or other to be prepared for it, as if it were a necessity, an inevitable complement of all war news, good or bad.' After Mons and Le Cateau 'Eve' of the *Tatler* wrote: 'Really now there is hardly a family among the people one knows that isn't more or less deeply in mourning.' The glossy magazines ran their own illustrated casualty lists, with studio photographs of fresh, handsome, clean-run menfolk under standing headlines like DEAD ON THE FIELD OF HONOUR.

The lists could not hope to reflect the day-by-day horror of the Somme. On the first day the British Army lost 19,240 dead and 57,470 wounded, three times its entire losses in battle in the Boer War. Publication of these names was spread over weeks. By the end of 1916 Britain's losses were greater than in all her wars since the Plantagenets were overthrown. After two years of strife Nancy Astor noted: 'We did not look at the casualty lists any more. There was nothing to look for. All our friends had gone.'

While the casualty lists deaden the imagination, there are tiny items in the 'News in Brief' columns which shock it back to life: items laconically indexed in *The Times* as 'Family Records', telling of domestic sacrifices beyond the call of honour, patriotism or even reason, and inconceivable in any other period of British history.

John Buchan has described how, when on leave in the Tweedside hills, he met a shepherd's wife who had four sons in the Forces. Jock was in France with the Royal Scots, Jamie was in a place 'called Sammythrace', Tam was on the Arctic shore and Davie was at the walls of Jerusalem. This mother was lucky that only one of her sons was in the trenches. Many a mother had twice as many sons serving, all of them on the Western Front. The age was nothing if not philoprogenitive and there were reports of families with a dozen or more sons in uniform. At the time of the Somme battle Mr and Mrs A. Skerman, of Ashwell, Hertfordshire, had eleven sons in the Army and a twelfth just called up. Their seventy-year-old father, busy at the hay harvest, said to the Hitchin recruiting sergeant, 'I'd better go to complete the lot.' In the year of Passchendaele William Bacon, of Mitcham, a retired postman who in days of peace had captained ten sons at cricket, had eight out of eleven in the trenches; all were married with families and all had worked for the Post Office. In the village of Bromley, near Rotherham, was a sixty-seven-year-old Army pensioner, not even named, with sixteen sons in the firing line. He was said to have reared thirty-one children, including twelve daughters.

A sort of contest developed to see which family could field most fighting men. The Barkers, of Kingston-on-Thames, claimed thirty-four (sons, grandsons, nephews and sons-in-law) of whom six had been killed. Mrs White, of Addleston, Surrey, claimed eight sons and nine nephews; Mrs G. Kerley, of Cranborne, Dorset, aged eighty-six, had eighteen out of thirty-eight grandsons serving. Sometimes the King telegraphed his congratulations to such families. At other times congratulations came from the military tribunals when debating whether to call up the last son of the family (see Chapter Fifteen).

These family records were reported quite baldly, without any headline. Nor were headlines brought out when the small print told of families of sons wiped out. All we read is: 'Mrs Hughes, who lives near Roscommon, has just been informed by the War Office of the death of her sixth son in action. Two of her sons came from America to join and two belong to the Australian forces.' Three sons of Mr and Mrs Macleod, of Mealabout, Isle of Lewis, died on active service to add to the two who had already been lost in the Boer War. Of nine Birmingham brothers called Restorick eight were killed in action and the ninth wounded, all in different regiments; father and mother were dead but there were four sisters living. The Empire was not behindhand: in Vancouver a widower called Ball with eleven sons had married a widow with five sons. All these had enlisted and ten had been killed in action.

The press was not encouraged to play up morbid angles. No breast-beating women journalists debated which was worse, to lose an only son or to lose five sons and have one left. There were no photographs of the home with a row of empty chairs. The enforced stoicism of the age will never be emulated. Most of the traditional indulgences and solaces of grief were ruled out. If a son died in hospital in Britain the Army would lay on a funeral by gun carriage, with a Union Jack and a bugler. But a father could lose all his sons in Flanders and be unable to follow any of them to the grave. All he had to show was a row of snaps on the mantelpiece and a handful of War Office telegrams.

The telegram was the terror by day. During the big battles the sight of a Post Office boy in the street caused agonies of apprehension; a sharp knock on the door was the signal for

panic. None has written more movingly of this ordeal than Vera
Brittain, who lost a lover and a brother in France. Years after
the war she was unable to work comfortably in a room within
earshot of the front doorbell. Barbara Cartland writes: 'We . . .
watched our mothers go pale and fight for control at the sight of
a telegraph boy coming to the door. We watched them open a
yellow envelope with trembling fingers.' Ernest Raymond mentions a mother who called for a maid to be present whenever she
opened a telegram, for fear she fainted. No servant would think
of handing a telegram to a mother with a child in arms. But the
opening words 'Deeply regret . . .' could be a false alarm; Lady
Gregory tells how the insensitive were capable of sending a
telegram about a broken engagement in those terms.

In Henry Williamson's novel, *How Dear Is Life*, a woman
asks a telegraph boy if he realises what the sight of his stopping
in a road can mean to a mother with a son at the Front:

> 'Don't blame me, ma'am. I don't know what's in me tele-
> grams. Only sometimes, like.'
> 'Were you the little boy who brought the telegram to Mr
> Bolton's this morning?'
> ' 'Im what's son was killed. Yuss, I did an' all. And the lady I
> just bin to's 'ad three killed, all together. I wouldn't take
> nothing from 'er, though she offered me a copper.'
> 'You are a good kind boy,' said Mrs Neville. 'Now you wait
> here, dear, and I will bring you a nice orange.'

In H. G. Wells's *Mr Britling Sees It Through* the telegram
announcing the death of Mr Britling's son is brought, not by a
boy, but by a girl in a pinafore. How much is he to tip the
messenger of death? He wants to 'give the brat sixpence' but has
only threepence and a shilling in his pocket. For Mr Britling this
is a real problem; it would be shocking to give her a shilling, 'and
he couldn't somehow give just coppers for so important a thing
as Hugh's death'. In the end he gives her the shilling. He is
convinced she knows what is in the telegram and will be shocked
at 'the gala-like treatment of such terrible news'. She seems to
be taking him in, 'recording him, for repetition, greedily, with
every fibre of her being'. Then he turns away and forgets her.

The messenger was a girl, we are told, because boys were now
doing the work of youths and youths the work of men. In

Parliament in July 1915 Herbert Samuel announced that where possible disabled men would be used to deliver telegrams.

In the earlier years the message would read: 'Deeply regret to inform you that 2nd Lieut . . . was killed in action on . . . Lord Kitchener expresses his sympathy.' After Kitchener's death the telegrams ended: 'The Army Council express their sympathy.' Sometimes there was a telegram from Buckingham Palace: 'The King and Queen deeply regret the loss you and the Army have sustained by the death of your son/husband in the service of his country. Their Majesties truly sympathise with you in your sorrow.'

Was a telegram the best way of delivering bad news? Readers of the *Daily Mail*, in January 1917, commended the French system, under which the news was sent via the local mayor, who was enjoined to see that his messenger conveyed it with all sympathy and delicacy, along with the nation's thanks. Each mayor had his own band of volunteers for this purpose and was required to report back to the Minister for War when the mission was completed.

For some, bad news came by post belatedly. In the earlier stages of the war a singularly harsh letter was sent by Infantry Records to the next-of-kin of soldiers who had been shot for cowardice or desertion: 'I am directed to inform you that a report has been received from the War Office to the effect that . . . was sentenced after trial by court-martial to be shot for . . . and that sentence was duly executed on . . .' The letter might well be signed by a second-lieutenant on behalf of a commanding officer. In 1917 in Parliament the War Minister was asked whether deaths of executed soldiers were announced in the casualty lists and was told that they were not; the next-of-kin were informed independently. James Hogge pressed for the name to be included in the casualty lists, to avoid embarrassment to next-of-kin. That, said Ian Macpherson, Under-Secretary for War, would not be stating the truth. 'It is a polite letter which is sent, stating what is necessarily a brutal fact.' To a suggestion that one or two words of sympathy could be added there was no reply. However, shortly afterwards Bonar Law announced: 'It has been decided that in future the communications made to the dependents of soldiers shot at the front should merely state that they have died on active service.' In post-war statements to the Commons the number of officers and men executed in the British Army was given as 287, out of 2,690 sentenced to death.

The telegram with the War Office's regrets was only part of the bereaved family's ordeal. After some days letters addressed to the dead man were returned to sender laconically stamped 'Killed in Action' or 'Deceased'. Most poignant of all were the letters from the dead, hidden in desks or entrusted to friends, which began 'You will only read this when I am no longer here . . .' or 'This is a letter I hope you will never read.' Then came the delivery of the dead soldier's effects. Vera Brittain tells how the family of her lover were sent his bullet-ripped tunic, a pair of blood-stained breeches cut open at the top by someone in a hurry and a once-rakish cap crushed out of recognition. Why, she asked, return these gruesome rags? The youth's mother directed that they should be burned or buried; they smelled of death. Among them was a notebook containing poems. Sir Oliver Lodge, who was to write a famous book about his dead son Raymond, received as part of the blood-soaked kit from Flanders a diary with its pages congealed together.

A more treasurable relic of an officer was his sword; but according to a correspondence in *The Times* early in 1915 under the title *The Swords Of Fallen Officers*, many a weapon, perhaps because badly labelled, had vanished on the way home. 'The pain caused to relatives by the non-receipt of a lost one's sword is great,' wrote one reader. In fact, the sword might well have been the cause of the officer's death, for it was a foolish weapon to flourish in trench warfare.

The death of an officer was followed by letters from his commanding officer and brother officers, praising his character and devotion to duty. They usually said that he had died instantly, whether he had or not (it was always 'shot through the head' or 'shot through the heart' according to Vera Brittain). The stretcher-bearers did all that was possible; he died in very fine company; he was killed while rallying his men; he was loved by all; the sun shone on his funeral; and so forth. For regimental officers not trained in the art of condolence it was a grim exercise, but at times they acquitted themselves uncommonly well (always they hoped that the next-of-kin would not pursue them for further details). Among the letters might be one from the dead officer's servant. Vera Brittain says that one such communication was 'extremely loquacious and illegibly expressed in pencil'; but that such communications should be sent at all illuminates the officer–man relationships of the day. After the Hon. Yvo Charteris, son of the Earl of Wemyss, was killed at Loos his soldier-servant Bates wrote to the family to ask if he might call on them during his leave. To Cynthia Asquith he was 'the greatest darling imaginable'; 'I have never seen such charm – extreme good looks and the manners of an ambassador.' Bates testified that his officer was always fearless and cool and that he had died instantaneously. Anita Leslie says that when Clare Sheridan's husband was killed, his wounded servant David arrived for a visit, spoke of the events of Sheridan's last day and his joy on learning that he had fathered a son; then, after some days, having made himself useful and agreeable, David returned to the Front, his wound healed.

In the summer of 1916 the cinema was called into service to show the people of Britain something of the ordeal their men were facing across the Channel. So far films from the Front had featured troops training or singing in cafés or kicking footballs about; now the War Office decided to release films taken during the Somme battle by its Military Director of Kinematograph Operations. These showed soldiers going over the top, falling back dead or wounded, stumbling into wire, being carried away on stretchers and receiving emergency treatment. Among those who queued for hours in London to see the films were the bereaved.

The Dean of Durham, the Very Rev. H. Hensley Henson, took the innovation very much amiss. Only recently, he pointed out in *The Times*, a proposal to film the Cabinet in session had been abandoned after protests that such a thing would insult the nation's self-respect; yet people were now crowding into cinemas, 'feasting their eyes on pictures which present the passion and death of British soldiers'. The Dean may well have been one of those who used to argue that to show a moving picture of a person after death would be an intolerable blasphemy. Thousands still found it hard to come to terms with the cinema. However, on the issue of the Somme films the Dean received little support. Sir Henry Newbolt wrote a poem praising them ('O living pictures of the dead . . .'). Many bereaved citizens wrote to the papers to say that at last they realised the degree of the sacrifice their loved ones had made and how proud they were to be able to share in some measure the great adventure with them. Any complaints tended to be about the trivial supporting programmes.

To forestall objections about cinemas making money out of the films the War Office insisted that forty per cent of the takings should go to charities. The King had already praised the films at a special showing in Windsor Castle and the Queen had pronounced them 'wonderful'. Lloyd George's secretary, Frances Stevenson, who had lost a brother at the Front, said that having seen what he had gone through she felt as the Greek playgoers of old must have felt – purged in their minds by pity and terror. By the standards of today the Somme films were masterpieces of restraint; but at least they did a little to bring the battlefields nearer. They were shown all over Britain, even in the remotest village halls. By January 1917 the *Daily Mail* had a full-page advertisement headed COME AND SEE THE TANKS ADVANCE AT THE FRONT. It was now the Battle of the Ancre. 'Take the wife and children,' said the announcement, adding, 'Nothing faked.' Among the sights to see were 'the sea of mud which covers everything and in which even the horses sink knee-deep'. Showmanship, it seemed, rather than pity was now in the saddle. Perhaps it was the Staff at General Headquarters which should have been goggling at the pictures of the great sea of mud. (Passchendaele was still to come.)

It was about the time of the Somme battle that the Government was persuaded that a death telegram, scrawled in an unlettered hand, was not really an adequate memorial to a dead soldier. France sent the next-of-kin a diploma expressing the 'homage and gratitude' of the nation. Perhaps some gesture, not too florid in conception, would be appreciated by those who had 'given their sons'? Eventually it was decided to produce a small bronze plaque bearing the words 'He Died For Freedom And Honour' and inscribed with the dead man's name and service record. One side portrayed Britannia with a rather meagre lion and a group of dolphins (symbolising sea power), and on the other side the lion was depicted slaying an eagle representing the Central Powers. The plaque did not go into production until just after the war, by which time Woolwich Arsenal was happy to secure part of the contract. Today specimens of the plaque are to be found in shops selling military souvenirs.

Meanwhile the working people had devised their own communal expression of remembrance: the street shrine. Usually it took the form of a tablet attached to wall or railings bearing the names of the neighbourhood dead (and sometimes of the serving), surmounted by crossed flags and with a shelf for flowers; or it might consist of a special structure erected at a street corner. Generals and admirals and their ladies were persuaded to tour the shrines; bishops blessed them; and the Queen laid her tribute of flowers beside memorials in Holborn and Hackney. War shrines were not found in sedate suburbs; they were a feature of those streets where life was lived communally. However, in essence a shrine of this type differed little from, say, the Roll of Honour which the House of Commons set up in St Margaret's, Westminster: a simple framed list of Members and officers killed on active service. In 1918, to mark four years of war, 20,000 people brought flowers to a large and controversial war shrine in Hyde Park, an obelisk flanked by two pylons, each capped by a cone supposedly symbolising eternity. There was talk of replacing this shrine with one by Sir Edwin Lutyens, but the conventional argued that the place for devotions was in a church.

Many families were eager that their dead sons should be commemorated by memorials within churches, but bishops and rectors pointed out, often in the face of displeasure, that a collective sacrifice would be better honoured by a collective memorial. The sometimes anguished and often ludicrous controversies over war memorials fall outside the scope of this book, but it is worth mentioning a forgotten proposal that a dead soldier's home should contain its own memorial to him. A body called the Civic Arts Association, created in the hope of ensuring that the dead should not be insulted by the sort of rubbishy street furniture erected after Queen Victoria's Jubilees, held a competition in which designs were invited for various kinds of memorial, including 'an inexpensive memorial for the home'. The idea seems to have been lost sight of, although at one time it appealed to Sir William Lever, the paternalist soap-maker of Port Sunlight. According to a biographer, he wanted to see a 'stained glass window' in every mourning home in his town, to consist of a coloured transparency, bearing the dead man's name, which could be affixed to any window the relatives might nominate. Lever was willing to foot the bill, but the idea was quietly abandoned.

For some, the Bible was not dead but uncomfortably alive. Pamphleteers in some profusion discussed whether Flanders was truly the great battlefield of the Apocalypse, the Armageddon where the powers of light and darkness would finally contest for mastery. They offered, among other titles: *Armageddon Foretold*, *Is It Armageddon?*, *This Is The Armageddon* and *Armageddon Not Yet*. Other theologians dealt with the Supreme Warlord: *Is The Kaiser Lucifer?* and *Is The Kaiser The 'Beast' of Revelations?* Then there was the question: would the war end in the Second Coming? Yes, according to *The Great War, The Herald Of The Lord's Return*; maybe, according to *Messiah's Advent: Is It Imminent?*; no, said *Christendom's Impending Doom*. None of this did any harm, not even *Why The War Will End In 1917*.

The war stimulated a trade in sacred emblems, scapulars, cauls, talismans and amulets. 'Touchwood, the Wonderful Eastern Charm', sold by the million. Suggested by the custom of touching wood for safety (which in turn stemmed from touching the Cross), Touchwood was a tiny, sparkling-eyed imp surmounted by a khaki cap, with his legs crossed. The imp's great day came when he was presented by the actress Delysia to 1,200 officers and men of the 36th Battalion City of London Regiment in Regent's Park, London; a seeming contravention of the Army regulation which forbids the wearing of trinkets.

Among Irish troops there was a clamorous demand for the Badge of the Sacred Heart, an oval piece of red cloth bearing the representation of Christ, which was sewn inside the tunic. Jesuits in Dublin, faced with huge orders from soldiers' relatives, warned that it was no talisman against shot and shell, but to no avail. Soldiers testified in public how, by wearing the badge and uttering a timely cry of 'O Sacred Heart of Jesus, have mercy on us!', they diverted shells from their course. Mothers of soldiers were not happy until their sons had been equipped with all available religious prophylactics. In a religious magazine was quoted a letter from a bereaved mother writing about her dead son who had served in the Royal Munster Fusiliers: 'Dear Reverend Father, I have heard from Father Gleason and he died with his rosary beads round his neck and reciting his rosary . . . I know perfectly well that it was owing to his having St Joseph's Cord about him that he got such a happy death . . . he also had

the Sacred Heart of Jesus, a crucifix and his Blue and Brown
Scapulars on him, so that I am content about the way he died.'
Sometimes soldiers twisted rosary beads round the barrels of
their rifles. Off the battlefield, a charm could still render useful
service. A resident of Mountmellick wrote: 'I have sent 147
parcels to prisoners of war from this town and not one was lost. I
put the Sacred Heart Badge in every parcel.'

Sir Philip Gibbs, the war correspondent, met numerous men
at the Front who believed themselves immune from sudden
death. A colonel in the North Staffordshires told him: 'I have a
mystical power . . . Nothing will ever hit me as long as I keep that
power which comes from faith. I go through any barrage
unscathed because my will is strong enough to turn aside explo-
sive shells and machine-gun bullets. As matter, they must obey
my intelligence. They are powerless to resist the mind of a man
in touch with the Universal Spirit, as I am.' Gibbs thought the
colonel might have been mad, but envied him his 'kink'.

There was a popular legend, perhaps not yet extinct, that a
British regiment served throughout the war without losing a
man, thanks to the assiduity with which officers and men repeated the words of the 91st Psalm, or *Psalm of Protection*. ('I
will say of the Lord, He is my refuge and my fortress . . . Thou
shalt not be afraid for the terror by night; nor for the arrow that
flieth by day. . . . A thousand shall fall by thy side, and ten
thousand at thy right hand; but it shall not come nigh thee. . . .')
This legend is traceable to the writings of the once-notorious F.
L. Rawson, an 'engineer' who, failing to extract gold from sea
water, found brief prosperity by conducting a 'prayer shop', or
'psychic bucket shop', at 90 Regent Street, London, which was
exposed by Harold Ashton in a series of articles in the *Daily
Mail* in 1917. He had already been under fire in *Truth*.

A prayer shop differed from a soothsaying or a mediumistic
establishment in that the staff undertook to say prayers on a
sliding scale of payment on behalf of anyone in trouble; an
intercession which any minister of the Gospel would have been
happy to make for nothing. In Rawson's prayer shop the person
interceded for did not need to be present or even to know about
the transaction; divine healing would simply flow from Regent
Street to the recipient. A number of presentable young women
('vestals', Ashton called them) sat at small tables interviewing

bereaved women, filling in forms for them and discussing how much they wanted to pay. Sometimes the well-dressed clients were privileged to have among them a young 'Colonel MacGregor DSO' in Black Watch tartan, one of those who, like Gibbs's mad colonel, had passed unscathed through shellfire. So had his regiment, according to Rawson. ('All of them?' – 'Very nearly all.') For a fee, the master held 'Audible Treatments', addressing his audience in mumbo-jumbo which seemed to derive from Mrs Eddy (though the Christian Scientists disowned him). He claimed to be able to divert Zeppelin bombs from their target and to evade blows from madmen. When he failed to stop a blow from the *Mail*'s investigator, the ladies present were indignant that anyone should make a scene in a prayer shop. One of them wanted to know why, with so much divine will-power waiting to be harnessed, they could not stop the war. It would need tremendous concentration by a great many, said Rawson; Jesus or Buddha could do it right away, but it would take him six months at the rate he was progressing. Meanwhile his acolytes were doing what they could, intervening on behalf of oppressed prisoners of war, regiments drafted to unpleasant places and soldiers whose rations were being delayed. Ashton kept his exposure going until the day when police raided the prayer shop and took away half a ton of records.

For Rawson, it was a setback but not a total disaster. In 1917, when it became imperative for Britain to grow more food, he published his *Divine Protection For The Garden And Farm*, describing how right thinking could restore sickly plants, stop plantains growing in lawns, keep tools sharp, prevent green-house fires going out, abate high winds and dematerialise harmful bacteria; the same right thinking which, he said, had enabled aviators to stop their engines faltering and postmen to keep savage dogs at bay. Some of his works were still being published after World War Two.

The rush to spiritualism began soon after the first big casualty lists came out. It soon became an obsession in all ranks of society and a great many opportunists set out to exploit it. Kipling, according to Charles Carrington, found 'peculiarly trying' the letters from mediums offering to get in touch with his son John, who died at Loos; his poem 'En Dor' mocks the pretence that the voice of a dead man can come only through a 'hireling's mouth'. Cynthia Asquith tells how, in 1916, her mother resorted to a medium with the excuse that 'perhaps one ought just to give a chance to the theory that the middle man may well be necessary for communication'. At other big houses table-rapping was tried out in a less reverent spirit. In 1916 Edward Marsh stayed at the house of the wealthy Mrs Duggan, who still kept four footmen. During the table-rapping (we are told by Christopher Hassall) the late Mr Duggan kept coming through and talking about the war in a confusing fashion, until his widow asked him 'quite nicely' to go away and let somebody else take over.

In 1916 Kipling wrote a short story called *On The Gate*, making gentle fun of the upsets caused to the bureaucracy of Heaven by the mass influx of dead from the battlefields. St Peter, though badly overworked, was doing his best to keep up standards of admission, though St Christopher was ready to admit 'anything that looks wet and muddy'. It is hardly surprising that this story was not published until after the war. For their part, spiritualists claimed to have special knowledge of the 1914 emergency plans prepared on the Other Side. According to one source, the spirit had been alerted in the summer of 1914 to prepare for 'a vast number of Servicemen' who were about to be 'hastily flung into the next world'. (This contrasted with the situation in 1939, when the spirits believed there would be no war.) It was even claimed that 'part of the plan' was that the *Empress of Ireland* should have a big contingent of Salvation Army officers on board when she sank in May 1914 (148 Salvationists were drowned). 'These were needed to form a good link between the military life and the religious life, for the special inter-world duties consequent on the war.' The Salvationists' experience of sudden death made them especially valuable for this purpose; and they did not need to be told that God works in mysterious ways.

Those who doubted in their hearts that the mass drowning of Salvationists could have been part of the divine plan were faced, in the winter of 1916, with the startling vision of the life of dead subalterns on the Other Side contained in *Raymond, or Life and Death*, by the scientist-spiritualist Sir Oliver Lodge, Principal of Birmingham University. Raymond Lodge, youngest son of Sir Oliver, typical of thousands of second-lieutenants, had been killed at Hooge Hill in 1915. His father sought to get in touch with him through the medium Mrs Osborne Leonard, whose control was a young girl called Feda. Some of the purported messages came in Feda's voice and other information was obtained from table-tiltings. Raymond, it appeared, was still feeling his way about, occasionally pinching himself to see if he was real. Such pinches did not hurt. New arrivals, if they so wished, were able to wear their familiar clothes, but they soon dressed in white robes like 'the natives'. The sexes seemed to have the same feeling for each other, but they had 'a different expression of it'. No children were born; procreation was performed only in the physical body, on the earth plane. Raymond was friendly with a golden-haired girl, who carried a lily. Some newly-arrived 'chaps', ignorant of the customs, asked for cigars and whisky-and-sodas, which were provided by the heavenly hosts, for there were laboratories which manufactured such things from essences and gases; but the taste for earthly consolations of this kind rapidly passed away. The spirit bodies of those who had been blown to pieces took some time to reassemble themselves; but Raymond knew a man who had lost an arm and had grown a new, rather better, one; he himself had grown a new tooth. Raymond warned that they were having 'terrible trouble' with arrivals who had been prematurely cremated, and urged a seven-day wait before a body was burned ('people are so careless'). Some newcomers with unfortunate tastes and voices went to a sort of reformatory, but the rest joined in the community life, which involved a good deal of singing, not necessarily of sacred songs, and a certain amount of skylarking; they also took an interest in the progress of the earthly war. There were trees and gardens on the Other Side and the heavenly mansions were made of bricks, fashioned from earthly emanations.

Sir Oliver Lodge well knew the risks he was taking in printing such material. He conceded that some of Feda's statements were humorous or absurd, but he felt it would not be right to pick and choose among her messages, since some of them were of confirmable evidential value. He acknowledged that Feda sometimes did a silly-little-girl act; she stumbled over big words while managing very well with subalterns' slang; and he agreed it was possible she had picked up some ideas from the plethora of spiritualist books or from other sittings at which she had assisted (the newspapers of the times were intermittently agitated over the risks of premature cremation and burial).

Raymond was a wild success, with printing after printing for the rest of the war. Many reviewers praised Sir Oliver's courage, if nothing else. The *Spectator* thought he had observed the spirit of Dr Johnson's dictum: 'Sir, to keep things out of a book merely because people tell you they will not be believed is meanness.' However, the journal thought the book would create bewilderment and that the picture of life on the Other Side would impress many as jejune and sentimental. Could there have been, the writer wondered, a terrific plot by the country's mediums: Lodge's son reported dead, all mediums alerted to devise plans for hocussing sitters, investigators sent out to pick up scraps of information from family and servants, relevant photographs circulated to all conspirators? All this was possible, but was it likely? 'To upset the mediums we have indeed to represent them as persons of unholy cunning endowed with a power of rapid ratiocination and also as drivelling idiots – which is puzzling at the lowest.' To the *Daily Mail*, then campaigning against psychic charlatans, *Raymond* was 'Sir Oliver Lodge's Spook Book: Half a Guinea's Worth of Rubbish'. The scientist had proved 'as easily credulous as the sad creatures who fall a willing prey to soothsayer and fortune-teller'.

The established Church was much put out over the success of *Raymond*. The Master of the Temple, Dr E. W. Barnes (later Bishop of Birmingham) deplored the vogue for communicating with spirits, especially under the cloak of science. He quoted the belief of Lord Halifax, who wrote a pamphlet replying to *Raymond*, that evil spirits had ensnared the young subaltern. A Swedenborgian, the Rev. E. J. E. Schreck, found in the book 'intrinsic evidence that the whole story was concocted by deluding spirits'. There was a good deal of mixed company between heaven and hell, he said, and it was possible in the early stages for the evil-minded to impose on the good.

In the columns of *Light*, the spiritualist magazine, Sir Oliver Lodge protested that there had been too much concentration on the miracle of the cigars and whiskies; persons on the Other Side did not occupy their time with such things, but newcomers were always puzzled and asked for what was unreasonable. In meeting their requests, the spirits were acting merely as clergy in a retreat would do if a stranger, mistaking the place for a hotel, asked for licensed refreshment. As for the power to manufacture such things, he saw no reason why the study of chemistry and physics should cease on the Other Side, any more than that the pursuit of art and literature should cease.

In a later edition of the book, *Raymond Revised*, Sir Oliver said some people had been upset because the dead generation were singing songs like *Irish Eyes* and bursts of ragtime, but youths 'shot out of the trenches' were not likely to become saints overnight. Let us be sensible, he said; 'sudden perfection is not for the likes of us'. The revised edition also told how the family invited the medium Mrs Leonard to stay at the house called Mariemont, where Raymond had lived. Waking in the White Room she heard raps on the wardrobe, saw a greenish light and recognised the young officer. In a later seance Raymond pointed out that they had put the wrong date on his memorial tablet.

Early in 1917 the *Daily Mail*, having disposed of Rawson, reported under the running headline THE FLIGHT OF THE SEERS how the West End of London was being purged of 'clairvoyants, psychic healers, palmists, massage and hypnotic specialists, psychometrists, astrologers, mediums ("trance" and "normal"), phrenologists, crystal-gazers and divine healers'. Three hundred of them, said the newspaper, had been marked down for attention; they included cooks, shop assistants and dressmakers, who had profitably discovered they had psychic gifts. A Madame Keiro complained in Marlborough Street Police Court that Lord Northcliffe had sent in seventeen spies after her. The heat was such that *Light*, with many heart-searchings and a prompting or two from Lady Mosley, decided to drop all advertisements by professional mediums and their kind; though it retained a prominent advertisement for the Vitic Rod, a highly charged piece of metal which 'gives vigour to the medium and should always be used before and after seances'. Some mediums held meetings to protest at being persecuted under the Witchcraft and Vagrancy Acts. They also had to combat allegations that they were part of the dread Hidden Hand conspiracy (see Chapter Twenty-One). Arnold Bennett, never one to miss an experience, attended a seance at this time and was told by the medium's son that there were 500 professed spiritualist soldiers at Aldershot.

In 1918 Sir Arthur Conan Doyle published his psychic testament, *The New Revelation*. His interest in spiritualism had been quickened by a woman resident in his household who convinced him she was receiving messages from her three brothers killed in Flanders. 'Nearly every woman is an undeveloped medium,' he said. 'Let her try her own powers of automatic writing. . . . What is done must be done with every precaution in a reverent and prayerful mood. But if you are earnest you will win through somehow, for someone else is probably trying on the other side.' He instanced Raymond's account of how dead boys were anxious to get their messages through to their people, but found ignorance and prejudice a perpetual bar.

The Church had another problem on its hands: what to do about the spiritual conversion of H. G. Wells. Late in 1916 appeared his semi-autobiographical novel, *Mr Britling Sees It Through*, which joined *Raymond* in the best-seller lists. Mr Britling, a prosperous and self-important writer too old to fight, much exercised by the moral issues of the war, loses his son in battle (as Wells did not) and suddenly discovers God. Brooding late at night he feels a Presence, 'a Presence so close to him that it was behind his eyes and in his brain and hands . . . it was the Master, the Captain of Mankind, it was God, there present with him, and he knew it was God'. For Mr Britling, religion was now the first thing and the last thing; 'until a man has found God and been found by God, he begins at no beginning, he works to no end. . . .'

Coming from the great scoffer and agnostic, this was apocalyptic stuff. Thousands rejoiced because a brand had been snatched from the burning. The timing was perfect; it was the dismal aftermath of the Somme and the bereaved were ready to welcome anything that strengthened their shrunken faith in the divine. Gratefully they echoed the sentiment of Mr Britling: 'Our sons have shown us God.' But not every churchman was happy. The Wellsian God, the Captain of Mankind, was merely the grandiloquently named ruler of Wells's Utopia, a world state president wearing a secular halo. Christian congregations were urged to think twice before worshipping such an idol. However, nothing could stay the sale of *Mr Britling*, which put its author in the same tax range as the munitions profiteers.

Wells followed up Mr Britling with *God, The Invisible King*, published in 1917; and in the same year William Archer teased him in *God And Mr Wells*. 'Where was the Invisible King in July 1914?' asked Archer. 'Or for that matter what has he been doing since July 1870?' The Invisible King, who apparently was not a figure of speech but as real an entity as the Kaiser or President Wilsor had 'made a terrible hash' of his opportunities all through the ages. In his *Experiment in Autobiography* Wells explains away his war-time lapse. What happened, he says, was that he had been revolted by the way in which men were being urged to die 'for King and Country' when they could have lived and died for a greater objective which he tried to personify in his Invisible King, making no concession to Christianity. He wished he had not fallen into this 'barren detour' and was sorry to have misled everybody.

CHAPTER 13

STRIFE IN THE FACTORIES

By modern standards, and even by the standards of the time, one of the more freakish creations of the war was the Dockers' Battalion of the Liverpool Regiment, raised by Lord Derby in 1915. The men, all volunteers, were subject to military law; they wore a light khaki uniform, learned how to form fours and were supposed to shave daily and polish their boots. However, their duties were performed strictly in accordance with trade union rules. Financially they derived the best from both worlds: they were paid the dockers' minimum of 35s a week plus the shilling a day paid to men in uniform. As a further comfort, the Battalion received an undertaking that it would never be posted abroad. The NCOs were drawn from the union's trusted officials, who enjoyed the right, on giving notice to the commanding officer, to inspect the men's cards and badges and demand the suspension of any whose contributions were in arrears.

Lord Derby stressed that the Battalion would never be used for strike-breaking, later qualifying this by saying he would not regard it as strike-breaking if the Battalion did the work of men who, by opposing their union officials, were holding up supplies for the Front. Lloyd George and Kitchener both supported the idea of the Battalion. The secretary of the Dockers' Union, James Sexton, claims that Lloyd George urged him to become its commanding officer; but, writes Sexton, 'I could not imagine myself wearing a Sam Browne belt and a sword – possibly even having to ride a horse.' He pleaded that the role would interfere with his trade union duties and Lord Derby assumed the command, which had probably been the intention all along. After its first review the Battalion marched off to work on an ocean liner, where some of the men changed their uniforms for rougher garb.

The Dockers' Battalion, according to Sexton, 'worked quite well', despite antagonism and deep distrust from other dockers. No records of court-martials or field punishments seem to have been handed down. Lord Derby thought highly enough of its performance to treat the men to supper in St George's Hall, Liverpool, at Christmas, 1916. But, significantly, there were no Miners' Battalions, no Engineers' Battalions, no Shipbuilders' Battalions. As a marriage of the military and the industrial it stood alone; and if any men were entitled to sing *We are Fred Karno's Army* it was these.

In the years just before the war industrial strife had been unusually rancorous. Woolwich Arsenal was closed by a strike in July 1914, an event which could hardly have gone unnoticed in Potsdam. Thanks to the Liberal Government in 1906 the unions had been granted immunity from the consequences of their actions and it was permissible, as the future Lord Birkenhead pointed out, for a hundred men to apply peaceful persuasion to one. The carried-over bitterness did nothing to assist the task of turning a feckless and fractious democracy into a totalitarian arsenal. If the employers were tempted to welcome the war as a means of bringing the unions back under restraint, they were soon disabused.

Almost all the forms of industrial militancy familiar today were practised in the years when the armies pulped each other in France. Generally it was the shop stewards ('a formidable element of disturbance', as Lloyd George called them) who chose the way of militancy, irrespective of their unions' advice. In 1917 and 1918 there was widespread comment on the incapacity of the engineering unions in particular to control their members. Mass strikes by miners and others were settled by giving in to their demands, while bravely pretending otherwise. However, the State was by no means without teeth, even if it was wary of using them. Scores of munitions tribunals had powers to punish workers for indiscipline; the hardiest agitators were 'deported' or gaoled; and under conscription the State had power to call up strikers, which proved a powerful weapon.

In the first flush of patriotic ardour the union leaders agreed to an industrial truce. This gesture distanced them from their flock, who were less eager to forswear the right to strike. In 1915 a Munitions of War Act made stoppages illegal and arbitration compulsory, but the Act was persistently defied, sometimes by as many men as would have filled six Army divisions. Legend has it – and perhaps it was more than legend – that at one time the Fleet was left with only a week's supply of coal. There was a black day in 1918 when the miners' leaders had to be called to Downing Street to look at the war map, a reminder of the other conflict in progress. There were weeks when *Punch* printed cartoons showing the British worker being offered the Iron Cross of Germany 'for services rendered', or advancing with a dagger to stab the British soldier from behind.

It has to be conceded that some Britons had more to fight for than others. The black and bitter squalor of the Welsh coalfields was not calculated to inspire the higher flights of patriotism and the cries of 'St George for England' did not go down well in the slums of Glasgow; yet this is the place to point out that Wales put more men into uniform, per head of population, than England, Scotland or Ireland, and that Glasgow provided one soldier for every 23 raised in England. Let it be conceded, too, that the strain of long shifts in munitions – working weeks of eighty or even ninety hours – could only be demoralising. The troops suffered worse conditions, certainly, but at least they were moved regularly into rest areas. And many a soldier would have thought himself well out of an overcrowded hell-hole like Barrow-in-Furness, which had all the classic elements of angry headlines (except that angry headlines were discouraged).

In the early months 'war factories' sprang up everywhere. There was no workshop so humble that it could not switch over to making cartridge cases. Garages and engineering shops turned their attention to arms components. A Hove historian tells how an organ builder changed over to making shell cases, a window-blind maker produced steel fittings for collapsible boats and a doctor converted his drawing-room into a factory for making fuse caps. A Ministry of Munitions did not come into existence until May 1915, after the shell shortage scandal had broken. At first Woolwich was almost the only place where shells could be filled, but by the war's end there were eighteen gigantic installations for this purpose.

For the workers, the bogey was not the Hun but the profiteer. No war could be just if the boss class were allowed to make money out of it. Yet what was a profiteer? Was he perhaps just a man whose lust for profit enabled him to give that extra push to the war effort? In February 1915 Members of Parliament were agog over the remuneration of Montague Meyer, sole purchasing agent for timber needed by the War Office. His contract entitled him to 2½ per cent commission, but since he had bought timber worth about £600,000 that meant he had received £15,000 already. For the War Office it was explained that Meyer was able to buy cheaper than anyone else and the sums he was saving the Government were infinitely larger than his commission. Nevertheless, a Member described it as 'one of the most terrible scandals that has ever occurred in the history of the British Government'.

On the ethics of profit-making in war the Cabinet was split. Lucy Masterman, whose husband C. F. G. Masterman was in the Government, tells how the Cabinet reacted to the news that speculators had bought a semi-derelict ship and in one voyage had made a 400–500 per cent profit out of bringing necessities to Britain. Asquith's comment, 'Disgusting', provoked a minister to say that this was simply the normal operation of trade; if these speculators had not done what they did, others would have jumped in, and they might not have sailed the vessel to Britain. 'I can see nothing disgraceful in the whole transaction,' he said. Asquith retorted: 'I did not say it was disgraceful. I said it was disgusting. You may leave it at that.'

Disgusting was the mildest of the adjectives used by the workers to describe their own employers' profits, as they fought unblushingly for a bigger share of them. Any feeling that workers ought not to be blowing other workers to bits – if it ever existed – was lost sight of in the fight for more money for making the weapons that were to blow other workers to bits. It became clear that if industrial strife were to be checked, the profits of industry would have to be controlled and this is what Lloyd George did in the spring and summer of 1915. As Minister of Munitions he inaugurated many forms of State Socialism; that is, he set up huge controlled establishments in which the State assumed responsibility for management, and he imposed controls on more than 700 firms, limiting their profits to pre-war levels. The State assumed the power not only to take over factories producing war material but factories which were capable of being so used. The Conservative Bonar Law thought these were the most drastic powers ever asked by Parliament. As Lloyd George told the Trades Union Congress at Brighton in 1915: 'I have seen resolutions passed from time to time at trades union congresses about nationalising the industries of this country. Well, we have done it.' (He was oddly slow in 'nationalising' shipowners, many of whom made staggering profits until they were controlled two years later.)

That summer 200,000 South Wales miners came out on strike. Lloyd George was accorded great credit for speaking to them bluntly and getting them back to work; in fact, he got them back by conceding almost all they wanted. According to Sir George Askwith, the Chief Industrial Commissioner and a skilled administrator, 'the example was set to strike first and apply to Mr Lloyd George, whatever ministers, officials, employers or union leaders might say'. The settlement 'did more to cause unrest during succeeding years than almost any other factor in the war'.

That Trades Union Congress in 1915 hardly knew what to think. The *New Statesman*, reporting on it, wrote of the most passionate feeling among the delegates at the way in which the wage earner was robbed by the one-tenth of the population which controlled nine-tenths of the wealth. With equal passion the delegates condemned the employers' determination to mobilise men but not money. Yet approval of Britain's participation in the war was endorsed in a crescendo of patriotic fervour, which 'made all the more impressive' the unanimous declaration against conscription. The 'silence could be felt' when Robert Smillie told how a French railway strike had been averted by a threat to call up the strikers. But at other times the silence was broken by the sound of delegates boasting how their kin were helping to win the war: one trade union secretary had four commissioned sons, another had three sons, four brothers-in-law and nine nephews in uniform.

The first big challenge came from the Clyde. According to Lord Shinwell, who was secretary of a seamen's union in those days, Glasgow's resistance to injustice and erosion of personal freedom became an inspiration; but if Glasgow's peculiar brand of industrial indiscipline had not been stamped out – as it was stamped out, firmly, in 1916 – the outcome of the war might have been very different. Much effort has been expended in an effort to show, socially and historically, why the men of Clydeside were, and are, so thrawn, bloody-minded and resistant of authority. The machismo which goes with fashioning large metal artefacts has something to do with it, but other regions of heavy industry were not scourged by the same irrational muscle-flexing. In this war it was inevitable that the Clyde's anti-disciplinarians, schooled in a dimly understood Marxism, would leap at any opportunity of conflict. Just as the Irish traditionally looked on England's peril as Ireland's opportunity, so there were those, like William Gallacher, who were willing to proclaim: 'The adversity of the capitalist class is the opportunity of the working class. Let us take advantage of it.' Gallacher was chairman of the Clyde Workers Committee, formed to protect the workers from the 'treachery' of their own unions. Its members fought to retain all their restrictive practices; they attacked the system of 'leaving certificates' which prevented skilled men moving to better-paid, if less essential jobs ('industrial serfdom'); and they opposed dilution, whether by men or women (there were opportunist employers who tried to introduce dilutees into factories not engaged in war work).

To the charge that their industrial indiscipline was betraying their comrades in the trenches, they retorted that their comrades would never forgive them if they lost the industrial battle. An early symbol of Glasgow's opposition was the burly figure of David Kirkwood, the shop steward who stalked about Beardmore's, the finest shipyard in the world, as if he owned it. 'Look here, Kirkwood, are these your works or mine?' was the not-wholly-jocular protest of Sir William Beardmore. Kirkwood, a member of the Independent Labour Party, disapproved of war. 'Yet I was working in an arsenal, making guns and shells for one purpose – to kill men in order to keep them from killing men. What a confusion! What was I to do?' What he did, while resolving that his engineer's skill should be devoted to his country, was to press on with his union's twopence-an-hour claim. Willing to forbid overtime but reluctant to call an all-out strike, he settled in the end for one penny, or a farthing more than the employers had offered. Some of the limelight was lost to the battling housewives of Glasgow who, with some justification, declared a strike against increased rents; when their menfolk realised they were on to a good grievance they swarmed in from the outer factories and invested the Glasgow Sheriff Court, where eviction orders were due to be heard. According to Gallacher, a 'white-faced' sheriff rang up Lloyd George and asked what he was to do. Whatever the answer was, the cases before the court were dropped and a rent control act followed.

There were many more grievances for the Clydesiders to exploit, notably 'industrial serfdom'. Though claiming the freedom of the works, Kirkwood pretended to be as much Beardmore's slave as if he had a letter 'B' branded on him, and he would trace the letter on his brow with his forefinger in case his audience had failed to grasp the point. This he did when Lloyd George arrived in Glasgow at Christmas 1915 in the hope of persuading 3,000 shop stewards to back the Government's policy on dilution. In his best bullying manner, Kirkwood introduced the Minister, saying they had no reason to trust him, that every Act associated with his name was tainted by slavery and that his words would be taken down and used against him. The shop stewards took their cue from their spokesman. Some of them demanded worker management, to which Lloyd George said this was not the time for social revolution. On Christmas morning he was shouted down at a mass meeting in St Andrew's Hall, Glasgow. When he appeared, a choir ill-advisedly began to chant *See the Conquering Hero Comes*, but the audience sang *The Red Flag* and urged him to get his hair cut. The Glasgow newspaper *Forward*, which carried an unapproved report of the event, was temporarily suppressed. It all served to underline the findings of an enquiry held that year into Clyde unrest: that trouble was caused by 'indiscretion or inconsideration on one side or the other' and 'irritation which spreads and feeds on adventitious causes'. The commissioners, Lord Balfour of Burleigh and Lynden Macassey KC, thought there should have been a mediator on the Clyde to stop disputes in embryo.

A showdown came after three officials styling themselves Dilution Commissioners arrived to enforce their will on the Clyde. Kirkwood did not oppose dilution so long as there were safeguards against abuse, but he was angry because his 'right' to walk about Beardmore's had been rescinded (the Government version was that he had demanded an extension of this freedom) and this supposed snub was made the pretext for a strike. At three o'clock in the morning of March 25, 1916, there was a knock on the door of Kirkwood's home and his wife said, 'That's them for ye noo.' The callers were four detectives, armed (so Kirkwood says) with revolvers. He gave them 'the dressing-down of their lives', with suitable allusions to the Czar's secret police, an ordeal they bore cheerfully. After a few hours in gaol he was brought before the Chief of Police and a Colonel Levita, who told him he was to be deported from Glasgow under the Defence of the Realm Act (his story that he had been court-martialled *in absentia* is nonsense). The Colonel, he says, told him he could go to San Francisco if he wanted, which may have been a jest; in Parliament Dr Addison, for the Ministry of Munitions, said he knew nothing about such a proposal. In the event Kirkwood agreed to be deported to Edinburgh; so with five other ringleaders he was given a single ticket to that city, with a ten shilling note, and put on the train, amid emotional scenes as though the party were being sent to Siberia. In Parliament Sir Edward Carson enquired: 'Has it been considered whether they are guilty of high treason?' Dr Addison replied that Carson's question was indeed being considered, but immediate deportation had been decided upon because of the inevitable delay in bringing a criminal trial.

Kirkwood's account of these events is full of posturing. He would have the reader believe that he thought he was going to be shot, 'as they had shot my friend John Connolly in Dublin a few days previously'. In fact he was treated with extraordinary indulgence. The courteous chief constable of Edinburgh merely required him not to go beyond a five-mile radius and to keep away from public meetings. His fellow deportees were offered work in England and took it, but Kirkwood demanded to be restored to Beardmore's. He was told this could be done if he would sign a promise of good conduct, which he refused to do, even though the written conditions grew ever lighter. One day 200 Clyde shop stewards travelled to Edinburgh to fortify his morale. When the military found that he had been planning to go to a Labour Party conference at Manchester disguised as a clergyman, they allowed him to go there undisguised – to receive a hero's welcome. This emboldened him to return, not to Edinburgh but to Glasgow. For reasons not apparent from his narrative he next moved to hydropathics at Crieff and Moffat, with a spell in a 'dungeon' in Edinburgh Castle, where he could hear the shouts of German and Austrian officers lodged in superior quarters above him. Gallacher's deflationary version of these travels is that Kirkwood was being supported by money raised by the workers. Eventually he was allowed back to Glasgow to see his wife, who had given birth to a baby, and his deportation order was revoked. Later he called on Winston Churchill, by then Minister of Munitions, who gave him tea and cake and arranged for him to take up a managerial post in Beardmore's Mile End shell factory, where he did wonders for production until the Armistice. At least Kirkwood summons up the grace to express thanks that he was living in Britain; anywhere else he could have been quietly dispatched as a nuisance and a traitor. 'Nuisance I may have been,' he says, 'traitor I never was.' One who rated him more than a nuisance was the veteran Socialist Robert Blatchford, who had a pulpit in the *Weekly Dispatch*. The deportees, he said, were 'a clique of malignants with no grievance', guilty of 'mutiny in the face of the enemy'.

While Kirkwood was nursing his ego in exile, James Maxton, William Gallacher and other wild men of the Clyde were serving sentences in Calton Gaol, Edinburgh. (Kirkwood claims to have waved to them, when they were on exercise, from Calton Hill.) Maxton, who totally opposed the war, had been incensed over the deportations. Addressing a meeting on Glasgow Green he cried 'Strike! Strike! Strike! Down tools and to hell with them!' and urged any police who might be present to take down his words. They needed no urging. In the High Court, Edinburgh, in April 1916 the fiery orator apologised profusely through his counsel for his 'quite inexcusable action' and begged leniency; but the judge, stressing the 'dastardliness and cowardice' of his offence, imposed a twelve months' sentence. Maxton's dog is said to have been stoned to death at Barrhead for his master's sins, a fate normally reserved in those days for dachshunds. In gaol he tried to persuade his warders to join a union. On release, barred from practising as a teacher, he worked in shipyards, which was usually construed as helping the war effort.

William Gallacher was gaoled in Edinburgh with two others after the appearance of an article entitled SHOULD THE WORKERS ARM? in the organ of the Clyde Workers' Committee. In his autobiography he advances the curious idea that a Zeppelin raid on Edinburgh had stiffened the jury into a determination to convict the Clyde rebels. John Maclean, the incorrigible Marxist agitator ('as sincere as sunlight and as passionate as a typhoon', to quote an uncharacteristic phrase from Kirkwood), received three years penal servitude in the same Scots court for making statements calculated to prejudice recruiting and spread disaffection. Four men who sang *The Red Flag* in court escaped gaol only by apologising. Maclean was released soon afterwards, but his sincerity and passion earned him another sentence, this time of seven years. All the Parliamentary prophesies of revolution if the Clydesiders were treated sternly were now shown to be hollow; the war within a war was over. Behind the policy of firmness was 'Willie' Weir, the hard-line Scots industrialist who was Director of Munitions for Scotland. 'His conception of a carefully timed and resolute resort to force caused the whole Clydeside revolt to collapse in abrupt and final defeat,' says his biographer. Such was rebel Glasgow, a city which – despite its 'malignants' – raised the astonishing total of 200,000 Servicemen.

Lesser offenders on the industrial front were dealt with by munitions tribunals, which heard charges of absenteeism, bad timekeeping, falling asleep, drunkenness, insulting the foreman and so on. Normally penalties were light. The tribunals lacked full judicial powers and concerted efforts were often made to make them look ridiculous. At Birmingham in February 1917 235 navvies were summoned for being absent from work on December 28, 1916. When the tribunal convened they cheered, jeered, kept their caps on, smoked and passed round bottles of beer. Police intervened only to prevent two of them fighting. A Navvies' Union official who appealed for quiet was told to shut up. Fines ranged from 10s downwards. Sometimes pedlars of radical literature moved about the courtroom crying their wares. At Huddersfield 280 munition workers, mostly apprentices, who had failed to work óver Whitsun, marched on the tribunal singing and blowing bugles; their fines ranged from 25s to 1s. Some disciplinary charges were brought in the police courts, where sharper penalties were imposed. Many munition workers, both men and women, were gaoled for smoking or possessing combustible material; it was also an offence to possess sweets, since sugar mixed with the appropriate acids could cause an explosion. Gaol sentences were sometimes imposed for spinning out work to get extra pay. Two munitions workers who fell asleep on duty, allegedly imperilling thousands, were fined two guineas each by a North Midlands court, a modest enough penalty compared with that dealt out by the Army to sleeping sentries.

The mass entry of women into munitions had to wait until the giant shell-filling factories had been built. Mrs Pankhurst fretted at the delay and, in July 1915, led tens of thousands of women, accompanied by ninety bands, through London demanding war work. It was a great feat of generalship. Lloyd George agreed with her that, at that time, Britain had only 50,000 women in munitions as against Germany's 500,000. Among Britain's 50,000 were a force of 'educated women of the leisure class', who had been enrolled to work at weekends in Vickers factories at Erith, relieving men who were putting in eight-hour shifts seven days a week; a stipulation was that they should not compete financially with the regular workers. Lady Scott, sculptor-widow of the explorer and a friend of Asquith, was one of them, her speciality being the making of electrical coils. In mid-1916, with the enforcement of dilution, women were to be found not only in the filling factories but at the benches of engineering works and shipyards, performing men's tasks and sometimes working harder than shop stewards thought reasonable. Many were former servants, exchanging a domestic tyranny for an industrial one, but at least the pay was better and the evenings were free. Some of the big factories undertook to look after babies.

Not all the women who marched behind Mrs Pankhurst would have relished the ordeal which faced women in certain explosives plants. According to Arnold Bennett's novel, *The Pretty Lady*, five thousand women in the Clyde factories had to strip off all their clothes in one room and run naked to another, where their special clothing was kept, as a precaution against explosions. Like their menfolk, the munitions women were liable to be hauled before tribunals for disciplinary offences, but women assessors tried to ensure fair play for their sex. In Glasgow four girls who refused to wear trousers appealed against dismissal, arguing that they were in no danger from machinery when wearing skirts; but the sheriff ruled that male attire was a condition of employment. There is a tale of a munition worker who refused to wear trousers, but did so for a royal visit. 'Yes, I'm a loyal woman, I am,' she said. 'I put 'em on to please the King, but I'll take 'em off again tomorrow.'

While women were never welcome in the engineering shops, they were free to turn themselves into scarecrows and blow their fingers off in the shell-filling factories. It was not the honest sons of toil whose faces turned a repulsive bright yellow, and whose hair fell out, but their plucky daughters. So hideous were the 'Canaries', as they were dubbed, that they were turned away from polite eating-places, as noseless beggars are spurned. Lloyd George in his *War Memoirs* finds time to pay tribute to these young women who laid down their looks for their country. He recalls Plutarch's account of the battle of Pharsalus at which Julius Caesar urged his legions to thrust their spears at the faces of Pompey's exquisite cavalry, who were willing to face bodily wounds but not facial disfigurement; and in the event they galloped off with their hands before their eyes. The hard core of women workers turned out to be of sterner stuff than Pompey's elegant extracts. To guard against toxic jaundice from trinitrotoluene they were supposed to coat their faces with grease and even wear respirators, but the precautions were nearly as unpleasant as the complaint and often a yellow face seemed the easier way out. The jaundice could be fatal; fifty-two women died of it in 1916 and forty-two in 1917.

Lloyd George praises also the courage of the women workers at Hayes who risked maiming and disembowelling when securing refractory fuse components in shells. In 1915, he records, there had been too many prematures and blinds in American shells caused by a component with a left-hand thread which came undone in flight; to prevent this happening, the part had to be stabbed in two places with a chisel, and if a trace of fulminate were ignited, the shell would explode. One day several women were killed from this cause at Hayes, but the rest went on stabbing away, singing cheerfully. Another feminine chore was filling shells with toxic gas. An account of Bristol's contribution to the war says that in 1918 some 1,300 women were more or less seriously gassed in a factory near Henbury, producing mustard-gas shells which were later used 'with excellent effect' against the Hindenburg Line.

The principle that women ought not to be called on in person to kill the country's enemies was well established, but no serious objection seems to have been raised to women making the wherewithal to kill the enemy. 'Woodbine Willie' (the Rev. G. A. Studdert-Kennedy) characteristically wrote of the rain of shells on the Western Front: 'By George, it's a glorious barrage, and English girls made 'em. We're all in it, sweethearts, mothers and wives. The hand that rocks the cradle wrecks the world. There are no non-combatants.' By the end of the war more than a million and a half women could be said to have blood on their hands.

The prosperity which existed in households where wives and daughters worked in munitions did not go unremarked. In a *John Bull* 'Bullets' competition someone won a substantial prize for adding to the phrase 'Child's Play' the comment 'Selling Pianos At Woolwich'. R. D. Blumenfeld wrote in his diary in July 1916: 'The British piano dealers have never been so prosperous as they are today. You cannot buy a cheap piano for immediate delivery. They have all gone into the cottages of workmen who have never made so much money.' One-time parlourmaids who were formerly paid £25 a year were now earning at least £2 a week and as a result, said Blumenfeld, the makers of gewgaws could not keep pace with demand. Other observers commented on the rage for furs and fancy nightgowns. Ironically, women who had escaped from the sweated 'parasite' trades were now becoming the mainstay of those trades. Pawnbrokers said that while their traditional business was slumping, their sales of jewellery were booming. Butchers found that workers were buying the best cuts of meat. In the summer of 1916 the newspapers expressed surprise, under headlines like MUNITIONS DUKES AT SOUTHEND, at the high prices paid for furnished holiday apartments by war workers. An article in the *Weekly Dispatch* on October 15, 1916, began with this statement from the head of a big store: 'The Somme battle has been the best tonic that business in this country has had since the war began.' It contained references to munitions workers buying furs. A year later the *Daily Telegraph* reported a court hearing at Kingston in which a soldier's wife was reported to be receiving over £3 in Army allowances and nearly as much in an arms factory, while her boy of thirteen was being paid more than £2 for munition work. 'Eight pounds a week!' exclaimed the Mayor. 'Four hundred pounds a year! It sounds like a fairy tale from the Arabian Nights.'

In the summer of 1917, shortly before Churchill was appointed Minister of Munitions, the engineers bloodied their noses in a direct challenge to the Government. A stoppage which crippled a whole string of major arms centres was caused by grievances over food prices, pay, dilution, the rules of exemption, the operation of the comb-out, and a general distrust of Government intentions, all subsumed in a general ferment bred of war strain. In some centres military pickets were turned out to prevent troops on leave, notably Empire servicemen, from attacking young strikers. Union officials opposed the strike but were impotent. The Government, after uttering a series of threats, arrested eight ringleaders and charged them at Bow Street, London, under Defence Regulations with promoting strikes and trying to delay war supplies, for which the maximum penalty was penal servitude for life. The engineers then went back and the eight men were freed.

The munitions empire which Churchill inherited included the wrecked area of Silvertown, in East London, where in January of that year a great multi-coloured fireball, followed by a stunning boom, had sent apprehensions of Doomsday through the capital; the explosion blew scores of munitions workers to bits and laid waste a square mile of houses. The Ministry which controlled these deadly townships was distributed over a range of fashionable hotels in London; it had fifty main departments and a staff of 20,000 (Lloyd George started it with little more than a table and a couple of chairs). The finest business brains, as Churchill relates, were working for honour alone, forswearing the huge fortunes they could have won as private contractors. One notable figure in the Ministry was Sir Eric Geddes, a former general manager of the London and North-Eastern Railway, who had put on a general's uniform to reorganise the railways on the British front in France and a vice-admiral's uniform to control the supply departments of the Royal Navy.

On the railways at home there was much bad blood. In 1917 the National Union of Railwaymen in Liverpool and Birkenhead called what is now described as a go-slow but in those days was designated a policy of 'ca' canny', 'slow gear' and 'working to the rules of the company'. This union was frequently at loggerheads over pay and conditions with the Associated Society of Locomotive Engineers and Firemen, as it is today. The enmity spread from the tracks to the law courts, where a group of NUR men sued the ASLEF general secretary for slander and libel. During one hearing the judge asked J. H. Thomas whether a man who took the place of a striker, no matter what the circumstances, was a blackleg, and the reply was yes. 'Even although he believes that the existence of a strike may be fraught with serious consequences for the country?' – 'Yes, my Lord.'

The unions' last fling, with Churchill forced to use his heaviest weapon against the engineers, is described in the last chapter.

CHAPTER 14

'COMING TO FETCH YOU!'

In the summer of 1915 a worried British citizen received a letter signed by a recruiting officer, bearing the Royal Arms and posted On His Majesty's Service. Its terms were such that he lost no time in passing it on to James Hogge, Liberal Member for East Edinburgh, who welcomed any opportunity to embarrass the Government. The letter, produced by Hogge in the Commons on July 7, read:

Dear Sir, Unless you have some good and genuine reason for not enlisting, which I am agreeable to investigate, I advise you to offer to join the Army before you are made to. This is an entirely private and friendly piece of advice. Compulsion may not be so far off as you think. I am only waiting the word to call up every man of eligible age and as you see I have you on my list. . . . I can only tell you that I have good reason to believe that you will be mightily sorry in the end if you wait until you are fetched. Not only that, but if it comes to fetching, those who are fetched will not be asked where they would like to go.

Yours truly,

Major, Recruiting Officer.

The President of the Local Government Board, Walter Long, assured the House that no authority existed for sending such letters and he hoped there would be no more of them.

Recruiting officers had always been encouraged to use their initiative and this one was only personalising the message of 'come willingly or we'll fetch you' which had been creeping into posters and speeches. In fact, conscription was not so imminent as he suggested, but some eight months' distant.

The Liberals in the Government continued to baulk at the idea of compulsion, which they thought would split the country, whereas what was beginning to split the country was the lack of it. Conscription, in Liberal eyes, was an infringement of basic liberties; it was undemocratic, a tool of tyrants; it was the resort of Jingos; it was a course urged by Northcliffe, which alone was enough to condemn it; and Kitchener did not appear to want it. They rejected the argument that France was no tyranny and France had conscription. They shut their eyes to the injustices of 'voluntaryism', which encouraged one family to send six sons to France and allowed another to keep six eligible sons at home; which required volunteers to go back into the Line no matter how often they were wounded; and which expected Territorials and Regulars to serve on indefinitely. There were even Liberals who argued that the volunteers in the trenches would refuse to serve alongside pressed men. However, inquiries made in France, says Lloyd George, showed that soldiers were all for 'sending for the shirkers'; they were realists who did not believe that 'the fewer men the greater share of honour'. From this distance the objections to spreading the burden seem perverse and grotesque. But it was the first time in British history that the concept of mass enrolment had been conjured up, as distinct from the raising of expeditionary forces. People knew that Napoleon had been seen off the stage without conscription; what they overlooked was the powerful part played by the press gang in manning Nelson's ships.

Tied up with the conscription issue was the controversy which perhaps for the first time in Britain set married men against single. In simple equity there was no reason why bachelors should give their lives for those who had chosen domesticity, or had it forced on them as a result of indiscretions in a haystack. If Jones had lost his girl to Smith, why should Jones lose his life for Smith as well? If Simpson was a none-too-robust bachelor of forty, why should he go to the trenches to defend Robinson, a healthy married scamp of twenty? If a man had given hostages to fortune, should he not be proud and ready to protect them, while the State lent them the necessary financial support? The Socialist Countess of Warwick introduced a eugenic argument, contending that married men were expendable. 'They have fulfilled, or partly fulfilled, the function upon which civilisation depends,' she asserted; her view was that the young men, the nation's breeding stock, should be worked hard in the factories but kept out of the firing line. Against all this, the married man was entitled to argue that family life was the backbone of the nation, and that the mass creation of widows and orphans was no way to build a better Britain. Indeed, Asquith put the case for him by quoting (on the 500th anniversary of Agincourt) the ballad in which Henry V says to the Lord Derby of his day:

> Go 'cruit me Cheshire and Lancashire,
>   And Derby hills that are so free,
> No married man or widow's son –
>   No widow's curse shall go with me.

It was an allusion that the Prime Minister must have regretted making, for his good intentions were overwhelmed by events. Perhaps the only real argument for keeping married men at home was that of the Treasury: it saved the country money. Single men were cheaper to kill.

By mid-1915 three million men had volunteered, yet it became increasingly obvious that if Britain was to produce the seventy divisions Kitchener wanted to match Allied strengths a system of compulsion was inevitable. Lord Derby, appointed Director of Recruiting in October, conceived a scheme under which men of military age were invited to attest their willingness to serve when their age group was called up on the Continental pattern. Built into the scheme was an ill-defined pledge that married men would not be called up before unmarried.

There was an encouraging rush to attest. Even men in holy orders tried to do so, but the Archbishop of Canterbury objected. The *Illustrated London News* had an inspiring drawing of an ardent, impatient throng of heroes in 'one of the hundreds of long queues of men eager to be attested – a scene in London by night during the last week of Lord Derby's scheme'. At City Hall, Hull, 12,000 men were interviewed in three days. Unfortunately it turned out that Lord Derby had been outwitted, or at least misled. Whole crowds of married men attested in the belief that they would not be wanted until all the single men – believed to be a million or so – had been pulled in; and the single men held back. By the time the unmarried volunteers had been weeded there were only 343,000 of them.

Late in 1915, despite heavy opposition, a Military Service Bill was drafted. If an unexempted single man between the ages of eighteen and forty-one did not enlist he knew what would happen to him: 'He will be deemed to have enlisted under the Military Service Act. On Thursday March 2, 1916, he will be placed in the Reserve and be called up in his class, as the military authorities may determine.' It was as simple as that. The Act forcibly enlisted younger married men as well. However, a month or so was enough to show that further powers would be necessary. A new Bill was introduced to make general and complete military service compulsory. Married men, who had formed an Attested Married Men's Union, howled about betrayal, even hiring the Albert Hall for the purpose. There they catcalled as a message was read from Lord Derby; he had sympathy for them, but pointed out that a million married men had already joined up without trying to make terms. The new Bill was law by the end of May, almost all Parliamentary opposition having collapsed at news of the Dublin Rising (conscription for the Irish was not authorised until 1918 and never enforced). Only Sir John Simon resigned and he later admitted his error. The union leader J. H. Thomas, who had prophesied industrial revolution, was left eating his words; Lloyd George called him 'the greatest bletherer ever'. C. P. Scott, editor of the *Manchester Guardian*, a frequent breakfast guest of Lloyd George, had also blethered about industrial bloodshed.

Britain was now full of men who were 'deemed to have enlisted', who lived in expectation of the knock on the door which would bring them their call-up papers. Mothers learned that it could be an offence to 'harbour' a son the Army wanted. Most men took it philosophically and were glad to have their minds made up for them; many sought exemption from tribunals (of which more later); a minute handful mutilated or doctored themselves to avoid service.

The recruiters who had threatened to 'come and fetch' the

laggards now made the most of the opportunities offered them.
In the summer and autumn of 1916 something very like the
press gang was revived in Britain, as police and military conducted sudden round-ups at railway stations and places of entertainment. One September morning suburban passengers
arriving at Marylebone Station found their exits from the ter-
minus blocked and an absence of taxis. All who appeared to be
of military age were shepherded into a roped space where their
documents, if any, were examined; those without papers were
marched in batches to the nearest police station for further
questioning. The surprised crowd took it all fairly calmly; when
one man wept, there was a cry of 'Cheer up, they can't kill you.'
After much anxious telephoning, relatives began to arrive at the
police station in taxis with documents. A wife was heard giving
her husband the serves-you-right-I-warned-you treatment.
Eventually some 130 wage-earners from Pinner and Harrow –
'all evidently of a superior class', according to the *Daily Mirror* –
reported for work with a new excuse for being late. The same
treatment was meted out at Golders Green Underground
Station to returning theatre-goers and 'revellers', some of
whom, seeing what was afoot, jumped on trains going back to
London. About 150 were detained for investigation.

A round-up at the Ring, in Blackfriars, produced a more
spirited reaction. Informed by the manager that they would be
screened on the way out, the sporting audience broke windows
and skylights and tried to rush the stairs, but were contained.
The soldiers were curt, the police polite, the recruiting officers
'bland but business-like'. Outside bluejackets looked on
cynically as professional pugilists were taken away.

Round-ups quickly became a hazard of the music-halls.
Ribald cheers would greet the warning notice flashed on the
screen. From the stage of the Edmonton Empire a lion-tamer
was taken into custody. In Tottenham High Road the press gang
descended on a whist drive and a musical soirée. A travelling
circus was raided at Camberley, the lights went out in the 'big
top' and the performance was abandoned. Bohemian clubs were
searched in London. In the provinces it was the same story.
Newmarket racecourse seemed to promise a fine haul of
shirkers, but after an hour police and Army only had two Irishmen to show for their pains. In Edinburgh police not only

combed places of entertainment, but also made house-to-house visits.

It all lent a grim spice to life. Arnold Bennett, conscious of his youthful appearance, began carrying his birth certificate and registration card (he was nearing fifty). Some with uneasy consciences changed their places of resort and took roundabout routes to their destinations. But it emerged fairly speedily that the results of the round-ups were not justifying the effort and inconvenience. Out of 280 people detained in two swoops at Golders Green Station, only one was chargeable under the Act. Specimen statistics were: Croydon Hippodrome and Empire seventy (one caught); Woolwich Hippodrome eighty (1); The Ring 145 (1); Eel Pie Island, Twickenham, forty (0); Hull football ground 215 (2). The operations invited the criticism that able-bodied men were being used to catch a few feeble-bodied. So round-ups diminished in frequency, but were still used to harass meetings where a high proportion of dodgers or 'peace cranks' seemed likely to be found.

More productive of recruits was the process known as 'combing out', the extraction of able-bodied men from civilian jobs which others were capable of doing, or which were inessential in wartime. Every industry was recommended sooner or later for this treatment; and Churchill, in May 1916, struck a well-directed blow with 'I say to the War Office, "Physician, comb thyself".' Perhaps he was thinking of all those hutments of clerks in Whitehall, or perhaps of what C. E. Montague called 'a kind of fancy dress ball of non-combatant khaki' staged in the streets of London – 'a lord lieutenant, an honorary colonel, a dealer in horses, a valuer of cloth, an accountant, an actor in full work, a recruiter of other men for the battles that he avoided himself . . .' James Sexton, the dockers' leader, said the threat of combing out caused much wailing among his members, but it was in the munitions plants that the greatest stir was felt. Major J. R. P. Newman, Member for Enfield, told the Commons in October 1916 that he had been helping to comb out a factory and had found that out of 650 men of military age all but 100 were single. 'The feeling of the country on this issue is very great,' he said. Was too much regard being paid, he wondered, to the discretion of the employer and the foreman? Were married men being released because they had not given the foreman a tip? He tried hard to find excuses for single men. Had they taken offence at the expression 'combing out', with its suggestion that they were ticks in the national fleece? Had they been misled by that poster of the soldier shaking hands with the workman into believing that they were doing as good a job for their country at £3 a week as the soldier at a shilling a day?

Meanwhile the more radical Socialists had discovered another army of shirkers: the clergy. Philip Snowden wanted the Archbishop of Canterbury to be prosecuted under Defence Regulations for urging men in holy orders – many of whom preached fiery pro-war sermons – not to enlist. In September 1916 Ben Tillett, the dockers' leader, complained to the Trade Union Congress that there were 20,000 able-bodied clerics, 'miserable cowards', engaged in 'non-productive employment'. Why, he demanded, should men 'so fond of talking about Heaven be so afraid to pass through its gates?' James Sexton, also a docker, asked why they should pick on the clergy from all the other exempt categories, but the Congress passed a resolution supporting Tillett. In fact, a number of clergymen defied their Primate and served in the trenches. A biographer of the Archbishop says that he was ready, when the last Military Service Act was passed in 1918, to agree to a call-up of the clergy, if pressed hard enough.

CHAPTER 15

BEFORE THE TRIBUNAL

To operate conscription, it was necessary to set up a grand network of military tribunals; that is, panels of ordinary men and women empowered to send Jones into the firing line while keeping Smith at home. Until then, only judges had been vested with powers of life and death over their fellow men.

It was soon evident that the tribunals could do no right. If they spared the widow's son they were reviled by Lord Northcliffe. If they gave short shrift to scrimshankers they were guilty of dumping unassimilable dross into the Army. They were accused of robbing industry and of allowing industry to hoodwink them. They were attacked for browbeating conscientious objectors and for allowing themselves to be browbeaten by them. From the Left a not untypical appraisal was this, by J. R. Clynes (soon to join the Government): 'Nervous wrecks, semi-idiots and consumptives were forced by red-faced presidents of tribunals to get into khaki, and dragged out to France to die, cursing the country which had enslaved them in a military despotism and in whose service they had been forced to swear loyalty.' This, he went on, was in obedience to an Act which laid down that anyone 'must fight when called upon in pursuance of any aims desired by any capitalist or land-seeking government temporarily in power'.

The first tribunals were set up in a hurry under the Derby Scheme, principally to consider applications by employers for exemption of skilled workers. Under the Military Service Acts

their duty was to take account of special hardship, grave business inconvenience, the usefulness or otherwise of the job to the
State and, trickiest of all, pacifist conscience. The members were
intended to be representative of their communities. In practice
they were usually the sort of persons who are thought best
qualified to sign applications for passports: middle-aged pro-
fessionals, churchmen, political party workers, even union
officials. They could not be expected to know much about law,
the hope being that they would use their common-sense and
worldly experience. Sitting with each tribunal was a military
representative, usually a retired officer, who was there to advise
but not to take part in decision-making. He could appeal against
exemptions.

The Local Government Board urged members to give heed to
the religious and moral beliefs of applicants and judge whether
they were sincerely held. The fact that they disapproved of those
provisions of the Act which allowed men to advance 'cowardly'
pleas was irrelevant; they were there to administer the Act as it
stood. However, with tribunals numbered by the thousand the
chances that all would dispense immaculate justice were slight.
The members brought with them the views they had absorbed
from the newspapers, or from friends who urged them to 'teach
the slackers a lesson'. Some even invited their friends, or their
ladies, to sit alongside them, as High Court judges used to do.

A common type of case was that in which an employer
pleaded the indispensability of a clerk, praising his qualities in
extravagant terms. 'How much do you pay him?' the chairman
would ask, and the embarrassed reply would be 'One pound a
week.' So, amid a light laugh, the under-priced clerk would be
sent off to the wars and his boss taught a lesson. Sons who
claimed to be the sole support of mothers and sisters were
sometimes found to be contributing little more than sympathy
and encouragement. Much depended on the nature, or even the
designation, of a man's occupation; if a chimney repairer could
convince the tribunal that he was a steeplejack his chances of
exemption were improved. Pleas like 'Ladies must have corsets'
and 'People must have clogs' were countered by the military
representative's 'The Army must have men'.

A mayor of Preston, Harold Cartmell, who chaired a tribunal,
says the members learned a great deal about trades and skills.

When an advocate representing a tripe dresser asked the tribunal to agree that tripe, trotters and cow heels were articles of food, the mayor said: 'We go that far, certainly.' Advocate: 'In fact they are essential foods.' Mayor: 'We have not gone so far as that.' Advocate: 'Tripe and onions are regarded as a very useful dish.' Mayor: 'Very delectable, I believe, but hardly essential, perhaps.' The applicant was given a short exemption, but only because of his father's temporary incapacity. A tripe worker who scraped animals' stomachs and a man who made black puddings vied with each other in making their trades sound so repulsive that no woman could be expected to practise them. The Preston tribunal exempted a man who could kill a fowl, pluck it and have it ready for market in two minutes and who had once skinned 1,200 rabbits overnight. They gave temporary exemption, too, to a knocker-up who rose at four, worked as a weaver in the day, ran a fish-and-chip shop in the evening and went to bed at midnight; he also worked the church organ on Sundays. The tribunal, like many others, was asked to believe that fathers who had handed over their business to sons were past work at fifty; many observers, says Cartmell, might have assumed that 'senile decay sets in at a very early age in Preston'. Another odd feature of Preston, and perhaps not only of Preston, was that sometimes wives would write in asking for their husbands to be called up.

Since the newspapers in the main reported only odd fragments of proceedings, it is hard to generalise on the tribunals' findings, but it is easy to be surprised at the degree of leniency extended, at the way exemptions were renewed and renewed again. At Eastbourne a tribunal questioned a church organist who applied for his exemption to be extended. 'Don't you think,' he was asked, 'that church music might be done away with during the war?' His reply, 'That is a question for the vicar,' brought the retort, 'I would rather hear bad music from a man who served his country than jolly good music from a man who had not.' Not a high level of dialogue, perhaps, but the applicant was given a further extension of twelve weeks provided he joined the Red Cross, which hardly constitutes oppression. A general asked the Isle of Wight Rural Tribunal to let him keep his thirty-eight-year-old married woodman so that he could have one able-bodied man on the estate and conditional

exemption was granted. Sylvia Pankhurst was not alone in thinking that the limit of tolerance was shown by the Southwark
Tribunal which granted exemption to twenty-one single men
working for Northcliffe's *Comic Cuts, Home Chat* and *Forget-
Me-Not*. Northcliffe's papers complained that farmers' sons
were less liable to call-up than farmers' workmen, an objection
not without some substance; yet a single young cowman at
Witham, Essex, was given six months' exemption on the plea
that he was 'doing more good as a milkman than he would do in
the Army'. This was too much for the military representative,
who said milking cows was women's work. 'It is perfectly sick-
ening,' he said, 'to sit here and see such things done. We read of
the big push our men are making in France and then refuse to
send this single young man to help them.' He gave notice of
appeal.

The question of whether an artist should be required to go to
war was raised by the case of Jacob Epstein. He was born in
America of Polish parents and was naturalised British; and in
1917 he was thirty-six, married with no children. One tribunal
refused him exemption on the ground that a sculptor suffered
only temporary inconvenience in the Army. A second gave him
temporary exemption with a recommendation that he found
work of national importance; however, 'the classes of work
suggested were not suited to his particular genius'. A third
tribunal thought he 'might win fresh laurels in the trenches'.
After this the Law Society Appeal Tribunal was assured that 'he
was a man who was quite unlike anyone else in the country and
in regard to national memorials his work was extremely valuable'. He hoped, said counsel, to get a commission to design a
Kitchener memorial in St Paul's. In short, 'it would be a great
loss to the world if so great a genius were sent into the Army'. To
this the military representative said the question was simply
whether or not he was a one-man business. This tribunal gave a
further exemption for three months, saying all depended on the
Army's needs. 'Would you like to join the Volunteer Training
Corps?' asked the chairman. 'I should not mind.' – 'Then you
shall.' That Epstein genuinely believed himself 'too important'
to be wasted in the Army is evident from a letter by him quoted
in Michael Holroyd's biography of Augustus John. Holroyd
describes how the notorious prankster Horace de Vere Cole

intensified the press campaign against Epstein by inspiring a crop of hostile letters in the *Sunday Herald*, which shows what a practical joker can do for his country in war. Eventually Epstein was drafted, became ill and was discharged.

The most tragic figure to go before the tribunals was the mother pleading for her only, or last, son. In November 1917 a widow asked Croydon Tribunal to let her keep her eleventh son, her sole support, while her ten other sons were serving. Five of them had been wounded, two were prisoners in Germany, one was a prisoner in Turkey. Granting exemption, the mayor congratulated the woman on her fine record. 'Moreover,' said the military representative, 'all her eleven sons are equally proud of their mother.' At Barking, when a transport worker sought exemption for a son, saying he had already sent eight into the Army and that a ninth was about to go, the chairman told him he was a brick 'and had handsomely done his duty to his country', a tribute which was greeted with cheers. The tenth son was given three months' exemption, provided he did work of national importance. At Hull an elderly infirm widow sought exemption for her son, a time-expired Regular whose twelve years service had included sixteen months in France. One of her sons had died of wounds, another had died in the Merchant Navy, a third lay with a crippled spine in hospital. The Regular did not make a personal application to the tribunal, not wishing to appear a slacker. Exemption was granted. These tribunals, one might think, could hardly have decided otherwise than they did, but some were stonier-hearted. The *Daily Mail* complained from time to time of tribunals which allowed themselves to be swayed by sentiment. All over the country, it said, last sons were being exempted and so were last partners in businesses. What sentiment had been shown in respect of single sons who were called up to their death? 'Their parents have lost all, and the parents of larger families must also be prepared to send all their sons to the Army.'

It is a comment on the times that applications by Jews were usually news. In March 1916, under the headline A COHEN MUST NOT FIGHT, the *Morning Post* reported that a teacher of Hebrew and of the Jewish religion had appealed at Hackney for exemption on the grounds that a Cohen was an hereditary priest and was forbidden by his religion to touch or be near corpses. He said that on the recent death of a member of the family all relatives had left the house to live elsewhere pending the burial. The applicant 'admitted that Jews ought to fight for England in return for the protection and freedom they had received, but not Cohens'. The chairman of the tribunal replied, 'We have the National Service Act here and it does not say anything about Cohens.' The appeal was refused. Next day Major de Rothschild told the London City Tribunal that he had a message from the Chief Rabbi saying that 'where the safety of the country is at stake no exemption from military service can be justly claimed by any person on the ground that he is a Cohen'. The tribunals also learned that the Chief Rabbi was ready to give dispensations to Jews who pleaded that Army food was unclean in terms of Leviticus XI. The London City Tribunal awarded six weeks' exemption to a Jewish baker who claimed that he alone knew the secret ingredients of Jewish bread, but told the head of the firm they were surprised that he did not know what went into his product.

The tribunals yielded comedy of a sort. At Shoreditch an applicant was granted exemption when he claimed to be very deaf. As he left court the chairman said, 'The guvnor's going to give you a rise next week', which produced only a puzzled 'What say?' 'Oh yes,' said the chairman, 'he's deaf.' The Law Society Tribunal were delighted to be faced with a cinema producer, whom they asked to define what he did. 'Everything from writing the scenario to superintending the production,' was the reply. The chairman, a Member of Parliament, said, 'Oh, I see. You arrange for groups of people to throw each other into rivers and that sort of thing. [Laughter] Work of highest national importance, no doubt.' (Laughter.) The applicant was informed he would be called up in fourteen days and that he could apply to the Civil Liabilities Board for a grant.

Colonel Repington, who sat on a tribunal at Hampstead, considered that the members were careful, sympathetic and thorough. Little shirking was evident, but there was 'an intolerable number of claimants for exemption' because there were so many excused occupations. He spoke on the subject to General Sir William Robertson, who thought the tribunals were working indifferently except in London. One tribunal in Wales was supposed to have exempted all but six out of 2,000 men. In

such cases Repington thought the Government should nominate new members.

Beatrice Webb was convinced that class bias and local job-
bery were rampant on the tribunals. Certainly there were some
highly questionable incidents; as when, at Huntingdon, a nurseryman stepped down from the bench to argue the case for his
own exemption, which he was conditionally granted, and then
ascended the bench again.

Conscientious objectors brought out the worst in some, but by
no means all, tribunals. In the early weeks of conscription there
were chairmen who boasted that, no matter what loopholes
Parliament had left for shirkers, they would ensure that none
escaped. They made it clear that they would operate only such
parts of the Military Service Acts as seemed reasonable, and the
clause they thought most unreasonable was that which allowed
men to produce religious, moral and ethical reasons for not
serving. At Gower a 'conchie' was told he was 'fit only to be on
the point of a German bayonet'. A councillor on a tribunal at
Shaw, near Oldham, told an objector that he was 'exploiting
God to save his skin, that he was a deliberate and rank blas-
phemer, a coward and a cad, and nothing but a shivering mass of
unwholesome fat'. At Nairn a military representative said, 'I do
not think we ought to waste time on conscientious objectors,'
and the chairman told them, 'You are the most awful pack that
ever walked the earth.' Elsewhere they were called blackguards,
asked how often they took a bath and whether they had ever
been in a lunatic asylum. At West Bromwich an objector who
sought permission to make a statement was told that if he
wanted to air his views he could hire the town hall and give the
people a treat. Other applicants were informed that the tribunal
was not a debating society and that there was no time for the
reading of speeches. A not unusual judgement was that the
applicant was too young and immature to know his own mind.
Numerous examples of these and other incivilities were quoted
in Parliament, notably by Philip Snowden and Philip Morrell.
(The latter said he had applied for a commission when the war
began.) The Government's view was that it was for the local
authorities who appointed the tribunals to weed out the offending members.

Very few objectors received unconditional exemption on grounds of conscience. Tribunals were prepared to listen to those who believed that war at all times was morally wrong, but it was no use trying to shelter behind membership of the Church of England, since Article XXXVII says: 'It is lawful for Christian men, at the commandment of the Magistrate, to wear weapons and serve in the wars.' The tribunals were not prepared to exempt those who were willing to fight only in defence of a world order of which they approved, proclaiming, 'I have no country, I am an International Socialist.' Broadly speaking, there were three choices for objectors: to undertake work of national importance, like farming and forestry; to join a non-combatant corps administered by the Army, which might or might not mean serving abroad; or go to prison. For 'absolutists', who refused to do any work which could remotely help the war effort, or which could release another man into the firing line, the prospect was an unlimited series of gaol sentences, on the cat-and-mouse principle which had been applied to the suffragists.

It is, of course, impossible for any tribunal to judge with certainty whether a man's beliefs, be they religious, ethical or political, are sincerely held. These inquisitors were faced by religious zealots, Quakers, latter-day Jacobins, Marxists, anarchists, voluble polemicists of every stamp, bluffers and self-preservationists. Sir Francis Meynell has described his appearance before the Marylebone Tribunal, where he explained that only for overwhelmingly good ends – 'and that for me means social revolution' – would he support war and killing. His objection was largely political, but still, he contended, a conscientious one within the meaning of the Act. In his support he quoted 'Gury-Ballerine' and 'Lehmkuhl', the mere names probably being enough to prejudice his case. The tribunal did not advise him to hire the town hall; they simply turned him down and so did the appeal tribunal. He surrendered to the Army, was gaoled, went on hunger-and-thirst strike and was discharged as unlikely to make an efficient soldier.

Idyllic by contrast was the lot of Herbert Morrison, secretary of the London Labour Party, who vociferously opposed what he called a capitalist war. He was called before the Wandsworth

Tribunal, the members of which he has described as 'courteous and fair'. He says he did not regard his summons as an infringement of personal liberty, believing that 'a democratic Parliament has the right to order its citizens about', though this was not what he said in his early anti-war propaganda. To the disgust of his more fanatical friends he chose to perform alternative service on the land (his blind eye would have spared him the front line). The hard work on a fruit farm at Letchworth was good for him and he met his first wife there; he was even able to keep on organising the Labour Party. Letchworth was a hotbed of primitive Socialism which welcomed not only accredited objectors but – according to one source – furnished hideouts for runaways. In 1939–45 Morrison was no longer anti-war and, as Home Secretary, urged a forgiving nation to 'Go To It'.

Kingsley Martin, the future editor of the *New Statesman*, went before a tribunal while still a schoolboy of eighteen at Mill Hill. His pacifist father and the commanding officer of the Officers Training Corps both attested the sincerity of his anti-war beliefs. No admiration for his stand was forthcoming from his schoolfellows, who turned him out of his study and persecuted him. He served in the Friends Ambulance Unit in France.

The famous question, 'What would you do if a German were about to rape your sister/mother?' was usually answered by 'I should try to put myself between them', which was what Lytton Strachey said, though he is traditionally supposed to have made a rude jest of it. At Keighley the dialogue went: 'What would you do if a German attacked your mother?' – 'I would get between the attacker and my mother, but in no circumstances would I take life to save her.' – 'If the only way to protect your mother was to kill the German, would you still let him kill her?' – 'Yes.' – 'You ought to be shot.' The Member for Hanley, R. L. Outhwaite, wanted the question banned on the ground that since Britain was in no danger of invasion the dilemma would never arise. Another Member, Major J. R. P. Newman, urged the censor to forbid the reporting of 'cowardly pleas' of this type, but got no satisfaction.

Just as there were families with six sons in uniform, so there were families with six sons who refused to put on uniform. One such surfaced briefly in the summer of 1918. The sixth son,

appearing before a St Albans tribunal, was described as a vegetarian who refused to kill even a worm. His five brothers would
not enter the business of their father, a hatter, because it employed felt. He was refused exemption, but what duties, if any,
this family undertook did not emerge.

There is a mass of literature, much of it recent, describing the
ordeals of the conscientious objectors of those days and contending, or suggesting, that they were the real heroes of the war.
Many of them were later honoured for services to the country
they chose not to defend. What cannot be overlooked here is the
almost universal discredit they attracted at the time. There was a
popular story about a prison visitor chatting to a woman outside
a gaol. 'I'm going to see a conscientious objector,' he said,
causing the woman to exclaim, 'Thank God my man's not one of
them. He's in for forgery.' Rowdies who threw ochre and pepper
at pacifist spokesmen were told by a magistrate to 'leave idiots
alone'. Without a doubt some objectors were barbarously
treated by the Army; everyone knows about the batch who were
shipped to France and sentenced to execution, the penalty then
being commuted to imprisonment. It is equally beyond doubt
that the sufferings of many objectors were grossly and persistently exaggerated, not least in Parliament; while some showed
fortitude in their cells, others displayed a great lack of it on their
farms. Too many of them courted animosity by their insensitive
behaviour in public, of which cocking snooks at press cameras
was only a trivial example. If they had a rough time at the
tribunals, there were many who thought that was the way it
ought to be, and Asquith and Lloyd George were among them.
H. G. Wells believed that unless their path was made difficult
there would be a stampede of shirkers. Beatrice Webb found
unpleasing the airs of the young men of the No-Conscription
Fellowship, 'saliently conscious of their own righteousness',
with their claim of 'We are the ones whose eyes are open'.
Aldous Huxley, who watched tribunals at Oxford, became
'extraordinarily irritated' by the International Socialists, who
were 'merely half-baked, crude and without any real opinions of
their own'. Only Bertrand Russell, it seemed, was ready to take
risks for 'conchies' and even he found many of them unlikable.
In 1916, pleading the case of an absolutist, he was prosecuted at
London Guildhall for making statements in a pamphlet likely to

prejudice recruiting. When he declined to pay a fine of £100 the authorities seized his books, which his friends bought back.

One who gave evidence against Russell was Brigadier-General Wyndham Childs. Half of his time and energy at the War Office, he has said, was expended in 'securing justice in accordance with the law for people whose sole object seemed to be to desert their country in time of peril'. For the Quakers he had much admiration; nearly all members of the Friends Ambulance Unit, though unwilling to take the lives of others, would have been willing to lose their own lives under fire. He noted that very few Jews objected to military service. But for the No-Conscription Fellowship, the militant body which Russell supported, he had no respect whatever; the leaders 'should have been dealt with under the Incitement to Mutiny Act'. The Fellowship openly invited prosecution; a *Morning Post* report of one of their meetings in Bishopsgate, in April 1916, has Clifford Allen declaring that married men who were in sympathy with the Fellowship were prepared to receive in their homes young men who deserted.

The conscientious objectors who were employed on the home farm at Garsington Manor, that promiscuous Eden in Oxfordshire, had a famously easy time. They were allotted their own house but did not always keep to it. Like most denizens of Garsington they abused the hospitality of their hostess, Lady Ottoline Morrell, expecting her to feed their friends and then complaining that the fare was poor. Had it not been for Philip Morrell they could have ended up on the bleak home farm at Dartmoor, yet they repaid him by neglecting his fields and his livestock. Presumably they were inspected to ensure they were performing work of national importance, but all that observers saw, or reported, was men loafing, larking and everlastingly arguing. Clive Bell was supposed to look after the cows, but found them incompatible; Gerald Shove, a Cambridge economist, was responsible for egg production, which declined rapidly. One self-pitying figure, who had ambitions to sing in opera, could not even chop firewood, and when asked to clear molehills found reasons for not doing so. A few men worked hard and were respected in the nearby village, but most of the villagers must have regretted the day they jangled the church bells to welcome the Morrells to the manor. Reporters from London hovered round and were not wholly put off by threats of libel writs. Shove, who was there at his own request, tried to rally his fellow objectors into a union, to oppose exploitation, but his demonstration collapsed ignominiously, like his hens. To the *literati* in residence these antics were a distraction from their philanderings in a colony which D. H. Lawrence had once hoped could become the Utopian 'Rananim' of which he dreamed, but which more closely resembled one of those medieval communities of voluptuaries frivolling while the Plague raged outside. It held a fascination for Asquith who, careless of his reputation, used to drop in with his guests.

Some farmers refused to have conscientious objectors, intellectual or otherwise, on their land; marginally preferable were German prisoners, who at least did not wear long overcoats and mufflers at their work. There were farm labourers who refused to work alongside objectors. The Government was driven to organising a network of camps for the unwanted, of which the most publicised was on Dartmoor, adjoining the prison. Here in the spring of 1917 a thousand men in overcoats, many of them newly out of gaol, were assigned to a land reclamation scheme on which they made indifferent progress. Their demands for ploughs instead of spades were not met; it became clear that the Government was content for the land to be worked the hard way and for men to do the work of horses.

In Princetown there was great indignation over the invasion of 'conchies', bringing disgrace on a famous gaol. The men were free to roam the town in the evenings and at weekends. Among complaints against them were these: they moved about in jostling, catcalling gangs, annoying women; they cycled in droves to the neighbouring villages, spreading political contagion; they paraded with 'Peace' signs, raised red banners and sang *The Red Flag*; they accosted young people, criticising the King and saying, 'we would be better under a republic'; they commandeered the warders' cricket ground; they bought up supplies in the shops, notably of sweets; they declined to stand for the National Anthem in Princetown Church; they refused to work in the quarries and jeered at those who did; they sent for their friends, who swarmed in the lodging-houses; and – this was more a criticism of the Government – they travelled on free rail passes at Easter when travel was officially discouraged, even for soldiers.

The people of Princetown and Plymouth needed no goading by Lord Northcliffe to hold mass indignation meetings and the Government was forced to take notice. Rules against spreading propaganda were tightened, visits to villages forbidden and some of the less tractable objectors were fed back into the military and penal machines. But there was never any lack of inflammatory news from Dartmoor. One objector shot another with a revolver, accidentally it appears, and decamped. There were mass strikes. A proposal to start a brass band was described by the Home Secretary, Sir George Cave as 'intolerable in present conditions'. Photographs of the 'Princetown pets', among whom were many politicals, scarcely suggest abused weaklings. One of the *Daily Mail*'s first pictures showed a mixture of cloth caps and Homburg hats, though disappointingly no topper. The *Mail* urged that the objectors be disenfranchised, as in Canada, on the ground that a person unwilling to fight for his country should be denied any say in its affairs; and in November 1917, on the motion of Sir George Younger, the Commons included a disenfranchisement clause in the Representation of the People Act.

The Dartmoor camp was topped up from time to time with inmates from other Home Office colonies. Wherever objectors were concentrated, whether on farms or forestry schemes or road works or in quarries, or in the open gaols of Wakefield and Warwick, there was friction. Cycling 'conchies' were a prime target. Some notable mêlées occurred at Knutsford, where a group of objectors who stood armed with sticks outside their centre were rushed by a crowd and belaboured with their own weapons. A few 'trusties' were allowed to work for low pay in Government offices, reporting back to casual wards at night; they attracted no sympathy from fellow clerks who had been exempted by virtue of their calling. Philip Snowden urged that objectors who had been trained as teachers should be allowed to continue in their profession, but was told this would not be in the best interests of education. From time to time *John Bull* protested at the employment of conscientious 'objects' in YMCA canteens and even in Army messes.

In all, there were about 16,000 objectors as against eight

million men who put on uniform. Some 1,500 absolutists, mainly 'politicals', served repeated prison sentences on the cat-and-mouse principle (they wore a special black garb with white broad arrows); many hundreds of others went to prison and then decided to take up work of national importance. A tiny handful lived in friendly attics or holes in the ground.

The foregoing may remind some readers of John Buchan's *Mr Standfast* (1918), in which Brigadier-General Richard Hannay, with 'a chest like the High Priest's breastplate', is ordered to doff his uniform and infiltrate the pacifists of the Garden City of Biggleswick, where treason is afoot. Hannay swallows his revulsion and proceeds to 'sink down deep into the life of the half-baked', cultivating 'the eager, vital people . . . puffed up with spiritual pride . . . at the head of all the newest movements' (like the League of Democrats Against Aggression). *Mr Standfast* is a fascinating period piece and there can be little doubt that Biggleswick is modelled on Letchworth.

CHAPTER 16

THE NASTIEST RUMOUR

In his autobiography *The Youngest Son* Ivor Montagu recalls that when he was a boy during the war his family used to be visited at Townhill Park, Hampshire, by a cousin, Major Hugh Pollard, who laughingly described how his branch of Intelligence had launched the legend of the German corpse factories, in which the dead from the battlefields were supposed to be turned into soap and margarine. 'The tears ran down his cheeks as he told us of the story they had circulated of a consignment of soap from Germany arriving in Holland and being buried with full military honours.' Pollard claimed to have thought up the corpse factory idea to discredit the enemy in oriental countries, where reverence for the dead was deeply felt.

Montagu says the family lost their appetite for the Major's tales after he became a Black and Tan. To what extent had Cousin Hugh been teasing his young relatives? Was he really the originator of the *Kadaver* legend, which helped to intensify hatred of the Hun and inspired Kipling to a set of 'unprintable' verses? If there were any rival claimants for the honour they seem to have kept quiet.

The story had that element of black comedy which characterises the most successful atrocity tales; it ranks with the reports of Belgian nuns suspended head downwards to serve as clappers in church bells. 'War,' as Woodbine Willie said, 'is best bought in the *Daily Mail* and read over breakfast. It goes very well with bacon and eggs.' However, the *Daily Mail* headline of

April 17, 1917 – HUN GHOULS: Oil, Fodder and Dividends From The Dead – may have caused even loyal readers to push their bacon and eggs aside.

Rumours of the existence of corpse factories had been cropping up long before that date. In Cynthia Asquith's *Diaries* an entry for June 16, 1915, mentions a discussion on the subject, ending, 'I suggested that Haldane should offer his vast body as raw material to Lloyd George.' Then, in the *North China Herald** of March 3, 1917, appeared an unobtrusive report from a Peking correspondent headed HOW GERMANS ALIENATED THE PREMIER. This Shanghai newspaper described how pressures had been applied by the Germans on Tuan Chi-jui to throw in his lot with the Central Powers. He had been unimpressed by news that the Germans had made a peace offer, which he regarded as a sign of weakness, and even less impressed when told that they proposed to put women in the trenches. 'But the matter was clinched when Admiral von Hintze [German Minister in Peking] was dilating upon the ingenious methods by which German scientists were obtaining chemicals necessary for the manufacture of munitions. The Admiral triumphantly stated that they were extracting glycerine out of dead soldiers! From that moment the horrified Premier had no more use for Germany. . . .'

At the time this report appears not to have attracted attention in Britain. However, public 'confirmation' of the rumours was not far off; for little more than a month later the British papers picked up from the Berlin *Lokal Anzeiger* a report by its war correspondent Karl Rosner:

'We are passing through Evergnicourt. There is a dull smell in the air, as if lime were being burnt. We are passing the Great Corpse Exploitation Establishment (*Kadaverwertunganstalt*) of this Army Group. The fat that is won here is turned into lubricating oils and everything else is ground down in the bone mill into a powder which is used for mixing with pigs' food and as manure.'

Rosner added: 'Nothing can be permitted to go to waste.'

This translation appeared in the column 'Through German

*The weekly edition of the *North China Daily News*, strongly pro-Allies (filed at British Library).

Eyes' in *The Times* of April 16, 1917. Next day the newspaper described it as 'the first admission concerning the way in which Germans use dead bodies', and said it confirmed striking accounts of 'this new and horrible German industry' which had appeared in *Indépendance Belge* in France on April 10, extracted from *La Belgique* of Leyden.

According to *Indépendance Belge* it had long been known that the Germans stripped their dead behind the firing line, tied the bodies into bundles of three or four and then sent them in wagons to the rear. Latterly they had been consigned to a new factory near St Vith, close to the Belgian frontier. If the results were good, it was proposed to set up another factory for corpses from the Eastern Front. The company conducting the operation was the German Offal Utilisation Company (*Deutsche Abfall Verwertungs Gesellschaft*) with a capital of £250,000.

There was a circumstantial description of the factory, which measured 700 feet long, was invisible from the railway, surrounded by thick trees and enclosed by electrified wire. When the corpse trains arrived men in oilskins and wearing mica masks used hooked poles to lift the bodies on to an endless chain. The corpses passed through disinfecting and drying chambers into a 'digester' where they were left for six or eight hours. Among the by-products were stearine and other fats used for soap. The men employed in this mechanised charnel-house were not allowed to leave and were closely guarded.

Not all newspaper readers were prepared to swallow these reports whole. Some were quick to assert that in German *Kadaver* meant an animal corpse; but others unearthed without difficulty examples of *Kadaver* used to describe a human corpse. A medical reader of *The Times* said that when studying at Berlin University he had been given a certificate by the Anatomical Institute in respect of dissections performed on a *Kadaver*. The controversy gained fresh impetus from the discovery of a German Sixth Army Order containing, among routine items, a paragraph directing that 'when corpses are sent to the *Kadaver* utilisation establishment, returns as to the unit, date of death, illnesses and information as to epidemics, if any, are to be furnished at the same time.' This document was photographically reproduced, with the sanction or connivance of the British Censor, to show its authenticity.

The letter columns of the newspapers continued to reflect the controversy. One writer told of a German prisoner of war who had referred to margarine as 'corpse fat' (much margarine in those days was of a quality to inspire grisly jests). The Maharajah of Bikanir said the revelations would only make Indian troops fight the harder; they knew that whatever happened to their bodies in battle death in a righteous cause ensured an early entry into Paradise.

By now the Germans were angrily repudiating the corpse factory tale. The *Lokal Anzeiger* said the reading of *Kadaver* as human corpse was the essence of stupidity. The German wireless press exposed the reports as 'loathsome and ridiculous'. Not even the French had stooped to spreading this rumour, said the *Frankfurter Zeitung*.

When Lord Robert Cecil, Minister of Blockade, was asked in Parliament on April 30 if he could shed light on the reports, he said they had been cleared by the usual authorities and it was no part of the Government's task to enquire what went on in Germany. 'In view of other actions by German military authorities there is nothing incredible in the present charges against them,' he said. This produced an explosion in the Reichstag, where the German Foreign Secretary was asked how he proposed to counteract 'this most pitiful of all English calumnies'. All he could do was threaten neutrals with criminal prosecution if they repeated the stories.

If the rumour was good enough for a Cecil, it was good enough for Kipling. He was provoked to write a parody of Thackeray's *Sorrow of Werther*, in which Charlotte spread her dead lover 'lightly on her bread'. *John Bull* had a cartoon of the Kaiser holding a newspaper with the headline THOUSANDS OF GERMANS DEAD, exclaiming, 'Never mind, they will make good pig food', and *Punch* showed the Emperor saying to a recruit, 'And don't forget that your Kaiser will find a use for you alive or dead.' The *Lancet* calculated that in a period of heavy casualties the factories would yield a material amount of glycerine – four hundredweight per thousand bodies. Thus the shareholders of the parent company should be quite happy. In the *Daily Mail* appeared an article by a colonel tracing back the Germans to a wolf tribe who threw their corpses to dogs; he also mentioned that the German heroes ate corpses at their banquets in Valhalla. *Truth*, normally sceptical, became convinced the charges were true after Welsh troops, storming Messines, were reported to have found 'unsavoury German corpses done up in bundles of three'.

The Department of Information did not circulate the story. Its Director, C. F. G. Masterman, was attacked for not doing so, but he and his staff found much of the published information unsatisfactory; in later life he prided himself on having left the rumour alone. Doubts must have been gathering in Fleet Street, for the story was soon abandoned. In any event the lie by now had 'time on its own wings to fly'.

In *Disenchantment* C. E. Montague says that in 1918 chance took him to a chamber of horrors in a subterranean room near Bellicourt. Two big dixies, or cauldrons, lay amid a shambles of bodies and parts of bodies. The explanation was simple: a shell had landed on a cookhouse, not a rare happening. An Australian sergeant who had heard that this was the scene of corpse boiling said, with some bitterness, 'Can't believe a word you read, can you?'

Little more might have been heard of the story had not Brigadier-General John Charteris delivered an unfortunate speech at a dinner of the National Arts Club in New York in October 1925. He was reported as saying that the story began as propaganda for use in China. Two photographs had been found on a German prisoner, one showing a trainload of wounded soldiers, another a trainload of dead horses labelled *Kadaver*. By switching the captions, a mischievously false impression was given, and the result was sent off to a newspaper in Shanghai. When the report of his speech raised a stir General Charteris hastened to deny what he called a wholly inaccurate report of a speech at a private dinner. He had not transposed any picture captions and would be as interested as the general public to know the true origin of the story. General Headquarters in France, where he served as head of Intelligence services, had come into the matter only when a diary faked to give substance to the story had been submitted for planting on a dead German, but the idea was rejected. The General maintained his innocence in an interview with the Secretary for War.

Charteris also complained of an incorrect version of the affair in *These Eventful Years*, a war record published by the Encyclopaedia Britannica Company. It contained an article on propaganda by Bertrand Russell, who said the corpse factory story was widely used in China when the country's participation was desired, in the hope that it would shock the population. 'The story was set going cynically by one of the employees in the British propaganda department, a man with a good knowledge of German, perfectly aware that *Kadaver* means carcase not corpse, but aware also that the misrepresentation 'could be made to go down'. Russell does not give any authorities for his statements.

Was the story of Admiral von Hintze's clumsy diplomacy in Peking planted on the correspondent of the *North China Herald*, or was the correspondent perhaps privy to the plot – if plot there was? Or, if the story was true, could the Chinese Premier have misunderstood the use of the word *Kadaver*? In any event, how did Cynthia Asquith come to hear about corpse factories in 1915?

In Parliament on November 23, 1925, Commander J. M. Kenworthy sought to obtain the facts about the rumour and 'the extent to which it was accepted by the War Office at the time'. The War Minister, Sir L. Worthington-Evans, expressed doubts whether, at that stage, the source could be established with certainty. He said that the reports in the *Lokal Anzeiger* and Belgian newspapers, taken in conjunction with the captured German Army order, were such that the War Office 'appeared to have seen no reason to disbelieve the truth of the story'. Pressed to disavow the reports, he said he was not concerned with whether they were true or not, only with the information on which his predecessors acted. However, on December 2, Sir Austen Chamberlain, Secretary for Foreign Affairs, said that the German Chancellor had assured him there was never any truth in the story. 'On behalf of His Majesty's Government,' he said, 'I accept this denial and I trust that this false report will not again be revived.'

The *Nation* said that many believed the story had originated in an honest blunder; if it had, an authoritative statement to that effect would help to clear Britain's name of an ugly stain. It has been suggested that shamefacedness over the corpse factory story may have made British editors wary of printing reports about Hitler's extermination camps in World War Two. In these establishments, as the world has often been reminded, the by-products of corpses were put to industrial and even aesthetic use.

CHAPTER 17

A WHIFF OF REVOLUTION

In March 1917 occurred the first Russian Revolution. 'Not since the Bastille fell has there been an event so full of splendid significance for men as the mighty happening of this week in Petrograd,' said the *Daily News*. 'A new star of hope has risen over Europe,' said the *Herald*, adding that 'those of our ruling classes who most bitterly detest freedom are already pale with anxiety lest Russia should become *too free*.' If so, they paled unnecessarily, for the British Revolution which some now thought to be inevitable proved an *ignis fatuus* and the man who, according to Lloyd George, would have been the British Kerensky, namely Ramsay MacDonald, suffered humiliation of an excruciating kind.

After the French Revolution radicals in Britain went around calling each other 'Citizen', dressing in unbuttoned French style and saying '*Ça ira*'. Now, with the fall of the Romanovs, their spiritual successors put on red ties and red blouses, sang *The Red Flag*, talked of going to the barricades and, in general, did their utmost to acclaim the grand event brought about by the war they had opposed. Seven thousand of them cheered a party of Russian sailors at a rally in Mile End. Ten thousand of them cheered Clara Butt, heroine of many a recruiting rally, as she sang *Give us peace in our time, O Lord* in the Albert Hall; but 'the most passionate applause of the evening' was reserved for the soldiers who had refused to shoot the workers in Petrograd. All that was necessary now, said George Lansbury, was for the troops of all armies to advance into no-man's-land and shake hands.

In the pulpits sermons were preached on the theme of a great nation rising in majesty and throwing off its shackles. A preacher more uplifted than most was the future 'Red Dean' of Canterbury, the Rev. Hewlett Johnson, then Vicar of Altrincham, who chaired a big meeting in Manchester 'to welcome the Revolution'. It was addressed by Bertrand Russell. By the Dean's account, a small military detachment was present to keep the peace and act as a brake on the exuberance of the speakers. 'The detachment got so interested in the speeches,' he says, 'that the officer, fearing penetration of Socialist ideas in the Army, formed fours and marched them out.' This sounds wildly unlikely. A *Manchester Guardian* report of a hail-the-Revolution meeting in Manchester, chaired by Hewlett Johnson and addressed by Russell, describes how a military detachment marched in during the speeches and obtained the chairman's permission to check the documents of the audience, an exercise which was greeted by boos and *The Red Flag*. In other words, it was an ordinary military round-up.

In Liverpool thousands attended a big open-air demonstration called to congratulate Russia. There were four platforms, from one of which spoke the veteran Socialist, Tom Mann. Open-air meetings of this type usually drew the disapproval of soldiers and this was no exception; they forced the organisers to haul down the red flag and aimed blows at speakers.

The spirit of the Cabinet was not exalted by news of the Revolution. It was vital to keep Russia in the fight, otherwise the Germans would be free to mass all their divisions on the Western Front. Even the American declaration of war against Germany, which came less than a month after the Russian upheaval, did not render less terrible this military nightmare.

At the close of 1916 the Russians had been solid with their Allies in rejecting the Peace Note put forward, via the United States, by the German Chancellor, von Bethmann-Hollweg. As peace notes go, it was markedly truculent. It said the latest events had shown that a continuation of the war could not break the Central Powers, who had only taken up arms to defend their own freedom; nevertheless, the Emperor, who had no wish to annihilate his adversaries but was much concerned to staunch the flow of blood, would be prepared for discussions on peace, provided Germany's rights and interests were safeguarded; if his approach was rebuffed, Germany would fight to the end, 'while solemnly disclaiming any responsibility before mankind and history'. The Allies decided, very quickly, that it was all a sham, a device to gain time, a plot to divide, an attempt to reassure Germany's home front, a propaganda exercise to impress neutrals, an attempt to negotiate while conditions were favourable. In the Commons Lloyd George said that anyone who wantonly prolonged the war 'would have on his soul a crime that oceans could not cleanse'; on the other hand, to give up through weariness or despair would be 'the costliest act of poltroonery ever perpetrated'. Three major objections to the Note were: it suggested the Allies started the war; it insisted that the Central Powers were victorious; and it gave no hint of restitution for Belgium. To reject the Note was, therefore, easy; though it would have been less easy if Britain and France had known that Russia was about to collapse. Along with the German Note, the Allies had rejected proposals by President Wilson of the United States that the belligerents should state their peace terms. His suggestion that both sides were fighting for the same objectives was ill received.

The city of Leeds was now to find itself unwillingly projected into the headlines. It was chosen as a meeting-place for those who, afire with libertarian ideas, yearned to accelerate the British Revolution. One of their main proposals was to set up soviets, or councils of workers' and soldiers' delegates, in every town and village in Britain. A circular issued under the unfamiliar aegis of the United Socialist Council was headed: 'Great Labour, Socialist and Democratic Convention to hail the Russian Revolution and to organise the British Democracy TO FOLLOW RUSSIA'. The convention, the circular said, 'will begin a new era of democratic power in Great Britain. It will begin to do for this country what the Russian Revolution has accomplished in Russia'. Among the signatories were Ramsay MacDonald, Philip Snowden, George Lansbury and Robert Smillie.

The United Socialist Council drew much of its support from the Independent Labour Party and the British Socialist Party

This full-page advertisement in the *Daily Mail* of January 11, 1917, promised the cinemagoer a sight of 'the sea of mud which covers everything, and in which even the horses sink knee-deep'.

Arsenal vista: women workers help to inspect the product.

Left: A London mother arrays flowers at a street shrine in honour of the dead from neighbouring streets.

Left: The axewoman: a recruit of the Women's Forestry Corps.

The sweep is called up: his wife carries on.

Below: Bring out your dead: a woman undertaker in war-time 'uniform'.

The Lady Superintendent of Woolwich Arsenal: Lilian Barker (later a Dame). She was responsible for the welfare of 30,000 women.

Conscription comes at last: laggards are 'deemed to have enlisted'.

MILITARY SERVICE ACT
1916

EVERY UNMARRIED MAN
of
MILITARY AGE
Not excepted or exempted under this Act
CAN CHOOSE
ONE OF TWO COURSES:

(1) He can ENLIST AT ONCE and join the Colours without delay:

(2) He can ATTEST AT ONCE UNDER THE GROUP SYSTEM and be called up in due course with his Group.

If he does neither, a third course awaits him:
HE WILL BE DEEMED TO HAVE ENLISTED
under the Military Service Act
ON THURSDAY, MARCH 2nd, 1916.

HE WILL BE PLACED IN THE RESERVE, AND BE CALLED UP IN HIS CLASS,
as the Military Authorities may determine.

Asquith's pledge not to conscript married men before bachelors led to difficulties – and bitter feelings. Married men formed themselves into a union.

THE PRIME MINISTER'S PLEDGE

To Married Men is now being redeemed by Parliament.

But let the young unmarried men themselves redeem that Pledge by joining under the Group System

TO-DAY.

DO NOT FORCE YOUR COUNTRY TO FORCE YOU TO FIGHT, BUT COME OF YOUR OWN FREE WILL

British seamen prevent Ramsay MacDonald from sailing to Petrograd to address the Russian Revolutionaries. From *Punch*, June 20, 1917.

Below: To avoid trouble with the law householders surrender hoarded food. From *Punch*, February 13, 1918.

HOIST WITH HIS OWN PETARD.

Mr. Ramsay Macdonald (*Champion of Independent Labour*). "OF COURSE I'M ALL FOR PEACEFUL PICKETING—ON PRINCIPLE. BUT IT MUST BE APPLIED TO THE PROPER PARTIES."

UNDOING THEIR BIT.

QUEUE OF CONSCIENTIOUS DISGORGERS PATRIOTICALLY EVADING PROSECUTION.

(both Marxist bodies) and was backed by the Union of Democratic Control and the National Council for Civil Liberties. In answer to its summons some 1,200 red-ribboned 'peace prattlers' (as the press called them) converged in June 1917 on the Coliseum Cinema in Leeds. They included members of trades councils, trade unions, reformist organisations, anti-war groups, adult schools, May Day committees, co-operative societies, women's leagues, ex-suffragists, communists, conscientious objectors, anti-vaccinationists and the church militant. Many of the delegates represented only themselves; others were uninstructed by the groups to which they adhered. The Labour Party opposed the convention, though many members attended.

The city of Leeds lacked all desire to become the British Petrograd. When delegates arrived at their hotels they were asked, 'Are you attending the convention?' and if the answer was yes their bookings were cancelled. Local Socialists opened a lodgings bureau, but scores had to sleep in 'dormitories' in the Engineers' Club. Restaurants were disinclined to serve the visitors. There was booing and jostling and some pelting, with shouts of 'Traitor!' The convention had been denied the use of the city's Albert Hall, for fear of disorder, and for the same reason a ban was imposed on open-air meetings. MacDonald fully expected the convention to be stopped by the military at the last minute. On the opening day, according to the *Yorkshire Post*, 'Leeds honoured itself by taking very little notice of the assembly in its midst', though the newspaper did not deny coverage to 'this sinister movement launched under cover of the Russian Revolution'.

The organisers had hoped to produce revolutionaries from Petrograd on the platform, but this was not to be. Predictably, the convention opened with *The Red Flag*. The chairman, Robert Smillie, who had two sons serving and a third who was a conscientious objector, said he was there to talk reason not treason. Britain's soldiers, he argued, needed a joint civil and military organisation to put forward their grievances and to safeguard their post-war treatment. As for peace, it must come not by a knock-out blow and the common people must have a chance to make it. More subversive was the advice to the workers from Robert Williams, of the Transport Workers'

Federation: 'Have as little concern for the British Constitution as the Russians you are praising had for the dynasty of the Romanovs.' Some delegates warned that the British soviets must not be destructive of military discipline, others saw them as instruments for enforcing peace. Whatever their role, Sylvia Pankhurst wanted to see women on them. Ramsay MacDonald and Bertrand Russell demanded freedom of speech, press and association. Ernest Bevin, representing Bristol dockers, said he was ready to act the role of pacifist, 'but only when Germany is ready to respond'. He complained of Philip Snowden's 'fatuous friends' in the Independent Labour Party, which did not go down well. A ranting voice from Clydeside, that of William Gallacher, warned that workers who made revolution did not do so in order that the bourgeoisie could take over.

Among those who tried to speak was the fiery Captain Edward Tupper of the Seamen's and Firemen's Union, who was all for getting on with the war and making Germany pay indemnities. Who else, he asked, would compensate the families of his members, the men who were drowned in an effort to keep the delegates fed? 'The British shipowners,' came the reply, along with inexplicable cries of 'Judas!' Impatiently, the meeting howled down the 'swashbuckling captain', which turned out to be a bad mistake.

After the convention, Philip Snowden drafted a windy message to Petrograd: 'The largest convention of Labour, Socialist and democratic bodies held in Great Britain during this generation has today endorsed Russia's declaration of foreign policy and war aims and has pledged itself to work through its newly constituted Workmen's and Soldiers' Council for an immediate democratic peace.' In fact, hardly any thought had been given as to how this Council, or its subsidiary councils, would be constituted. As will be seen, such efforts as were made to transform the wish into reality were quickly frustrated.

Strangely, as *Truth* pointed out, the newspapers which reported the convention did not mention the wrecking and looting of the Jewish quarter of Leeds by 'hundreds of youths and men'; coverage of this was left to the *Jewish Chronicle*. Many of the delegates to the convention were Russian Jews.

Lloyd George suspected that the convention's organisers were wary of moving until they had gauged the effect of their oratory on the country. 'Had the workmen rallied to the proposal of establishing a Soviet in Britain on Russian lines, then the Leeds meeting would have inaugurated a British Revolution and Mr MacDonald would have been our Kerensky,' he has written. As it was, the conference was widely assailed as ridiculous even by many who took part in it. Herbert Morrison called it hysterical and unreal, 'an anti-climax to all the exhilarating revolutionary talk, and most of us knew it'. Russell's view was that 'nothing was lacking except leaders'. James Sexton, the dockers' organiser, called it 'the most bogus, the most dishonest and the most corrupt conference ever created by the mind of man', a judgement quoted with approval by Basil Thomson, the Assistant Commissioner of Metropolitan Police, whose men kept close watch on the organisers' subsequent moves.

According to Will Thorne, Labour Member for West Ham, who was a guest at Buckingham Palace, the King was 'greatly disturbed' about the Leeds episode and feared the day might come when he would follow the Romanovs. Thorne replied that there would never be 'a physical, violent revolution in the country', though there would have to be political and industrial change. 'This,' says Thorne, 'seemed to relieve his mind.' Thorne was the hero of the gasfitters' union and was sometimes seen in the uniform of a lieutenant-colonel commanding the West Ham Volunteers. He had also been seen in Petrograd on a goodwill visit wearing a fine fur coat presented to him by Sir F. E. Smith (who had two more at home).

When the Convention broke up, Ramsay MacDonald was more concerned to visit Russia than to organise a soviet at Lossiemouth or Leicester. When it was learned that he had obtained a passport for Petrograd, Members of Parliament wanted to know why it had been issued; they were told that Russia wished to greet representatives of minority workers' opinion in Britain and the Government was reluctant to antagonise them by a refusal. What many MPs feared was that MacDonald would make an unauthorised call at Stockholm, where the International Socialist Bureau (a new version of the International) was trying to convene a meeting of world Socialists, including German Socialists, to discuss peace proposals. This would have meant sitting down with the King's

enemies, as the law officers of the Crown pointed out; but the
Labour Party repeatedly pressed to be allowed to do so.

MacDonald's plans were dashed when leaders of the Seamen's and Firemen's Union told him that if he wished to visit
Russia he would have to swim there; none of them would serve
on a ship which allowed him on board. This was the union's
revenge for the shouting down of their man at Leeds. In the
main seaports tub-thumping speeches were delivered in
justification of the ban. At Cardiff there was a demand that the
articles of all Russia-bound ships should be endorsed, 'No peace
cranks to be carried'. Sadly, the *Herald*, which was normally in
favour of militant union action, pointed out that this strike was
levelled not only at the Government but at the Labour Party
and, even worse, against the new Russia.

MacDonald tried to run the seamen's gauntlet. He was slip-
ping into King's Cross Station to catch a train to Aberdeen when
a union picket said, 'Good evening, Mr MacDonald.' Thereafter
the wires hummed and thousands gathered on the Aberdeen
wharf whence the ship was due to sail. MacDonald made only
one attempt to board, desisting when the crew lined up and
made it clear they would put on their coats and go home. He
then returned, through a picket line, to his hotel, where he rang
Lloyd George, on a very bad line, and asked him to help. The
Prime Minister had already been warned by the union that if
MacDonald were given a naval crew they would call a general
seamen's strike. He had also received a telegram from
Emanuel Shinwell, Clydeside organiser of the British Sea-
farers' Union, offering to provide a crew to take MacDonald to
Russia; but Shinwell never received a reply.

Lloyd George tried gentle pressure on Havelock Wilson,
president of the Seamen's and Firemen's Union, but to no avail.
In his *Memoirs* he notes with some satisfaction that the sailors
were giving the Member for Leicester 'some taste of what a
general strike, such as he subsequently advocated in 1926,
would be like'. So MacDonald was reduced to sending his
apologies to Petrograd, explaining that 'unworthy members' of
a union had performed malicious acts, had wilfully lied and had
displayed ignorance, hooliganism and blindness of passion. No
Marxist could have put it better. The ill wind blew a beneficial
gust to a competitor in *John Bull*'s 'Bullets' contest: a prize of

£1,000 for appending to 'Ramsay MacDonald' the phrase
' "Swab" Sailors Won't Carry'.

Confinement to Britain left MacDonald free to speak in
Parliament on a Vote by the Reichstag (a body with no executive
power) urging peace negotiations on a basis of mutual under-
standing and reconciliation. His motion urged that the British
Government should make an answering gesture and that, as
Russia suggested, 'representatives of the peoples' should take
part in any peace talks. Asquith pointed out that the Reichstag's
'ambiguous generalities' said nothing about withdrawal from,
or reparations for, Belgium. The motion was lost by 148 votes
to 19.

Meanwhile, the attempts to create British soviets were found-
ering. Bertrand Russell was passively involved in an affray in the
Brotherhood Church in Southgate, London, where proposals to
form such councils were to be discussed. Inflamed by leaflets,
newspaper editorials and drink, a mob of workers and soldiers,
with attendant womenfolk, stormed the church, smashing the
windows and wrecking the interior. Russell says the mob
included viragos armed with nail-studded boards. The police, he
claims, looked on calmly, unmoved when informed by a lady
that he was a man of learning but exerting themselves when
told he was the brother of an earl. One pacifist was brought to
bay in the pulpit and another had to leap from the organ loft. At
length a Canadian soldier called to his comrades, 'This is God's
house, and we must respect it.' Similar meetings were broken up
in Swansea and Newcastle, with Empire troops to the fore, but
at Leicester, Bristol and Norwich there was no trouble.

On Merseyside that summer would-be revolutionists, allied
with disgruntled ex-soldiers, naturalised aliens and conscientious objectors, shattered the calm of the Liverpool Abercromby
by-election. Lord Stanley, son of the War Minister, Lord Derby,
was expected to slide into the seat with ease, but huge embarrassment was caused when Stanley, a twice-wounded officer in
the Grenadier Guards, was opposed by a one-legged ex-private,
claiming to be the discharged soldiers' champion but apparently
the catspaw of others. The War Office was deeply unhappy at
the prospect of a serving officer being heckled by angry and
shell-shocked other ranks. As they feared, the barracking was

ugly. However, Sir Archibald Salvidge, the Liverpool brewer who was Stanley's agent, had a flash of inspiration. 'I got a handbill out,' he says in his diary, 'showing that the twenty signatures on [the ex-private's] nomination papers included the names Lazarus, Isaac, Fineberg, Chishelsky, Kesler, Pochinsky, Neurick, Myer and Skulnick. That did it. The ex-soldier support of our opponent largely melted away and left us with only the revolutionaries to cope with.' On polling day Stanley won comfortably. Salvidge makes no apology in his diary for these tactics.

In November 1917 Kerensky was overthrown and the Bolsheviks took over. By December 15 they had made peace with Germany, which was free to concentrate men and metal on the Western Front. It made a frightening end to a dismaying year; yet the country, despite pockets of unrest, was still contemptuous of 'peace cranks', whose end-the-war gatherings were always liable to be invaded and turned into patriotic rallies. Even Lord Lansdowne, the Tory elder statesman, was execrated as a peace crank when, in a famous letter to the *Daily Telegraph* on November 29, 1917, he said the waste of blood had become so intolerable that there must be a negotiated peace, otherwise the fruits of victory would not be worth having. The peace party in Germany, he argued, would be strengthened by the knowledge that the Allies were not out to annihilate the Fatherland, impose any form of government on it or wreck its commercial future. He was ostracised even by those members of his party who, privately, thought the letter made sense.

The Russian upheavals caused some agonising in the East End of London, where 25,000 Russian Jews of military age were congregated. Some were fugitives from the Czar, some had fled Menshevism and Bolshevism, but many had been born in Britain. Since the advent of conscription there had been complaints in Parliament that these eligible aliens were shirking military service, that they were ready enough to manufacture khaki cloth but not to wear it. Throughout 1916 the Home Secretary, Herbert Samuel, was kept busy explaining that the Russians, if they did not wish to return to their homeland, would be required to serve in the British Army, unless exempted by tribunals. He pointed out that French, Italians and Belgians of military age had been sent from Britain to their parent countries, and that the Russian Government was content to see its expatriates serve in the British Army. Yet Samuel was continually baited on this issue. 'You do not dare to treat Irishmen in that way,' said Philip Morrell, 'you do not dare to treat Indians in that way.' The Government's policy, he suggested, would bring infamy on the name of Samuel. To this, the Home Secretary spoke of the bitterness in the East End where businesses had been closed and trades crippled by the call-up, while thousands of able-bodied young Russians, many of them born in Britain, were making no sacrifice. This situation was impossible for a Home Secretary to ignore, especially a Jewish one.

The March Revolution changed the situation overnight. With the Czar overthrown, would not the Russian exiles wish to hurry back to their country and fight for freedom? In the event, a great many did, though others were quick to say that conscription was a violation of the rights of sanctuary. That summer the *Daily Mail* described conditions in the happy and flourishing tailoring establishments in the East End. The Passover celebrations, the newspaper said, had been characterised by wealth and plenty. Refugees in Petticoat Lane had been scrambling for Surrey chickens and paying highly for 'rich, sticky Passover confectionery'. The West End had been alive with the gaiety of young Russians enjoying their holiday. One headline ran: MUCH TOO HAPPY TO FIGHT. In October of that year Parliament was told that four-sevenths of the Russians in the East End had applied to be shipped home and the rest were available for service in the British Army. 'There is no question of sending further shiploads to Russia,' said the Government spokesman.

Suggestions were made for the formation of a Jewish Pals Battalion, a Jewish Regiment and even a Jewish Legion, but such proposals drew the criticism that tens of thousands of Jews were already serving in the Forces and it would be wrong for Jews as a whole to be judged on the performance of a single unit. Nevertheless a Jewish Regiment was raised, doomed to be known as the Jordan Highlanders, but officially embodied in the Royal Fusiliers. One of its battalions marched through the City of London in February 1918 and the Lord Mayor took the salute. It was the first time a military unit composed wholly of Jews had marched under the British flag.

CHAPTER 18

MORALITY AT BAY

In *The Queen's Gift Book*, published in 1915, the novelist Hall Caine took it upon himself to define the role of Woman in relation to Man. She was:

> Not his temptress, not his slave-mate, not his subject, not his squaw,
> But his helpmeet and his angel by the right of God's own law.

And what was God's own law?

> If He dowered the man with passions which the grosser instincts move,
> He reserved it to the Woman to uplift his lust to love.

And the following two lines served as caption for a picture of a wartime heroine of the wards:

> Hers the conflict, hers the conquest, hers the flag of life unfurled.
> Hers the sorrow, hers the suffering, hers the love that rules the world.

These were reassuring, high-flying sentiments that people looked for in royal gift books. Outside the gift books women were floundering in a world that was brutal, bawdy, heroic and innocent all at the same time; basically a man's world, still enshrining the 'double standard' of conduct; a world in which the Army gave each man a slip for his pay-book bearing

Kitchener's advice to 'avoid any intimacy' with women – and then sanctioned his visits to vetted drabs who were unlikely to uplift his lust to love; a world in which, none the less, there were still youths in plenty strong enough to resist 'the things of night' and 'the shameful doorway' (Ernest Raymond's phrases) and who, when their hour came, threw aside *Comic Cuts* and the *Magnet*, went over the top and died as virgins.

Before 1914, as Harold Macmillan observes in *Winds of Change*, a young lady of good position could not walk in the street without damage to her reputation. To be seen going down St James's Street in London would put her beyond the pale. The London magistrate George Denman laid down that a woman appearing in Regent Street after ten o'clock must expect to be molested. The West End was not, of course, representative of London. The Right Rev. Claudius Billing, Bishop of Bedford, was said to have told mothers who were worried about their daughters working among the East End poor, 'See her as far as Temple Bar and then she will be all right'; but not all parents believed him. Many middle-class mothers were ready to regard a daughter as compromised if a man, even a fiancé, took her to a restaurant. If the daughter travelled anywhere unchaperoned she was expected to send a telegram announcing her arrival. Barbara Cartland assures us that girls of respectable family were not allowed to look at the newspapers.

By 1917, according to a contemporary observer, women of 'a strange and quite distinct type' were to be seen abroad in London: 'women, many in uniform, and with high boots, who walk through the streets of the Metropolis at midnight unprotected, unmolested, safe in the new-found confidence that war work has given to their sex. Two and a half years earlier every other man would have considered them fair game and one in three would have spoken to them.' In cafés once frequented only by tarts sat young flappers who, according to the same observer, showed no more refinement than prostitutes and sometimes less. 'Granted that [the flapper] has not made a trade of love, is her mind so very wholesome, has it much more of real purity than the daughters of joy, who sin boldly and pay the price of their transgressions without a murmur? Listen to the conversation of the flapper and it will not be her chastity, but her circumspection, that will impress you. She knows everything and knows it all wrong. Precocity has prevented her growing up, innocence has long gone.'

There is more than a touch of the Fleet Street moralist here. However, complaints about noisy girls behaving shamelessly are not hard to find in the newspapers and householders were indignant about the cheeky, rebellious creatures who sought employment as maids. The Salvation Army eventually began to advertise facilities for the reclamation of 'unruly girls, whose numbers are daily increasing owing to the abnormal conditions'. Very probably 'unruly' was a euphemism.

In *Disenchantment* C. E. Montague tells how the first dedicated volunteers in Kitchener's New Armies 'kept an unwonted hold on themselves during the months when hundreds of reputable women and girls round every camp seemed to have been suddenly smitten with a Bacchantic frenzy'. Commenting on this frenzy, Mrs Helena Swanwick, of the Women's International League, explained that 'it was the natural female complement to the male frenzy of killing'. She went on: 'If millions of men were to be killed in early manhood, or even boyhood, it behoved every young woman to secure a mate and replenish the population while there was yet time. It was an outbreak of primitive instinct, if you will, and no more beautiful in its manifestations than many primitive instincts are in a sophisticated world; but it all fitted together.'

This did not mean that Nature should be allowed to get away with it. Women of Mrs Swanwick's background, responsible matrons and spinsters of the middle and upper classes, lost no time forming purity patrols to combat 'khaki fever' wherever it manifested itself. In their dark blue uniforms and hard felt hats these volunteers were prepared, as the police were not, to rout couples from under bushes, from long grass, from shop doorways and all the dark corners of urban civilisation, not to mention the wide open spaces of Hyde Park and Richmond Park. Wielding little more than the authority which had always quelled servants, they told soldiers to be ashamed of themselves, marched drunk girls home and even forced soldiers' wives to turn their randy pick-ups out into the street; and the hardier among them did not shrink from raiding brothels and harrying pimps. Among these masterful women was Margaret Damer Dawson, motorcyclist and Alpinist, who recruited many upper-class suffragists to her banner; she was co-founder of the Women's Police Volunteers and later became Chief Officer of the Women's Police Service. One of her colleagues was Mary Allen, who had been gaoled for suffragist activities, and whose hobbies were driving and flying; she wore jackboots and breeches and usually had a monocle dangling on her chest. Damer Dawson, as she was known, was proud of having cleared certain West End streets of prostitutes. 'Young officers, boys of seventeen and eighteen, who have hardly left their mothers, are taken to these streets by women who ought to know better, but when they see the policewomen they bolt,' she told an interviewer. Mary Allen, faced with a young officer who said the two disreputable women with him were his cousins, replied, 'Very well, you are an officer and a gentleman and I must accept your word.' Five minutes later he touched her arm and said, 'I am sorry to have told you a lie. I thought you might like to know I am going back to camp.' Less easy to shame were prosperous civilians lacking a code of honour, however temporary.

Great emotion was generated over the problem of 'war babies'. The Archbishop of Canterbury, Dr Randall Davidson, voiced his displeasure to the Cabinet over proposals to pay the same separation allowances to unmarried women as to married (even in World War Two there were protests at the State's support of 'concubines'). The Archbishop did not wish unmarried mothers to starve, but at the same time he was anxious that they should not be placed openly on the public payroll. Lloyd George's view was that if the State was prepared to send men to fight it should be prepared to support their women. His secretary, Frances Stevenson, doubted whether the country should enquire into a man's morals before sending him to die for it. Fortunately the State was under no obligation to enquire into the morals of those who directed its destinies.

As things turned out, it was the number of marriages that shot up, rather than the number of bastards. If the *Tatler* is right, women were saying, 'Better to be married a minute than to die an old maid,' which is different from saying, 'Better a minute's wicked bliss than to die an old maid.' By the end of the war the illegitimacy rate had risen by only thirty per cent, and some of the babies would have been legitimised if the fathers had not been killed in action. (Princess Christian, Victoria's third daughter, is supposed to have pulled wires to have one of her gamekeepers brought back from the Front to make an honest woman of his fiancée.) Christabel Pankhurst wanted her suffragists to rear war babies in ideal conditions and her mother was all for starting with a pilot scheme of fifty little girls, but enthusiasm for this cause was not high and Mrs Pankhurst at length settled for four.

There were some, like Ronald McNeill, a diehard Tory Member of Parliament, who felt that the State should gratefully adopt war babies. Here he was in sympathy with the Socialist Countess of Warwick, who pleaded the war babies' case in the radical press. She was keen that regimental officers should parade their men at the end of the war and urge them to marry the girls they left behind them, with a Government assurance that the child would then be legitimised. Too many of those fighting were single. 'I have looked in vain through the speeches of statesmen,' she said, 'for a single recommendation to our defenders to marry and leave behind them some pledge of their affection, some asset for the real national treasury that does not consist of gold. . . .'

For reasons more sentimental than eugenic, there were parents who worried lest their fighting sons should die without leaving 'some pledge of affection'; though there may well have been others who feared this very eventuality.

In London certain institutions which catered for the raffish continued to flourish in war. One of them was the private upstairs dining-room, which could be hired for a meal for two in fashionable restaurants and hotels. The room would have a couch for after-dinner diversions and the elderly waiters were said to be unshockable. Among hotels with easy-going reputations was the Cavendish, the proprietress of which, Rosa Lewis, went to great lengths to give officers from the Front all they wanted, including a 'nice clean tart' and a parcel of luxuries when they left. Part of her war effort consisted of not cashing the cheques of those officers of whom she approved and, says Daphne Fielding, she finished the war with thousands of pounds' worth, though losses were partly recouped by overcharging rich civilians and foreigners. More impersonal hotels relaxed their rules cautiously, but cashed all cheques; the joke ran that they would eventually instal plaques 'To all the women who fell here during the Great War'. The main haunt of Bohemia, as always, was the Café Royal, where in due course Augustus John, exempted from service thanks to the equivalent of housemaid's knee, held court in the khaki of a Canadian major. (Sent to France as an artist, he was sent back for striking a fellow officer.) In uniform he retained his beard but not his earrings.

Much more exposed to criticism were the music-hall promenades which continued to offer men-about-town the pick of London's prostitutes. In their atmosphere of luxury and respectability the 'soiled doves' looked anything but soiled, and there was nothing exceptionable in their manners; but, as the *Contemporary Review* explained, they contributed to 'the physical collapse through sexual sin of an extraordinary number of men who would otherwise be playing their part in the fighting but instead are an encumbrance in hospitals and homes'. The military began to worry about the loss of officers from this cause. A senior Canadian officer, blaming the promenades for the condition of his men, is supposed to have said to the Bishop of London, the Right Rev. A. F. Winnington-Ingram, 'I tell you, sir, the mothers of Canada will hold *you* (meaning the people of England) responsible for this.' The Bishop wrote to *The Times* in July 1916 attacking the promenades as 'an insidious and deadly evil' and received strong support from that newspaper. He had already been trying to ginger the London County Council into action.

Lending support to the Bishop was Northcliffe's *Weekly Dispatch*, edited by Hannen Swaffer. Its investigators had been informed that the presence of the promenade ladies was worth £150 a week to the theatres concerned. They described how the Army's provost staff made regular visits to see how officers were behaving under temptation. The Alhambra, earlier that year, had been acquired by Sir Oswald Stoll who – the *Dispatch* revealed – was conducting a clean-up campaign. This included removing the seats on which ladies clustered, out of sight of the stage; if they could not see the stage, why were they there? As a result of his reforms, Stoll was now said to be attracting a respectable family trade. Belatedly the London County Council tabled a resolution that in future all premises licensed for music, dancing or the cinema should be subject to a condition that prostitutes should not habitually use them. Before this could be debated Alfred Butt announced that the Empire Theatre, the one most vigorously attacked, would close its promenade. News of this decision was borne in triumph to the Carshalton home of Mrs Ormiston Chant, who had campaigned against the Empire in the famous 'Prudes on the Prowl' controversy of 1894. The tidings were most graciously received.

Critics continued to attack the music-halls for the sniggering indecencies in which the performers specialised. Week after week General Sir Horace Smith-Dorrien was given lavish space in the *Weekly Dispatch* for this purpose. Sir Harry Lauder contributed a virtuous article saying that he had taken £1,635 in one week in Glasgow singing only clean songs expressive of a healthy sentiment. Eventually Smith-Dorrien found himself apologising in court to the Alhambra; he recognised that it was not always possible for a management to control every artist and the company piously agreed that entertainment should be unobjectionable.

Simultaneously with the attacks on music-halls was waged a war on night clubs, which were also denounced as nests of infected harpies, though the *Sunday Pictorial* found in them 'nothing to move the moralist to tears'. Not only were these sources of expensive cider-cup multiplying in the West End but they were spreading through the suburbs and along the Thames. In October 1915 night clubs were ordered to close at the same hour as restaurants. This was known as the 'beauty sleep order', the supposition being that subalterns would now go off to their beds; in fact, the clubs went underground, along with a number of gambling clubs, and their patrons followed them. Army officers were not allowed to wear uniform in night clubs, though Navy officers were.

For the Bishop of London it was a Sisyphean fight. He was the driving force of the London Council for the Promotion of Public Morality, otherwise known as 'the Bishop of London's Council'. In September 1916, wearing chaplain's uniform with peaked cap and Sam Browne, augmented by a shepherd's crook, he mounted the open-air pulpit attached to St James's, Piccadilly, a well-sited perch from which to denounce the wickedness of the West End. He asked his lunch-hour listeners: 'What are we to say of the male hawks who walk up and down this very Piccadilly night by night with twenty or thirty helpless and trembling girls under their surveillance and who take from them the very money the girls earn by their shame? I am not a bloodthirsty man but I say shooting is too good for them.' The parks, he continued, were not opened at great expense to be used as open-air brothels in the evening, but he declined to 'foul his hearers' minds' with the sixteen pages of evidence in his possession. To refute what he called a widespread misconception he quoted doctors as saying that 'no one was ever the worse for living a strictly moral life'. The sexual instinct (he called it 'the instinct involved') was 'an instinct implanted for a special purpose, which can be left unused for the whole of your life without the least injury to health'. A week later, resolute to 'free London from the curse of lust and sin', the Bishop addressed home-going workers in the Grove, Hammersmith, and urged them to keep away from 'the rubber shops', the existence of which he viewed as a scandal. (Their numbers, small at first, multiplied during the war.)

The Bishop was sadly aware that morality had been toppled from her throne even in London's teashops. Before Guildhall magistrates in July 1915 appeared a woman accused of allowing disorderly conduct in her lavishly furnished, dimly-lit *salon-de-thé* in Copthall Avenue. It consisted of one large room divided by heavy curtains. The six waitresses, with names like Fifi and Pepi, were said to be expensively dressed, or undressed, in low-cut blouses and short skirts, liberally bejewelled. 'What has that got to do with the case?' asked defence counsel and the magistrate, Sir George Truscott, said 'Oh, I think it has a great deal to do with it.' The conduct of the girls, police testified, was of a scandalous and disgraceful character, and seems to have consisted of fondling and kissing the customers on couches. On one occasion the manageress was said to have stood in front of the waitress and a customer while misbehaviour took place. It was customary for the waitresses to bring, along with tea and sandwiches, glasses of milk for themselves, which the customer had to pay for; and all parting customers were kissed as they left. The magistrate, on being told that there were a large number of teashops in the City where these things happened, said it was a pity in dark days that young men should have time to waste in such frivolities. He fined the accused woman £5 for each offence charged and said he wished he could have gaoled her. In 1918 similar evidence was still being given about fun-seeking officers and naughty waitresses in the tearooms of London; obviously such institutions fulfilled a popular need.

Blameless by contrast was the *thé-dansant*, a West End institution to which the war gave considerable impetus. A mere halfcrown bought music, flirtation and physical propinquity; if it did not add up to a subaltern's dream of sin, it was a tender, tantalising memory to carry to the Ypres Salient next day. However, 'tango teas' were open to objection. The tango was a mere licence for touching (*tango*: I touch), said the *Bystander* in 1914. It was 'in fact, sensuality and the worst kind of it; mild flirtation, suggestive titillation of the senses. Nothing even healthily indecent about it. Just the licence of those who are afraid.' The *Manchester Guardian* concurred. In 1917, it reported, tango dancing in the casino at Deauville had led to a ban on all dancing in the Calvados Department. In war, the problem was to indulge pleasures of the right sort. The dance, normally, was an excellent means of 'restoring the rhythmic balance of the spirit. But a thing neurotic and bizarre like the tango in some of its developments is a gratuitous perversion of the dance and if the only way to banish it from Deauville was by banishing all dances, there is something to be said for letting all dances go.' In Byron's day similar things were said of the waltz.

The cinema did not escape investigation. Soldiers, it was very apparent, were finding in the back stalls those cuddling facilities denied to them at the YMCA. But what else went on? A delegate told the Wesleyan Conference in July 1916 that assignations were being made in the dark. Other vigilantes reported molestation of children, goings-on in boxes and the indiscriminate admission of unsavoury characters. The result was that in 1916 the forces of morality set up a Cinema Commission to hear these and other complaints.

According to the Chairman of the Cinematograph Exhibitors Association, F. R. Goodwin, half the people in the country visited the cinema once a week and half of these took seats under threepence. He said that when complaints were investigated 'it was usually found that the alleged misconduct was no more than the privileged manifestation of affection between the sexes'; most married couples, he explained, sat close together, held hands, linked arms or encircled each other. Vigilance workers had visited 248 halls without finding any indecency. However, he conceded, it was different in the West End of London, where 60,000 prostitutes operated, 40,000 of them alien. (The Home Secretary later described these figures as exaggerated and said all German prostitutes had been deported.) The darkness in cinema vestibules, said Goodwin, made it exceedingly difficult to judge the character of women seeking admission. His Association favoured issuing cards for all females over fourteen and any woman convicted of prostitution would have her card clearly endorsed.

The Censor, J. Brooke Wilkinson, assured the Commission that 'scenes depicting the realistic horrors of warfare' were never screened (he was speaking long after the 'realistic' Somme films had been shown). There had been 'a growing tendency to develop stories turning on sexual relations, some of which had been very daring in their conception'. A Howard League spokesman, Cecil Leeson, said that children in trouble had learned to say, when asked where they got their wrong ideas, 'At the pictures, sir.' The Commission questioned a number of children on their tastes in films and on what went on in cinemas. There was some pulling of girls' hair, explained a schoolboy, 'but they seem to like it'.

Very slowly, the nation was bracing itself to utter the words venereal disease. When the Duchess of Marlborough mentioned the subject in her Priestley Lecture in 1916 on infant mortality, several old ladies rose 'and with horrified glances at my scarlet face turned their backs and walked out'. However, *The Times* thanked her the next day for her courage. To lighten the general ignorance on the subject the Lord Chamberlain was allowed, early in 1917, to lift his ban on the plays of Eugene Brieux. Lady Cynthia Asquith went to see *Damaged Goods* (*Les Avariés*) with a party of friends, two of whom walked out after the first act. 'I must say I was quite interested,' she says '. . . the play was unavoidably unpleasant, but not gratuitously so.' It ran for nine months. Arnold Bennett saw *Les Trois Filles De M. Dupont* and found it much worse than he expected, extremely crude throughout, but 'a great tract for those who need such things'. Those who needed such things, said the *Sporting Times*, included sixteen-year-olds of both sexes, and urged that they be admitted. Both plays were staged by the showman C. B. Cochran and ran in adjacent theatres.

In the eyes of the law venereal disease was a woman's disease. Early in the war the Women's Freedom League had protested against an Act which allowed wayward young girls to be sent to reformatories and women to be imprisoned under suspicion of infecting soldiers. This Act was replaced by Regulation 40D of the Defence of the Realm Act which laid down that no infected woman was to have sexual intercourse with any Serviceman; suspects were liable to be remanded for a week for medical examination. Several women's organisations took umbrage at this insult to women; it smacked too much of the Contagious Diseases Act under which women were harried in seaports and garrison towns in Victorian times. It was also, said these critics, a first step in the State regulation of vice. If soldiers wished to escape disease they had an easy remedy: to lead a clean life. Throughout the war women were gaoled for infecting Servicemen and, indeed, they were still being gaoled after the Armistice. Treatment of venereal disease was both painful and inefficient. In 1917 the Government passed a filleted Venereal Diseases Act which put some 5,000 quack pox-doctors out of business by preventing them from advertising. There were objections from upholders of the right of a patient to choose his own doctor, however ignorant, and also from chemists and medical herbalists.

The occasional society scandal helped to keep the public mind off the war. In the summer of 1916, during the long-drawn slaughter on the Somme, rumour had it that a lady of high birth and advancing years had interceded to obtain a commission for a young infantry sergeant of whom she was enamoured, only to find that he rejected her advances; in retaliation for which she used her influence with a variety of generals to have him posted to the Front. It sounded remarkably like the story of Potiphar's wife and Joseph, in *Genesis*. A Member of Parliament, Sir Arthur Markham, pressed for an enquiry and a special Act was passed for this purpose; Lloyd George, at this time Secretary for War, was not opposed to a sideshow which would embarrass the generals.

It all came out at great length in a Parliamentary Paper in January 1917, summarised in the press under headlines like YOUNG OFFICER'S ORDEAL. Potiphar's wife was not, as some gossips had thought, Lady Randolph Churchill, but Mrs Cornwallis-West, mother of the Duchess of Westminster and the Princess of Pless. At the age of sixty-three the *châtelaine* of Ruthin Castle had formed 'a more than ordinary interest' in Sergeant Patrick Barrett, aged twenty-six, of the Royal Welch Fusiliers and had represented to his battalion commander that he was worthy of a commission, a suggestion which that officer was happy to endorse. However, Second-Lieutenant Barrett, having 'consistently failed to respond' to her advances, eventually wrote her a letter of remonstrance, which she then sent on to his battalion commander. The lieutenant-colonel took the view that it was a disciplinary matter and recommended to the War Office that Barrett be transferred. He also censured Barrett twice, first in the presence of his adjutant and then before his company commander. When news reached Mrs Cornwallis-West that Barrett's friends were taking up his case she appealed to her old friend Lieutenant-General Sir John Cowans, the Quartermaster-General, to use his influence, but by then Barrett had been posted to another battalion. Cowans was not too busy feeding and supplying three-and-a-half million men (a task he performed superbly) to telegraph and write to the lieutenant-colonel, although the matter was outside his jurisdiction. He also disclosed confidential facts to Mrs Cornwallis-West and said he would fight for her if opportunity arose.

The official report, signed by Field-Marshal Lord Nicholson, said that General Cowans had been guilty of a departure from official propriety and had been informed of the Government's displeasure, but that in view of his distinguished service he would be retained in his post. The lieutenant-colonel had behaved hastily, harshly and improperly, in consequence of which he had been relieved of his command. 'We regret to think that, under the influence of a lady of position in the county, he allowed himself to deny justice to one of his junior officers,' said the report. However, he was cleared, as was Mrs Cornwallis-West, of any imputation that the purpose of transferring Barrett was to send him to the Front.

For the woman whose beauty had once dazzled Edward VII the Commission of Inquiry had no mercy. They thought she had exaggerated her influence with Cowans and that she had injudiciously boasted of her power at the War Office; they described her conduct as highly discreditable and said she had proved vindictive and untruthful; and they even regretted that she held important positions in the county associated with war work.

That a *grande dame* should bite the dust was no bad thing. Mrs Cornwallis-West was not the only society lady who pulled wires at the War Office, looking on military appointments as a legitimate sphere of influence. Her husband said it was all a storm in a tea-cup. *John Bull* under the headline THE WICKED WOMAN OF WALES printed purported letters to Mrs Cornwallis-West from the lieutenant, which showed him as very much the callow innocent. The *Sporting Times* (the *Pink 'Un*) produced a crop of squibs and limericks, mostly 'low in the neck', one of which ran: 'There was an old lady who pressed / Her love on a gentleman guest, / Then for vengeance did turn / When he would not adjourn / To her little grey home in the West.' Mrs Cornwallis-West, recalled the *Sporting Times*, had been one of the first 'professional beauties', like Lillie Langtry, whose photographs had been sold alongside those of jockeys; the suggestion seemed to be that it served her right. For her exonerated victim there was a Parliamentary display of sympathy. Lord Derby, the new War Minister, wished him a speedy recovery from an illness brought on by the strain of his ordeal.

With millions of men forcibly separated from their wives it was inevitable that there should be the occasional *crime passionel*. In September 1917 came the sensational case of Lieutenant Douglas Malcolm, who had dared to do what others would have liked to do: he had returned from France and settled accounts with the scoundrel, and an alien scoundrel at that, who had been leading his wife astray. To mark their approval of his conduct, an Old Bailey jury, amid wild excitement, acquitted him of murder. The victim was Anton Baumberg, variously described as Russian and Polish, with the self-awarded title of Count de Borch, which had a certain aptness. Over-dressed and apparently over-affluent, he was often seen at fashionable tea tables. His sources of wealth and his activities in general were mysterious enough to interest Scotland Yard. According to Sir John Simon, defending Malcolm, the dead man was 'one of those pieces of human refuse that are carried along on the tide of great cities, lunching at the best restaurants, sleeping in cheap lodging-houses, and carrying on an existence with the aid of such women as had his acquaintance'. One of these women, said Simon, was 'an infamous German woman who has since been dealt with in France as a spy'.

Malcolm, an officer of position and means, adopted an old-fashioned attitude towards the man he described as 'the cur who was luring my wife to destruction'. He began by horse-whipping him so severely that he was unable to go out for some days, and at the same time he challenged him to a duel, with pistols or swords, in France if need be. He talked to a friend about buying him off with £5,000, but was persuaded not to try. When Baumberg still pursued his wife, Malcolm obtained his address from Scotland Yard and went with a riding crop to Porchester Place, gaining entry by pretending to be a Scotland Yard inspector. In the resulting fracas Baumberg was shot dead with a pistol which, according to Malcolm, the impostor kept in a drawer. There was no evidence that Malcolm fired in self-defence.

Sir John Simon was careful not to invoke the unwritten law. His client chose not to give evidence, a fact upon which Mr Justice McCardie commented. However, the jury clearly felt that a French verdict was expected of them and the public would not have had it otherwise. The important thing was that a rascally scented alien with 'short soft legs' (as police evidence showed) had got his deserts at the hand of a British officer and gentleman, a patriot who had joined up three days after the declaration of war. The *Daily Telegraph*, describing Malcolm as 'a man of fine honour and lofty spirit', and his wife as 'like a dumb creature fascinated by a beast of prey . . . faltering, paralysed in mind and will', thought the case had all the elements with which great artists were wont to excite the imagination: 'true love and deepening passion, hideous villainy, miserable weakness, the strength which shrinks from no danger and admits no defeat'. As for the verdict, the case 'was judged according to law'. The *Manchester Guardian* was obviously worried about the outcome. Simon's plea of self-defence had put 'a tremendous strain on the facts'; it thought 'a verdict of guilty followed by a pardon would not have caused surprise'. Malcolm was to be commended for the purity and sincerity of his passion for his wife, but he was 'Gallic rather than English in his temperament' with 'none of the phlegm that is supposed to be part of our character'.

Two months after Malcolm's trial a jury at Bristol Assizes acquitted a private soldier who shot an unfaithful wife. He had spent his leave with her and they were standing in Temple Meads Station waiting for the train when she fell dead from a shot fired by her husband's rifle. Witnesses said that after she collapsed the soldier just stood stolidly and did not attempt to go to her aid. In court the plea was that it was an accident and the husband did not know the weapon was loaded. A letter from him to his wife, sent from France, was read in court: 'You see, Bess, my love, you have brought sorrow on us all. Could you not see this when this dirty cur of a fellow was after you?' The courts were being treated to many similar readings from letters by soldiers who had been alerted by neighbourly intimations that 'your wife is not behaving as she should'.

It is not difficult to find instances of private soldiers, convicted of murdering their wives, being reprieved. Most wifely betrayals, of course, led to the divorce courts rather than the criminal courts. FRAIL PARTNERS: BIG LIST OF CASES IN THE DIVORCE COURT: WIVES IN THE MAJORITY AS RESPONDENTS was a typical set of *News of the World* headlines in 1918. A reporter explained: ' "Another non-access case" is the familiar phraseology of counsel in explaining its nature in the briefest possible words to the judge. It is the case of a child born during the period of a husband's absence that leaves no doubt that the responsibility for bringing the little one into the world has to be looked for elsewhere.' That often meant seeking another Serviceman, untraceable. However, the dominating interest of the *News of the World* in 1917–18 was bigamy, a wave of which – perhaps the last big wave – was sweeping Britain. Everywhere judges were vowing to stamp out this new national pastime. One Recorder at the Old Bailey said he would always treat Kitchener's men leniently, but others made no concessions to Servicemen. On one page of the *News of the World*, in January

1918, were three bigamy reports featuring New Zealand soldiers. The soldier's excuse was usually that he was bored and far from home and that women would 'give you nothing' unless there was a promise of a ring. To that extent bigamy was a recognition of female virtue. But not only soldiers were contracting unlawful unions: at the Old Bailey a bigamous baronet in holy orders was given eighteen months hard labour.

At least one biographer has described Lloyd George as living virtually the life of a bigamist during the war. His time was deftly divided between his wife and his secretary, Frances Stevenson (whom he later married). One of the quainter entries in the Stevenson *Diary* consists of a protest in February 1917 at an article in the *Strand* portraying the Premier as a model family man. It was rare for the press to be other than hypocritical about the private lives of public figures.

In August of 1917, the House of Commons decided that the Ladies' Gallery need no longer be covered by a grille. The purpose of this had been to preserve Members from the distraction of female scrutiny, or perhaps to protect women from the bold stares of legislators. Its removal was hailed by some as symbolic of the new openness between the sexes and also as a gesture to those who, a few months earlier, had been promised the vote at thirty. By now women were well into their revolution; not only were they behaving differently, but their whole appearance was altering. In token of emancipation they were bobbing their hair, a fashion borrowed from the Slade School 'cropheads', which did nothing to sanctify it; it was even adopted by the Duchesses of Marlborough and Sutherland. Skirts, as the newspapers were always pointing out, were becoming ever shorter; from floor length in 1914 they ascended to eight inches from the ground in 1918. At the same time working women, spending their money on 'finery' and cosmetics, were becoming less frumpish, though they had much to learn in the art of face-painting. However, there were critics aplenty of the new freedoms. That summer the Headmistresses' Conference at Hammersmith expressed concern at the way young girl flag-sellers were accosting officers. 'To get good custom [a girl] must exercise her powers of fascination and the more fascinating she makes herself the more money she earns,' ran the complaint.

Soldier husbands could be as old-fashioned as anybody. One young officer bought a copy of the *London Mail* and found his wife's photograph on the cover, captioned '*The Whitsun Girl*'. It had not been supplied by his wife. Encouraged by his colonel, he laid proceedings and convinced a court that the magazine was putting forward his wife as 'a girl whom any man could pick up on his Whitsun holidays'. His counsel pointed out that the issue contained a picture of a naked woman sitting on a champagne bottle. The officer was awarded £110 damages. There were risks also in aspersing the morals of girls in khaki. Two well-dressed young women in Portsmouth saw two girls in Queen Mary's Army Auxiliary Corps approaching and one said to the other, 'Oh, here comes the pride of the Army. I would not lower my dignity to wear that uniform. We are respectable.' One of them added that WAACs got £15 for each child. The two women were fined £5 and £3 for making statements prejudicial to recruiting and were told that only their delicate health had preserved them from prison.

Outwardly, the high spirits which had characterised the West End of 1915 had now largely subsided, partly because of air raids and transport economies, partly because of the pessimism which had followed Passchendaele. On the social front 'studio parties' or 'jollies' were now the safety-valve, noisy and harmless for the most part. Arnold Bennett's *Journal* shows that he was worried about the degeneracy of the theatre, with actresses throwing themselves brazenly into the portrayal of tarts (as they have always done). His observations seem odd in the light of the stir caused by his novel, *The Pretty Lady*, published that year. The pretty lady was 'the accidental daughter of a daughter of joy' who plied her trade in the promenade of a Leicester Square music-hall. It shocked some of his faithful readers, angered Roman Catholics and was attacked by critics who did not like to see authors throwing themselves brazenly into the portrayal of tarts.

That observer who deplored the lost innocence of flappers wrote of 'secret meeting places and obscure flats where cocaine is obtained and injected; where opium smoking is practised amid surroundings of Eastern magnificence; where men and women indulge in strange exotic pleasures as alien to our race as the secrecy that covers them'. The last part leaves us guessing, but perhaps the writer was guessing too. Traffic in cocaine had been widespread enough to attract restrictive legislation in July 1916. According to the Sunday papers, it was available in West End hotels in halfcrown packets and even soldiers were buying it. Opium could be obtained, like everything else, from the less fastidious chemists. It was smoked in hotel rooms and in theatrical flats, with young actresses passing the pipe of peace; but there were also fashionable sorties, as there always had been, to the dens of Poplar and Limehouse, where the surroundings laid no claims to Eastern magnificence. Many other drugs were being freely used, including veronal, chloral and those substances which helped men to deceive medical boards. 'The Strand at this time,' says Commandant Mary Allen, 'was at night a veritable Devil's playground. White slavers crowded there. Drugs were bought and sold with the freedom of confectionery. Scenes of indescribable disorder prevailed.' She never doubted that drugs taken to dull bereavement, or to lessen apprehensions of the next spell in the trenches, soon drove their addicts to vice and crime.

For a further hint of unspecified dark doings one must turn to the author Stephen McKenna, who dates the collapse of morals from the beginning of 1918. 'In degeneracy, as in crime,' he says, 'it is usually the inexpert who is detected, and anyone who lived in London during those feverish months had forced upon his notice a spectacle of debauchery which would have swelled the record of scandal if it had been made public but which is mercifully forgotten because it is incredible. . . . The restraints of modern civilisation were burst on the resurgence of primitive man. Honourable, kindly, fastidious, gentle and reserved spirits, dragged back across the ages, lied and cheated, fought and bullied in an orgy of intrigue and self-seeking, of intoxication and madness . . . the bravery of the savage emerged hand in hand with the savage's ferocity, his licence, his superstition and his credulity.' Happily 'the panic rush of mob-madness passed quickly'. All of which adds a new sting to the question: 'What did YOU do in the Great War, Daddy?'

For young women, the days of disintegrating morals coincided with fierce unsettling resentment at the loss of their menfolk. Some became the wild ones of the 1920s, the rootless 'surplus women'; others, if Professor Paul Fussell, of Rutgers

CHAPTER 19

MOST EXCELLENT ORDER

In the summer of 1917, the summer of Passchendaele, Britain introduced two new Orders of Chivalry. One, the Order of the Companions of Honour, was for the distinguished few (only seventeen names appeared in the first list). The other, which caused great talk, was the Order of the British Empire and there was apparently no limit to the numbers who could be admitted to it. By tradition, Orders require a superlative to describe them. Those already existing included Most Noble, Most Noble and Ancient, Most Illustrious, Most Honourable, Most Exalted, Most Distinguished and Most Eminent. The new Order was styled Most Excellent. There were cynics who said it would have been better described as Most Unnecessary.

It was to be 'Democracy's Own Order', with prizes in the form of post-nominal letters distributed on a generous scale to those who could never aspire to the Garter or the Bath. It was to be the first Order of Knighthood to admit women on equal terms with men and it introduced a new rank for women equivalent to that of knight: the rank of dame.

As the King saw it, the Order ('For God and Empire') would reward those who had rendered important services, mainly non-combatant, to the embattled Empire, either as civilians or in the Services. Also eligible were foreigners who had helped Britain in her adversity. The King was not, at first, in favour of degrees of knighthood in the new order, but he yielded for the sake of uniformity with the accepted five-class system. There was also a medal, intended mainly for munitions workers. The classes ran as follows: Knights and Dames Grand Cross (GBE); Knights and Dames Commander (KBE); Commanders (CBE); Officers (OBE); Members (MBE); and Medallists (BEM). Even in 'Democracy's Own Order' the social gradations were carefully observed; whether one received a 'C', an 'O' or an 'M' depended very much on the nature of one's occupation, civil service grade or military rank.

To create a new Order, at a time when the nation was bitterly critical about climbers buying their way into the existing Orders, impressed many by its foolhardiness. However, to have expanded or democratised existing Orders like the Bath or the St Michael and St George would have caused deep distress in the upper ranks of society. As it was, many who had aspired to old-established honours were incensed when they found they were being fobbed off with the new unexclusive Order. What colonel would wish to retire to Cheltenham with a CBE instead of a CB? Little or no criticism was directed at the admission of women. But was 'Dame' the best name that could be devised for a female knight? Was there not a touch of the pantomime about it? Were dames to be tapped on the shoulder by the Sovereign's sword? It turned out that they would be required merely to curtsey and kiss hands.

The first list of awards, published in August 1917, and containing 320 names, aroused mingled pleasure, irreverence and incredulity. 'Some of the new KBEs are laughing-stocks', said the *New Statesman*. 'One had the impression that the general level of merit rose the lower one went in the grades.' Most of the dames turned out to have titles already, which did not mean that some of them were undeserving of another, to mark their labours for refugees, hospitals and the Red Cross. The Bank of England seemed more than adequately represented, with a GBE for the Governor, a KBE for the Deputy Director and a CBE for the Deputy Chief Cashier. Other KBEs went to the impressively styled Chairman of the Pyrites Sub-Committee of the Explosives Supply Department and the Chairman of the Clyde and Tyne Dilution Commission. Trade union leaders were honoured at 'C' and 'O' level; there was even a CBE for Havelock Wilson, whose seamen had prevented Ramsay MacDonald from sailing to Russia. The *Herald* said that most of the thirty-two men honoured had been 'notoriously henchmen of the Government'; here was 'an order of chivalry from which it is the highest honour for a Labour man to be excluded'.

With the second list, in January 1918, the deluge began: the names in small print filled three-and-a-half pages in *The Times* and were an extraordinary reflection of the intensity and variety of the nation's war effort. There were awards for censors, inspectors of prisoner-of-war parcels, chairmen of forage committees, adjudicators of prize courts, assessors of cotton claims, organisers of 'smoke funds', promoters of egg shows for hospitals, activists of the One-Man Business Preservation Scheme, members of the America and Argentine Remount Commission, tractor representatives, lady superintendents of YMCA huts and women who lent their homes for hospitals. Citations testified that so-and-so 'originated the use of goat-skins in the British Army', 'supplied a whole battalion with iodine capsules', 'conserved the economy of the Public Purse', 'worked late on HMSO accounts throughout the war', 'increased the cultivable area of the county by 32,000 acres', 'devised new methods for the preparation of bacteriological sugars required by Navy and Army' and 'took a hospital to France in 1914'. Secretaries, both public and private, male and female, paid and unpaid, were rewarded, among them the shorthand typist of the British Embassy in Norway and the honorary secretary of the Kobe Ladies Patriotic League.

The citations for Medallists told of acts of resolution or presence of mind in war factories or of steadfastness in repairing warships in battle; standing firm in a rain of molten metal, turning on drenchers in fires, descending into gas mains and boilers, running through dense gas to close valves, extracting comrades from machinery, fishing up valuable tools dropped in cooling ponds. The degree of hardihood varied. Winifred Burdett-Coutts was rewarded 'for courage in that, after losing a finger and badly lacerating her hand with a circular saw she went away quietly to have it treated, in order not to unnerve her fellow workers'. Herbert Janes 'returned to work immediately after his hand had been dressed on account of his losing three fingers in a shearing machine'. Some received the medal simply for keeping going with a broken thumb.

Among workers who earned the Medal without losing their extremities were seventy-four-year-old Thomas Harper who, having retired and gone to Australia, returned at his own expense and put in an average of fifty-four hours a week, sometimes fainting but refusing to go home, 'stating that he could not rest whilst he thought his country wanted shells'. William Gilchrist persisted in dangerous work though in great pain from an incurable disease; and Thomas Jones showed courage and high example 'in doing hard work for very long hours in spite of his age (79)'. Lizzie Robinson's devotion to duty consisted of not losing any time in a whole year's service in a projectile factory, 'although the factory had been working at very high pressure'. Could Lizzie have been unique in this respect? Another girl was rewarded 'for intelligence and courage' in securing the arrest of a suspicious character in a filling factory. There is a touch of a *Girl's Own Paper* adventure about the citation for Ella Trout: 'While fishing accompanied only by a boy of ten, she saw that a steamer had been torpedoed and was sinking. Though fully realising the danger she ran from enemy submarines she pulled rapidly to the wreck and succeeded in rescuing a drowning sailor.'

The Communist William Gallacher regarded the award of medals as bribes to the workers to abandon the class war. He says that on the Clyde the workforce were invited to select their own 'heroes', and that in a torpedo factory near Greenock the employees unanimously chose the lavatory attendant. 'What a roar of laughter shook the Clyde!' he writes. Perhaps even the lavatory attendant, convinced of his worthlessness, joined in.

Inevitably, the public made invidious comparisons. A knighthood went to a director of the Trench Warfare Research Department at the Ministry of Munitions, a CBE to a member of the Trench Warfare Advisory Committee and an MBE to an official in Trench Warfare Finance, at the same Ministry. It must have been news to the men at the Front that trenches had to be researched and have their accounts made up; certainly no knighthood went to anybody for fighting in a trench. However, knighthoods were conferred on those who supplied men for the trenches, with citations like 'raised several batteries of artillery' or 'raised the Salford Brigade of five battalions'. The highest award in the Order went to a recruiter of the church militant, the Very Rev. Thomas Strong, Vice-Chancellor at Oxford for three years and later Bishop of Ripon. He was a stalwart of the Officers' Training Corps at the University and reputed a great judge of fighting men. 'Thousands of officers of the best class have come from Oxford,' said the citation, 'largely owing to the great assistance rendered by Dr Strong.' No doubt many looked for the name of Bottomley among the great recruiters, but it was not there.

No one was surprised to see knighthoods bestowed on the armaments manufacturers, some of whom had lent a hand at the Ministry of Munitions. The most notorious 'armaments king', 'the mystery man of Europe', Sir Basil Zaharoff, was admitted to the highest class of the new Order, as also to the highest class of the Bath; on paper, his services consisted of founding three professorships in aviation (Paris, Petrograd and London) and two in French Literature (Oxford and Paris). He is said to have been an intelligence agent at the highest level. Among the more controversial of the knighthoods were those handed out to war correspondents, whose accounts of battles never failed to amaze and amuse those who had taken part in them. This was a mistake not repeated after World War Two.

Criticism ran from top to bottom of the lists. While men won medals for working on at the bench with broken thumbs, soldiers with legs and arms blown off were forced to recognise that valour is its own reward. To stay at one's post in the Ypres Salient was the least that could be expected of a man; to stay at a switchboard during a Zeppelin raid on London merited a decoration. For the military it was a sore point that their service in remote lands, and even their acts of bravery were rewarded in the same list with swill contractors and canteen-keepers. In 1918, to meet this complaint, separate military divisions were established for all classes, but there were still objections that an Order in which bravery played a minor part should take official precedence over the orders of gallantry.

The real criticism was that the awards in the middle ranges were excessive in numbers. 'There is no doubt that many of the recipients of appointments in the Order of the British Empire had not done anything sufficiently important to deserve an Order of any kind,' says Brigadier Sir Ivan de la Bere, secretary of the Central Chancery of Knighthood, in *The Queen's Orders of Chivalry*. For some reason the OBE attracted more derision than the other classes. It was rendered as 'Order of the Bad Egg', 'Other Beggars' Efforts' and 'Order of Bloody Everybody'. A poem circulating at the end of the war went thus:

> I knew a man of industry
> Who made big bombs for the RFC,
> Who pocketed lots of LSD,
> And he (thank God) is an OBE.

> I knew a woman of pedigree
> Who asked some soldiers out to tea,
> And said, 'Dear me' and 'Yes, I see',
> And she (thank God) is an OBE.

> I knew a fellow of twenty-three
> Who got a job with a fat MP,
> Not caring much for the Infantry,
> And he (thank God) is an OBE.

> I had a friend, a friend – and he
> Just held the Line for you and me,
> And kept the Germans from the sea,
> And died without the OBE,
> 　　　　　　Thank God!
> He died without the OBE.

There was sniping in Parliament about the Order. Colonel Josiah Wedgwood suggested that the grant of honours gave more dissatisfaction to people who did not get them than satisfaction to those who did. 'Is there any limit to the possible number of these honours?' asked P. A. Harris (ironical cries of 'No!'). 'Will the Government consider the fixing of 47,000 or some such number?' The National Union of Clerks demanded that the Order be wound up forthwith. In the *New Statesman* an appeal was made for the issue of supplementary lists of persons who had refused the honour. Even more interesting would have been a list of the many who put forward their own names for recognition. After a flood of awards there was sometimes a small list of persons who had asked for their names to be removed; perhaps because, like John Galsworthy's request to be excused being made a knight bachelor in 1918, the refusal had been sent in too late.

Among those who spurned the GBE was Neville Chamberlain, who had served as director of an ill-starred scheme to attract volunteers to industry. 'I have never ceased to congratulate myself that I did not figure among that rabble,' he said. Kipling took care not to become one of the new knights but only narrowly escaped being made a Companion of Honour. Arnold Bennett, who ended up the war giving orders to generals from the Ministry of Information, declined a knighthood for war work, while hinting that he might some day accept an award in recognition of his services to literature. When the offer was renewed, he said, 'Give it to Harry Lauder.' Lauder accepted a 'K', but George Robey, who had helped to raise £500,000 and had put on officer's uniform after the theatre to ferry servicemen from railway stations, felt that a 'C' was enough (his 'K' came in 1954). Clara Butt claimed to have been made a dame against her will; according to her biographer, the King told her he had received so many letters asking for her to be honoured that he could hold out no longer, or people would think it was his fault. Dora Black, later Bertrand Russell's wife, went with her father on a mission to Washington, where she met Northcliffe. 'No doubt,' she has written, 'I owe to him the not very welcome MBE with which I was decorated for my services in crossing the Atlantic at a time of danger.' Northcliffe recommended honours in profusion for his entourage and his own family fared uncommonly well in the general distribution; which did not stop him deploring the scramble for honours by others.

A remarkable onslaught on the new Order came in a letter to *The Times* in August 1918 from twenty-five much-decorated citizens, mostly peers, among them Lord Salisbury and Lord Balfour of Burleigh. A recent *London Gazette*, they said, had sixty quarto pages filled with names of recipients. While there was no suggestion of corruption, the wholesale scale of distribution made effective control impossible by the Minister responsible. 'Honours,' they said, 'may come to be regarded as dishonours, leaving no way out except their entire abolition.' An

untitled Member of Parliament retorted that their lordships'
indignation would have impressed him more had not every one
of them inherited a title or accepted one cheerfully in his own
person.

That letter has to be taken in the context of the scathing
attacks on the Honours system in general which were being
mounted in press and Parliament in the middle years of the war.
Early in 1917 the *Morning Post* expressed the view that 'if Judas
had lived in the present epoch he would have been made a
baronet or a Privy Councillor, or even a peer of the realm.' In
other words, he would have paid his thirty pieces of silver into a
secret party fund to obtain his title (about £25,000 for a
baronetcy, £15,000 for a knighthood). *The Times* wanted to see
the auditors called in to the party war chests and the real reason
for every award clearly stated; it considered the ranks of
political climbers, in wartime, a public outrage. However, in a
debate in the Lords in August, 1917, Lord Curzon tried to
invoke sympathy for the British plutocrat. The soldier was
rewarded for his valour, the artist for this talents, the industrialist for his enterprise. There were men whose only asset was their
wealth, who lacked political ambition. Were they not to contribute to political funds? 'Is no preferment ever to come their
way? Are the doors of the Temple of Honour to be perpetually
banged and barred in their faces?' Curzon conceded that the
sale of honours was despicable, but insisted: 'It is not a dishon-
our to subscribe to party funds or to receive an honour in the gift
of which a contribution to party funds may have played a part.'
What critics objected to was the arrangement by which a candi-
date for an honour was invited to an interview with a party whip,
who intimated that a contribution to the cost of fighting a given
number of seats, at so much a seat, would be very welcome. It
was not quite a conditional sale, but there was a risk that the
honour would be overlooked if no cheque arrived.

The public was ready to jeer at the procession of profiteers
taking their titles, but it choked at the spectacle of profiteers
who had been convicted of flouting wartime laws following each
other into the Temple of Honour. The immediate post-war
years offered some alarming examples. In 1921 a baronetcy
went to a Gosforth shipbuilder who had been fined £600 in 1918
for food hoarding. In the following year another baronetcy went

to a shipowner who had been found guilty in 1915 of trading with the enemy. The King protested angrily at not being informed of the background to such awards. However, the honours traffic continued until it received a sharp check with the trial and conviction of Maundy Gregory, the honours tout, in 1933.

CHAPTER 20

'EAT SLOWLY'

The Four Horsemen of the Apocalypse were War, Strife, Pestilence and Famine. Pestilence, in the form of Spanish influenza, reached Britain at the eleventh hour, but Famine sheered away after giving the nation a bad fright.

Lord Lee, who was Director of Food Production, says that at the worst period, in the spring of 1918, the country had only two weeks' supply of food left. 'This was the deadliest secret of the war at that stage, and to the very few of us who were in the know it was as ceaseless and nerve-racking an anxiety as the powers of hell could devise.'

In the first days of war, as we have seen, there was some panic buying of food. A shame-faced normality soon returned, but the threat of privation as a result of U-boat sinkings was always in the background. Schoolchildren learned to recite Kipling's *Big Steamers*, with its ringing catalogue of imperilled food imports.

There were few attempts, as in World War Two, to interest the public in strange foods like macon (mutton bacon), snoek and whale. Manufacturers were put under pressure to produce a cheap, popular margarine, but had some difficulty in making it palatable; however, by 1918, housewives were clamouring in the streets for the stuff.

Asquith's Government held out against compulsory rationing, as against compulsory enlistment. It would be bad for morale, said Lord Runciman in October 1916, if the British were to regard themselves as a blockaded people, scrambling for bread tickets and meat coupons. In the following month, however, came a dribble of sumptuary laws. Bread was to be standard; no more white flour was to be milled; no more whole milk was to be fed to pigs. It was probable, admitted Runciman, that further measures of State control would cause discomfort and discontent in some quarters. The first Food Controller, Lord Devonport, a rich grocer, was appointed. 'We don't exactly control food,' *Punch* made him say, 'we give hints to housewives and we issue grave warnings.'

In mid-December diners in restaurants and clubs were limited to three courses at meals served between six pm and nine-thirty pm and two courses at other times. There was nothing to stop anyone eating a meal in one establishment and a second meal in another, or even eating two meals on different floors of the same restaurant, though it required a certain hardihood to do so. Soon the screws were tightened on restaurateurs: they were ordered to observe a meatless day a week, to serve no potatoes on five days a week and to limit bread with meals. A meatless day at Romano's in the Strand went thus: *hors d'oeuvres; veloute de crevettes Normandes; omelette aux champignons, œuf sur plat Portugais; bouillabaisse Marseillaise; nouilles Napolitaines; saumon braisé au vermouth avec pommes nouvelles*; bread and butter pudding; jam roly-poly.

On February 1, 1917, unrestricted U-boat warfare began. 'We will frighten the British flag off the face of the waters and starve the British people until they, who have refused peace, will kneel and plead for it,' ran the Kaiser's threat. This the Germans might well have done if the Admiralty had not adopted the convoy system, which it did with reluctance under the bludgeonings of fate and Lloyd George, who was perhaps better at browbeating the admirals than the generals. In April 1917 the total losses of Allied and neutral ships reached 866,610 tons, well over the Kaiser's target of 600,000 tons a month. In May came a call from the King to his people to eat less bread, couched as a Royal Proclamation:

'We, being persuaded that the abstention from all unnecessary consumption of grain will furnish the surest and most effectual means of defeating the devices of our enemies . . .

[earnestly exhort] all those of Our loving subjects, the men and women of Our realm who have the means of procuring articles of food other than wheaten corn, as they tender their immediate interest and feel for the want of others, especially to practise the greatest economy and frugality in the use of every species of grain: And We do for this purpose more particularly exhort and charge all heads of household to reduce the consumption of bread in their respective families by at least one-fourth of the quantity consumed in ordinary times, to abstain from the use of flour in pastry and moreover carefully to restrict or wherever possible to abandon the use thereof in all other articles than bread. . . .'

The Proclamation went on to urge those who kept horses not to feed them with oats or grain without a licence; such luxuries were to be given 'only where it is necessary to do so with a view to maintaining the breed of horses in the national interest'. Finally came this injunction:

'And we do hereby further charge and enjoin all ministers of religion in their respective churches and chapels . . . to read or cause to be read this Our Proclamation on the Lord's Day for four successive weeks after the issue thereof. Given at Our Court at Buckingham Palace this second day of May in the year of Our Lord one thousand nine hundred and seventeen in the seventh year of Our reign. God Save The King.'

The wording followed very closely the language of a similar Proclamation made by George III in 1800, calling for a reduction of one-third in householders' consumption of bread. This had been reproduced in *The Times* a month earlier and had clearly struck a responsive chord at Buckingham Palace. The King did not content himself with issuing the Proclamation; he urged his loyal subjects to write their names on sheets headed:

'We, the undersigned, members of this household, hereby pledge ourselves on our honour to respond to His Majesty's appeal.'

Soon, outside hotels and in the windows of private houses, began to appear such pledges as, 'IN HONOUR BOUND we adopt the scale of Voluntary Rations.' The scales, which were 'on no account to be exceeded', were always changing and they sometimes involved calculating two-sevenths or five-sevenths of a pound of different foods, which must have made scrupulous obedience difficult.

The King's appeal to the better off to eat items other than wheaten corn was more or less in keeping with the argument propounded in the Northcliffe press that the rich should concentrate on consuming luxury foods which the poor could not afford or which they found unpalatable. In this unselfish and patriotic spirit the rich had been buying, among other things, tins of imported larks.

In the week of the Proclamation Colonel Repington, that hardy diner-out, noted 'a curious example of the way the poor live'. Sitting on one of his tribunals he encountered a woman with five children who had a modest greengrocery business, supplementing her separation allowance. She admitted taking in six loaves a day or eighty-four pounds of bread a week, when her proper allowance, under the voluntary rules, would have been twenty-four pounds. A member of the tribunal told him that 'people of her class ate bread at all meals as it was the easiest kind of food to eat and needed no preparation'.

The more affluent did not find it easy to stop eating bread with meals. Arnold Bennett took a tip from H. G. Wells and left the bread on the sideboard, so that those who wanted some had to get up and fetch it. Nor did the middle classes take kindly to the disappearance of muffins, tea cakes and light pastries, or of sugar bowls in restaurants. Going out for afternoon tea was discouraged by an order which said that no customer was to be charged more than sixpence a meal between 3 pm and 6 pm, unless it contained meat, fish or eggs; and that no customer should receive more than two ounces of bread, cake or biscuit.

The Royal Proclamation was rendered down into easy language for the masses. perhaps by the same craftsmen who simplified the recruiting appeals. Guzzlers were urged: 'EAT SLOWLY – YOU WILL NEED LESS FOOD.' Another advertisement ran:

> I am a slice of bread.
> I measure three inches by two-and-a-half and my thickness is half an inch.
> My weight is exactly an ounce.

I am wasted once a day by 48,000,000 people in Britain.
I am 'the bit left over'; the slice eaten absentmindedly when really I wasn't needed.
I am the waste crust.

If such slices were collected for a week, the leaflet proceeded, it would make the equivalent of nine shiploads of good bread – 'as much as twenty German submarines could sink – even if they had good luck.'

When you throw me away or waste me you are adding twenty submarines to the German Navy.
Save me and I will save you!

The campaign against wasting bread produced reports of prosecutions almost as bizarre as those of husbands buying drinks for their wives. At Thames Police Court in September 1917 an East End baker was gaoled for twenty-one days for selling fresh bread – in other words, bread which had not been made for at least twelve hours. Fines were imposed on citizens who threw rice at weddings, gave crusts to seagulls or fed stray dogs (which were to be handed over to the police). Launderers could be prosecuted for using too much starch.

Munition workers who now had ample funds to indulge their craving for sweets were disappointed to find that sweet manufacturers were ordered progressively to cut back production to half and then a quarter of the amount produced in 1915. The *Glasgow Herald* in May 1917 published a letter from a sweet manufacturer who wrote to the Ministry of Food for permission to use one hundredweight of malt in making toffee. The reply ran:

'With reference to your letter of the 13th April I am to say that you cannot be allowed to use your stock of one hundredweight of malt for the manufacture of toffee. You are recommended to sell it to a local brewer, if possible.'

The *Spectator*, commenting on this, wondered if perhaps the obedient servant who signed the letter had his tongue in his cheek. Certainly the temperance bodies were unamused by the Food Ministry's policy in this field. An advertisement by the Strength of Britain Movement in *The Times* in January 1918 asked:

'Why should you do without sugar?

'There is quite enough to go round. It is the Brewer more than the German submarine that is taking it from you. You could get enough sugar for your purpose if he did not waste it. Write to the Food Controller . . . and tell him it is a lie that the Working Man will not give up his Beer so that his Children may have food. Sugar gives the necessary heat in cold winter time. Why let your children be robbed of it?'

Belatedly, in 1917 came the order to plough up Britain, to turn the green fields brown; to cultivate not just waste lands and hill slopes but paddocks, ancestral parklands and ornamental gardens, not excluding Kew Gardens. Lloyd George had stormy meetings with Britain's 'landowner Junkers', men who were fiercely patriotic in their fashion but saw the order as the biggest challenge since the break-up of the feudal estates. Was it for this that their fathers had enclosed the family lands? The Prime Minister's chief executive was the thrusting Arthur Lee (later Lord Lee of Fareham, donor of Chequers to the nation). As Director-General of Food Production he rattled the Junkers exceedingly; his policy, they complained, was 'prison or plough'. There were not enough motor ploughs to carry through a national transformation, but Lee learned from the *Scientific American* that Henry Ford was experimenting with a new model. Here, perhaps, was salvation; however, Ford was a pacifist and the 'peace ship' he sent to Europe in 1915 had been bitterly derided (the *Sunday Pictorial* refused Ford advertisements). Why should he help? Without too much difficulty, Lee was able to convince Ford that non-belligerents were in danger of starving and won from him a promise to supply 10,000 tractors in six months. Ford built a new factory for the purpose, first refining the design of his experimental model. Lee made mistakes; some tracts were ploughed which could never grow crops. But obstructionists discovered that the Government was prepared, not only to punish them, but to take away their land for others to till.

Meanwhile Suburban Man was setting an example to his betters. Before 1916 allotments were virtually unknown. By the end of that year the Board of Agriculture had gained wide powers to acquire land and was using them. Armies of allotment

diggers flocked at weekends to parks, golf courses, deserted
gardens, tennis courts, rubbish tips, building land, railway
embankments and all those sites held vacant in the hope that
their value would increase in an environment improved by
others. By mid-1917 there were half a million plots under
cultivation. Some enthusiasts wanted to know whether it was the
right thing to dig on Sundays, to which the reluctant episcopal
answer was usually, 'Yes, if you go to church as well.' In some
areas services were held on allotments, the diggers gathering
together, heads bared, as if attending conventicles. For stiff-
collared urban man it was a regenerative experience, a belated
and even anxious awakening to the pageant of the seasons; and
if Londoners wanted to know what a good allotment looked like
they had only to peer through the wire at the internees' plots
outside Alexandra Palace. Politicians and public men judged
it advisable to join the movement, if only by urging their
sometimes unwilling servants to dig. Lloyd George let it
be known that he grew potatoes at Walton Heath. Many
citizens began keeping poultry and learned how to store
eggs in isinglass. At Guildford there was a patriotic proposal
to start a rabbit warren, something more easily advocated than
achieved.

Eating out continued to provoke controversy. A Director of
National Kitchens appeared on the scene and launched four
cheap eating-houses in London, which were popular enough to
be copied in other cities. Reporters sampled the sixpenny meal
in Poplar and thought the vegetable soup, fish pie and baked rice
were good value. One reporter's meal which caused embarrassment in Whitehall was consumed by Francis Meynell in the
West End in November 1917 and described by him in the
Herald under the headline: HOW THEY STARVE AT THE RITZ. It
consisted of hors d'oeuvres, 'a rich soup', sole and lobster,
chicken (half a bird per person), three rashers of bacon and
three tomatoes, fruit salad and coffee. 'We demanded whipped
cream to add to our soup – a bowl was produced; a cream sauce
was served with the fish; cream flowed plentifully over the
macédoine des fruits; and a jug of cream came with our coffee.'
Meynell forced himself to eat four rolls 'and there would have
been no difficulty in obtaining more'. The bill for two, inclusive
of a bottle of the 'cheaper champagne' at 14s and a tip, came to

£3. 'As we were bowed out of the door,' the article concluded, 'we saw under the arches at the front of the hotel three old women huddled up in their rags for the night.' With this blow-out, Meynell, who wrote anonymously as a '*Herald* representative', could be said to have made up for his hunger strike as a conscientious objector. That same month the Lord Mayor of London's banquet was on a more modest scale than usual, but ran to clear soup, fillets of sole, casserole of partridge, roast beef and sweets, with punch, champagne and port. The Ministry of Food's recommendation for Christmas Day dinner, 1917, was: rice soup; filleted haddock; roast fowl and plum pudding with caramel custard.

General rationing came only after a succession of ugly demonstrations and industrial threats, mostly in the winter of 1917–18. In many areas shoppers found butchers closed for lack of supplies; one winter morning 4,000 queued outside Smithfield meat market, from two am onwards, in snow. Elsewhere women queued for horseflesh, consumption of which caused no apparent harm to the Belgians. In Manchester a procession of several thousand munition workers (the *Annual Register* says 100,000) waited on the Lord Mayor to complain that they could not stand shortages much longer. At Chesterfield miners threatened to strike unless their meat ration was guaranteed and Nuneaton miners forced a food committee to order a shop to sell its newly arrived consignment of margarine. In Tottenham a crowd of women who had queued only to be informed, 'No margarine', besieged the Food Control Office, where they were told that women were worse off in Germany. In some areas police dispersed angry housewives. It was a cold winter for queueing – and queueing, save for paupers, was not yet an accepted part of the British way of life.

The Parliamentary Secretary to the Food Ministry at this time was J. R. Clynes, whose constituency sponsors, the Independent Labour Party, disapproved of his joining the Government, but the thought of battling with food profiteers seems to have overcome Clynes's scruples. One evening early in 1918, by his own account, he said to Lord Rhondda, the Food Controller, 'Will the country stand for wholesale rationing?' Rhondda, he says, replied: 'Without rationing we're done. It might well be, Clynes, that you and I at this moment are all that stand between this country and Revolution.' So rationing arrived, first in the form of meat cards in London and the Home Counties, to be followed in midsummer by a general issue of ration books for meat, bacon, sugar and fats. By then the war, though nobody guessed it, had only about three months to run.

Once the principle of fair shares for all had been belatedly acknowledged, unrest died. The less well-off were further cheered by the sight of wealthy citizens being hauled before the courts for food hoarding. One of the first was Marie Corelli. The seven persons under her roof at Stratford-on-Avon were entitled to 32 pounds of sugar for the period in question and she had obtained for them 183 pounds; and in the same period the butler had signed for 43 pounds of tea. The novelist exploded with anger at the suggestion that she was hoarding and prophesied not only the fall of Lloyd George but revolution within a week. The court imposed a fine of £50. A worse offence was that of a Unionist Member of Parliament with a house at Godstone and a town house in Eaton Square. He was fined £600 at Oxted for hoarding among other things 102 pounds of sugar and 435 pounds of flour. At Watford a £350 fine was imposed on a hoarder with 134 pounds of sugar, 352 of bacon, 56 of cocoa, 60 of biscuits, 425 of breakfast oats, 297 of rice, 98 of syrup, 28 tins of condensed milk and much else. There was a household of twelve persons. The defence plea was that the householder acquired most of the food in an invasion scare in 1915 and wanted to do what she could for the poor of the district. The biscuits were for her boys on vacation from Eton and represented a saving in bread. On the court's direction ninety per cent of the food was confiscated.

An offer of an amnesty for food hoarders was made by Lord Rhondda, but it produced no notable surrenders. Some culprits were thought to have buried tins of food in their gardens, some probably destroyed their stocks and some made anonymous gifts to hospitals. Worried citizens rang up food officers for advice. At Hammersmith a woman who had bought a case of tea in 1916 was allowed to keep six pounds; a Cheshunt woman with ten pounds of tea, and a family of eight, was told to give up eight pounds. A Camberwell man said he had in storage sixty partridges, eight pheasants and a few teal shot on his estate the previous year; he was told they must go to a hospital (where they no doubt met the usual welcome). In some areas the atmosphere was like that of a spy scare, with people denouncing their neighbours and causing much unnecessary investigation.

One by-product of the U-boat war (as in World War Two) was the strewing of Britain's coasts with tins of food from wrecked ships. If the metal was not too rusty, the contents were usually eatable; the problem, since the labels were washed off, was to know whether any given tin contained flesh, fish or fruit. If there were fizzing noises when the tin was opened, it was discarded. Another odd windfall for many homes consisted of parcels of butter bought at local markets by their men in France. This greasy traffic, running into hundreds of pounds of butter a week, posed problems for the Post Office's great hutted camp in Regent's Park and had to be stopped.

Rationing was not confined to food. Fuel shortages had the effect of hitting the rich in their mansions harder than the poor. The slogan 'Keep The Home Fires Burning Low' seemed to cancel out that other slogan 'Keep Warm – You Will Need Less Food'. In late 1917 the coal ration was two hundredweight weekly for three to five rooms, four hundredweight for six to seven rooms. Because so many coalmen had been called up, householders had to fetch their own supplies, which meant using perambulators, barrows and sacks – or hiring taxis. In industry big fuel savings were effected by the introduction, in the summer of 1916, of Daylight Saving, or Summer Time, after much curiously obtuse opposition in Parliament from those who held that changing the clock was not only blasphemous but impractical. Germany and Austria had already changed their clocks on May 1 of that year and the German press was jeering at Britain's inability to make up her mind. Sir Frederick Banbury spoke for many when he said that 'if the Germans have done it, it is a very good reason why we should not do it'. Lord Balfour of Burleigh asked his fellow peers to consider the plight of a woman giving birth to twins during a backward change in the clock, with the result that the second-born might be held to take precedence over the first-born for inheritance purposes.

Restrictions on the use of petrol were imposed early in the

war and were steadily tightened. In 1916 an outsize poster in Piccadilly ordered: DON'T USE A MOTOR-CAR FOR PLEASURE. The newspapers often sent out reporters to log the incidence of joy-riders at various points in London: 'a large man with an officer and a young girl', 'a two-seater with a second-lieutenant and flapper with a double pigtail', 'a large car with two men and three women luxuriously furred' and so on. By late summer of 1917 'joy-riding' became semi-respectable with the advent of gas-bag propulsion. Gerald Biss, the *Tatler*'s motoring correspondent, was most enthusiastic about the innovation. All the driver needed was a wooden superstructure on his car to carry a miniature Zeppelin and six feet of pipe for recharging at wayside gas points. Cars started more easily on gas than on petrol and the saving, said Biss, could be sixpence a mile. In an emergency the driver could nip over a cottage wall and ask for a refill, or even connect illegally with a convenient lamp-post. The gas-bag idea was popularised by an Eastbourne firm anxious to keep its *char-à-banc* fleet on the road. Once the New Forest had shown the way the Midlands and the North soon followed suit. An exhibition of more than forty types of vehicle adapted to the new system – including a troop-carrying *char-à-banc* – was organised by the *Commercial Motor* and a firm of balloon-makers began to turn out 1,200 containers a week. The British Commercial Gas Association issued maps showing the location of fuelling points. It was, of course, too good to last and in January 1918 the Board of Trade began to limit the use of gas for motor cars.

There were not so many cars that Whitehall could abuse them on any great scale. In his life of Lord Derby, Randolph Churchill prints some remarkable letters showing how the 'King of Lancashire' in the spring of 1917 began to harass Lord Curzon over the use of the ministerial car. He complained to Bonar Law that Curzon was behaving disgracefully, ferrying people to dances and allowing his wife to use the vehicle for shopping. In January 1918 Derby caught him out again over Christmas misuse of an official car at Montacute and elsewhere and obtained a diary of journeys by the Army driver. This document was passed to the abashed Earl for his comments.

A year earlier the *Observer* had apologised for saying that the Curzons had given many smart dances up to pre-war standards at No. 1 Carlton House Terrace; they maintained they had given no dances since the war began. There was nothing noticeably run-down about the town mansion, however. Visiting Curzon in April 1917 C. P. Scott was received and escorted through marble halls by numerous flunkeys 'apparently of military age'.

CHAPTER 21

THE UNSEEN HAND

One of the great delusions of the war was that there existed an Unseen (or Hidden, or Invisible) Hand, a pro-German influence which perennially strove to paralyse the nation's will and to set its most heroic efforts at naught. Here was a classic case of a metaphor getting out of control; it was as if a people promised 'pie in the sky' had come to believe that a real pie hovered in the firmament. As defeat seemed to loom, as French military morale broke and Russia made her separate peace, more and more were ready to believe that the Unseen Hand stood for a confederacy of evil men, taking their orders from Berlin, dedicated to the downfall of Britain by subversion of the military, the Cabinet, the Civil Service and the City; and working not only through the Establishment but through spiritualists, whores and homosexuals. Some even believed that the Unseen Hand was a single individual, inconceivably malign; they did not rule out Lucifer himself.

In *Disenchantment* C. E. Montague says that when Kitchener's New Armies were being raised there was an 'imp of frustration' about. One of his jokes was to slip into the War Office or Admiralty and tear up any letters he found from people offering cars, yachts or training grounds. The Unseen Hand would have scoffed at such simple sabotage; his speciality was to ensure that great offensives were entrusted to the least competent generals, that allies should default and that people should be cozened into clamouring for a shameful peace.

In London during the winter of 1916 crowded meetings were held to demand Government action against this intangible menace. One of them, called by the Women's Imperial Defence League in the Queen's Hall, was chaired by Kitchener's sister, Mrs Frances Parker, who was not convinced that her brother was dead. (One theory was that he was a prisoner in Germany, another that he was deep in an enchanted sleep in a Northern cave, awaiting his country's next call.) A resolution was passed demanding an immediate Royal Commission into the Unseen Hand, coupled with a demand for the dismissal of all British diplomats with German links. In Parliament Herbert Samuel asked Members to try to dispel this 'foolish myth', but the protest meetings continued. As Michael MacDonagh relates, these were not without hazards for reporters. A man from *The Times* writing old-fashioned shorthand was denounced by a woman who said she knew Pitman's when she saw it and this wasn't Pitman's – 'Mr Chairman, there is a German spy here!'

Belief in the Unseen Hand was not lessened by the release that winter of a patriotic film *It Is For England* (later reissued as *The Hidden Hand*), in which a young Army chaplain, reincarnated on the battlefield as St George, comes to England to harangue the nation on the Teutonic peril; he addresses not only Parliament (real MPs appeared in this scene), but City businessmen and industrial rebels. The film, backed by the Navy League, also featured the spy devices that made *The Man Who Stayed At Home* so popular.

One passionate believer in the Unseen Hand, who may have seen himself in the role of St George addressing the Commons, was Noel Pemberton Billing, a middle-aged 'knut' who wore a monocle and drove rakish cars. An aviator, inventor and at one time an actor, he joined the Royal Naval Air Service but resigned his commission in 1916 to stand for Parliament. His address to the Mile End electors was written, for £100, by Horatio Bottomley and rewritten, for nothing, by Hannen Swaffer, in spite, or because, of which he failed to win the seat. However, he was returned the same year as Independent Member for East Hertfordshire, pledged to clean up public life and speed the prosecution of the war, notably in the air. On flying and technical matters he was well-informed, but he was ready to believe that wireless spies were using a note 'so high that it is impossible for any official wireless machine to tune up to it'. Much of his excessive energy was fed into a scandalous journal he ran at his own expense, the *Imperialist*, later called the *Vigilante*, which was to become famous overnight.

Northcliffe was never one to discourage his editors from referring to the Unseen Hand (he is supposed to have scanned the Personal Column of *The Times* for spy messages). Outside his camp were a clutch of editor-publicists who believed, or found it convenient to believe, in the phantom influence. They were Bottomley, editor of *John Bull*, which blamed the Silvertown explosion and the 'murder' of Kitchener on the Unseen Hand; Leo Maxse, editor of the *National Review*, which fulminated against German financiers and 'the German Metal Octopus'; Dr Ellis Powell, editor of the *Financial News*, who was an influential figure in Fleet Street, a bachelor of law and a doctor of science, but whose Achilles heel was an interest in the psychic; and the septuagenarian Arnold White, a credulous popular journalist and Jew-thumper who had several times failed to get into Parliament. All made it a practice to take in each other's washing and commend each other's courage.

In 1917 White published a farrago called *The Hidden Hand*, in which he listed, as examples of the Hand at work, the Curragh Mutiny of 1914, the loss of Cradock's squadron at Coronel, the Gallipoli failure and the unrest in Ireland. (There were arms hidden in seventy-six localities in Ireland, including convents and Catholic laundries 'which are sacrosanct by law'.) With some satisfaction White noted that the military had commandeered the National Liberal Club, 'the spiritual home of every pro-German crank in the country'. The book did not mention the author's other obsession: the supposed campaign by the Germans to destroy Britain's manhood by turning her into a nation of homosexuals.

White was uncertain whether the Unseen Hand was 'an individual of supreme ability, working through astute agents, to many of whom his identity was unknown', which was Dr Ellis Powell's theory, or a network adroitly directed by agents of the German Government. The Powell theory is set out in the *National Review* for February 1917. Recommending to his readers this article by a 'courageous and patriotic contributor', Leo Maxse ends with the piquant question: 'Is the Unseen Hand a Right Hon?' (The right hon most frequently attacked in the *National Review* was Lord Haldane.)

Dr Powell asked, in effect: how could there *not* be an Unseen Hand? 'The hypothesis of a self-constructed clock, or of Paradise Lost as the chance result of printers' "pie", would not be more repulsive to the intellect than the accidental functioning of such an apt and closely coordinated system of philo-German perfidy as Britain has been compelled indignantly to witness for the last two-and-a-half years.' Why, then, was the Hand not more clearly recognisable? Dr Powell had to confess that it was 'all-pervasive, but intangible', while possessing 'the capacity to strike hard at those who sought to unveil its identity, or to paralyse its treacherous machinations . . .' In short, the Hidden Hand created politico-socio-economic chaos with 'a consummate skill hitherto attributed to only a single Practitioner, and he with ages of experience in deluding mankind into damnation'. Or, on a slightly lower level, he was 'an operator beside whom Richelieu and Metternich were but as babes'.

After recapitulating the Unseen Hand's activities in the City, Dr Powell mentioned the recent 'farcical' court proceedings against Trebitsch-Lincoln, the one-time curate of Appledore, Liberal Member for Darlington and self-proclaimed German spy gaoled at the Old Bailey for dishonesty. His 'fidelity to the Unseen Hand (when he could have betrayed its identity) had doubtless made him a rich man for life'. One 'arch-patriot' who was hard on the scent of the Hidden Hand had been hustled out of the country: namely, 'Billy' Hughes, the uncouth demagogic Prime Minister of Australia, whose outspokenness had set Ministers' nerves on edge.

'The Unseen Hand is undoubtedly an individual person,' concluded Dr Powell. 'If the whole of the colossal secrets of German intrigue had been committed to a body of agents, there would long ago have been a leakage.' Though versed in the law, the Hand was not a lawyer (which seemed to let out Haldane) but just conceivably was a woman. Powell put the income of the Lucifer figure at £10,000 a week in English notes supplied by the naturalised German colony.

How, then, was the Unseen Hand to be countered? Dr Powell could only urge a strong judicial tribunal on the lines of the Parnell Commission, sitting in camera, with no politicians or ex-politicians on it, but perhaps some lords justices of appeal. One thing was sure: the revelations of the Parnell Commission would 'appear as trumpery trifles by the side of the catalogue of devilry unveiled by an Unseen Hand Commission to a flabber-gasted world'.

Dr Powell's article appeared only a month before the out-break of the Russian Revolution, a triumph for the Unseen Hand if ever there was one. In that same March a public eager to be flabbergasted by conspiracies of evil was able to read reports of a trial at the Old Bailey of four persons accused of conspiring to murder Lloyd George and Arthur Henderson with poisoned darts. In this case it was evident that the Unseen Hand – if indeed he was involved – had been bested by the half-seen hand of the Secret Service.

The accused were described by the Attorney-General as 'a very desperate and dangerous body of people – people who were bitterly hostile to this country, shelterers of fugitives from the Army, and who did their best to injure Great Britain in the crisis in which she found herself'. These desperadoes were a Derby secondhand clothes dealer, Mrs Alice Wheeldon, aged fifty-one; her daughters Harriet Wheeldon and Winnie Mason, both teachers; and Alfred Mason, husband of Winnie, a chem-ist, who had 'made a special study of poisons'. Mrs Wheeldon had a son who was in custody as a conscientious objector and Mason was said to be trying to evade call-up.

It emerged that two secret agents had been employed by Major Melville Lee, of the Ministry of Munitions (a brother of the future Lord Lee of Fareham) to win the confidence of the Wheeldons. One of them, calling himself Comrade Best, posed as an Army deserter and a member of the 'Industrial Workers of the World'. He said that Mrs Wheeldon spoke to him of the need to kill Lloyd George. 'We suffragettes,' she was alleged to have said, 'had a plot before when we spent £300 in trying to poison him.' Their idea had been to enter his hotel and drive a poisoned nail through his boot, but he left for France before this could be arranged. There had also been a plot to kill Reginald McKenna by sending him a skull containing a poisoned needle; this had been abandoned for fear of killing an innocent party. Mrs Wheeldon's ultimate proposal was to fire a poisoned dart at the Prime Minister from an air rifle on Walton Heath golf course.

There was evidence of phials of strychnine and curare being sent by Mason from Southampton to Mrs Wheeldon in Derby. Her explanation was that poison was needed to kill guard dogs at the 'internment camps' where conscientious objectors were held, but it appeared that dogs were not used for this purpose. Under questioning she agreed that she hated Lloyd George, as the man behind the Military Service Acts. 'Would you like to do him a mischief?' she was asked, and replied, 'He's not worth it.' However, she agreed it would be a good idea if his public career were brought to an end. She also admitted saying that 'another who ought to be done in is George of Buckingham Palace'.

Mrs Wheeldon was unlucky in her counsel who, after complaining that a vital witness had not been produced, asked the judge to order a trial by ordeal:

'That the ladies should walk over hot ploughshares or something of that kind – is that it?'

'I do suggest that, my Lord, in order that they may prove their innocence.'

'If you have anything serious to suggest, I should like to hear it.'

Found guilty of conspiracy, soliciting to murder and intending to murder, Mrs Wheeldon was sentenced to ten years' penal servitude; Alfred and Winnie Mason, convicted of conspiracy only, were gaoled for seven and five years; and Harriet was acquitted. The foul language habitually and admittedly used by the three women (Harriet, although a Rationalist, taught Scripture) distressed the judge, who told the jury that he wondered whether elementary education was such a blessing after all. After the trial Mrs Pankhurst was allowed to deny that her suffragettes had ever planned to kill Lloyd George. In the climate of the times the convictions were inevitable. It is tempting to join those who now say these clownish dissenters were gaoled on flimsy evidence; yet traffic in poisons was admitted, only the purpose being disputed. A highly disaffected family dabbling in curare could hardly be left to its own devices.

By the end of 1917 the Unseen Hand was beginning to fight for headlines with the linked menace of Boloism, a word which obtained wide currency in the press but has failed to achieve an entry in the dictionaries. Paul Marie Bolo, latterly known as Bolo Pasha, was one of those overblown adventurers, like

Trebitsch-Lincoln, for whom the early years of this century were a fertile breeding ground. A rogue from boyhood, briefly a dentist, he survived charges of theft and bigamy to found banks in South America. In 1914 the Khedive made him his financial agent in Paris, where he cultivated Joseph Caillaux. When the pro-German Khedive was thrown out of Egypt, Bolo tried to acquire French newspapers with a view to spreading German propaganda. Money provided for this purpose was traced through the Deutsche Bank. Accused of trafficking with the enemy, Bolo was shot in February 1918, wearing white gloves and with his moustache specially curled for the occasion.

Boloism, therefore, was the distribution or receipt of funds calculated to assist the act of treason. The word Bolo, with its affinity for 'Bolshie', then undergoing a vogue, was made for headlines. 'Who is the British Bolo?' asked the Northcliffe papers. It was suggested that Potsdam gold was finding its way to Britain's pacifists; how else could they subsidise their expanding propaganda? How much German money had entered Britain via the Deutsche Bank, still not yet wound up? How much German money was being fed to spiritualistic mediums to spread despair? The Labour press angrily denied that they took Potsdam gold, as later they were to deny receiving Moscow gold; they tried to suggest that the 'Jingo press' was also being corruptly subsidised, but could not suggest by whom (a special Bolo Number of the *Herald* lifted no lids). In Parliament Richard Lambert invited the Home Secretary to say that it was in the offices of Jingo newspapers in France that treasonable transactions found fertile soil, as also among company promoters and society ladies. Would he see what he could find in 'similar ruts' in Britain? To this Sir George Cave replied that police were making enquiries and to say any more would be assisting the enemy. The Chancellor of the Exchequer, Bonar Law, was asked whether the accounts of the Deutsche Bank had been examined for traces of Bolo funds sent to individuals in Britain. He replied that the police and military were in touch with the liquidator, the indefatigable Sir William Plender.

Efforts to keep the Bolo affair alive were made by Pemberton Billing, who became seized of the idea that Sir Cecil Spring-Rice, British Ambassador to Washington, had met an unnatural death in Canada. It was with the aid of evidence

provided by Spring-Rice that Bolo was prosecuted. A Govern-
spokesman assured Billing that the Ambassador had died of
heart failure and that there was no need of an inquest. Nobody
ever did find a British Bolo.

The best, or worst, was yet to come. In the early summer of
1918 the Unseen Hand was revealed as a Potsdam-based conspiracy to propagate in Britain 'those vices which all decent
men thought had perished in Sodom and Lesbos'. (This was in
addition to rendering the Army ineffective by spreading
venereal disease.) These allegations emerged from a private
prosecution brought at the Old Bailey against Pemberton Billing by the actress Maud Allan, who had been unpleasantly but
ambiguously attacked in Billing's journal for undertaking to
play the role of Salome in Oscar Wilde's play. Much has been
written about this grotesque trial. In *Salome's Last Veil* Michael
Kettle links the case with the politicians-versus-soldiers
intrigues which led to the dismissal of Major-General Sir Frederick Maurice. Pemberton Billing was less concerned to justify
his libel on Maud Allan than to expose the enormities of the
Unseen Hand. His attack on the actress in the *Imperialist* had
been linked to a reference to a supposed Black Book, compiled
by German agents, listing 47,000 British subjects of perverted
tastes and hence of vulnerable loyalty. The names were said to
include those of Privy Councillors, Cabinet Ministers and their
wives, diplomats, bankers, poets, newspaper owners, members
of the Royal Household and even youths and ladies of the
chorus. Mr Justice Darling, the 'jesting judge', allowed Billing,
who conducted his own defence, to hurl accusations against
public figures as he chose. The Black Book could not be produced, as it was assumed to be in Germany. Captain Harold
Spencer, a former intelligence officer of doubtful sanity, claimed
to have seen it in the *cabinet noir* of Prince William of Wied,
briefly King of Albania in 1914; apparently the Prince showed it
to Spencer as a curiosity. The roster of names, said Spencer, was
prefaced by descriptions in German of the unnatural vices by
which the parties could be entrapped. Mrs Eileen Villiers-
Stuart, later to be gaoled for bigamy, claimed that two British
officers had shown her the Book, at her request, over afternoon
tea in a hotel at Ripley. These officers had since been killed –
mysteriously, she insisted – in Palestine.

After a bickering match with the judge, Billing sprang his first mine by shouting at Mrs Villiers-Stuart, 'Is Mr Justice Darling's name in the book?' and the witness replied, 'It is.' Three similar questions elicited that the names of Asquith, his wife and Haldane were in its pages. Captain Spencer also named a famous name; referring to supposed peace talks with Germany, he said that Mrs George Keppel, one-time mistress of Edward VII, had visited Holland as a go-between. The allegation was flatly denied by Mrs Keppel, but she was not allowed to make her rebuttal in court. Billing's defiance of the judge was flagitious; after evidence about a homosexual brothel in London he shouted, 'It will take more than you to protect these people, my Lord.' Among witnesses who made fools of themselves was the fashionable priest, Father Bernard Vaughan, who knew not the first thing about the laws of evidence and shook Billing by the hand as he left the box; and Dr John Clarke, who said the play *Salome* should be stored in a museum of sexual pathology and 'even then it might corrupt medical students'. Throughout the hearing the gallery were on Billing's side, accepting him on his own valuation as the only man who dared to bring the country's secret enemies into the open. They also enjoyed the way he made the law look silly and spoiled the judge's jokes. (These were, in any event, lamentable. When a witness spoke of someone 'talking the language of sodomy', the judge said, 'I suppose you found it interesting, as the language of Sodom was a dead language, to find it being talked.')

If Billing was a tool in a generals' plot to unseat Lloyd George and to foul any chances of peace (as Michael Kettle argues), the secret was well kept. For six days the court was in a state of hysteria, with more neurotic balderdash talked to the reported inch than seems conceivable. During those six days a ferocious drive by the Germans on Paris was held and blunted by the British Army; what nobody knew then was that this German failure presaged the end of the war. On the sixth day the judge, having allowed any number of questions about the Black Book, said in his summing up that it had nothing to do with the case. The jury returned a verdict for Billing, sparking off chaotic jubilation in court. Outside the Old Bailey the crowds hurled flowers at their hero, while a policeman sardonically observed, 'I expect Mr Billing is in the Book himself.' Six hundred telegrams arrived, one of them offering Billing the same rate as Charlie Chaplin for a lecture tour of America.

For Stephen McKenna the Billing case was a distillation of the general wickedness of 1918. He complained that the press had used its educational powers 'to secure that a hundred thousand villages should be made acquainted with the bewildering nomenclature of infamous vices'. (Even judge and counsel had to have explained to them terms of which few are ignorant today.) Northcliffe, who was living in a Gloucestershire town, was unelated by the sight of cyclists riding in from miles around to fetch the evening papers; the 'horrible case' was not his idea of a great news story and his papers bravely forebore to print the more clinical words. Many commentators assailed Mr Justice Darling for trying to joke his way through a disgraceful trial. The *Daily News* described the case as sinister and humiliating, 'exceeding in its frenzied silliness anything ever conceived in the fertile brain of Titus Oates'. But just as people had believed in the Popish Plot, so they were ready to believe in the Black Book; there were plenty who went about saying they had always suspected the grossest wickedness in high places. Whether any Black Book ever existed is highly doubtful; but, as some journals pointed out, every secret service may be expected to keep details of vulnerable people in the opposite camp. The *Spectator* feared that another Billing case might be the end of civilisation. The French Revolution had been born in 'a perfect cloud of suspicions', starting with Marie-Antoinette, and 'the recent Russian Revolution began with suspicions about the ways of the Court'. The journal wondered whether a court of honour in the form of a select committee should be appointed to investigate Billing's charges against Asquith.

As a method of exposing the machinations of the Unseen Hand, if that is what was originally intended, it was a bizarre operation. Billing's excuse must be that no one took any notice of his magazine and that the Treasury benches were always empty when he spoke. (Three months before the trial he had told the House that men and women in high places were being blackmailed by the German secret service.) He continued to call meetings to denounce the Unseen Hand. In July when the Commons debated the question of aliens Lloyd George caused a surprise by saying, 'There has never been a case of a British setback when I have not had letters crowing over it – letters bearing British postmarks and obviously written by Germans; indeed, they say that they are Germans. Where are they? I feel that that sort of business has got to be stopped.' During that debate the Home Secretary at last announced steps to wind up the German banks, which he described as 'practically dead', and to distribute their assets. An MP cried, 'After four years!' Sir George Cave also announced action against three German schools which had been kept up, as a Member alleged, by subscriptions from naturalised Germans.

In August Arnold White felt able to reveal to a British Empire Union meeting how the Unseen Hand had disposed of Kitchener. Twenty-four hours before the *Hampshire* sailed it was decided to alter her course. A cablegram sent to Holland in clear English read: 'Shall Herbert enter the legal academy next December?' The first censor passed it, the second wondered why the sender had gone to the expense of cabling 'the'. It was then found that the initial letters spelled Shetland. The ship was lost off the Orkneys.

That same month a giant 'Intern them all' demonstration was held in Hyde Park, with angry speakers haranguing the crowd from five platforms. A petition signed by a million people was carried to Downing Street, escorted by bands. The fury against aliens was now greater than it had been in the early days of war. But in a very short time the lies and malignancies of war would give way to the lies and malignancies of peace.

In World War Two the Unseen Hand became the Fifth Column.

CHAPTER 22

'VICTORY IS OURS!'

A curiosity of the last year of war was the truly prodigal amount of advertising space taken up in the newspapers by the Pelman Institute. One day big headlines would announce that 'Thirty-Six Generals And Eight Admirals' had signed on for this memory-training course; a few days later it would be 'Forty-Eight Generals And Ten Admirals', and so on. One general was quoted as saying that such a grand and beneficial enterprise ought to be nationalised. A captain said he owed to Pelmanism 'Three stars, a Military Cross and a Clearer Head'; a lieutenant-colonel wrote from Salonika, 'As a direct consequence of Lesson Two I have got a step in rank'; and a 'captain of a fine cruiser' thanked Pelmanism for his command, having been promoted over the heads of senior officers. From the ranks of business and industry came similar testimonials. The claims of Pelmanism even began to enthuse the editors in whose papers they were printed. Lord Northcliffe, who hated giving free space to advertisers, had to rebuke Hannen Swaffer and others for admitting puffs.

Among famous men whose support was sought for Pelmanism was Arnold Bennett. His biographer, Reginald Pound, refers to the brisk business the firm was doing with the young officer classes hoping for promotion. After all, the war looked like lasting for ever and the thing to do was to make the best of it, as the civilians did. The happy-go-lucky first wave of officers, long since wiped out, would have had no truck with memory-training, but the new, less patrician breed, sometimes dubbed 'TGs', or Temporary Gentlemen, evidently took their military careers more seriously.

For millions the war was something that one went to, or got on with, or tried to forget. If some worried about 'war aims', or how the victors proposed to divide the spoils, the aim of most was simply the defeat of Germany, if not that year, then the next or the next. The nation had grown to distrust high-faluting sentiments, but its resolution, though badly bruised, was intact. Doggedness may be sullen and disillusioned, but it is still doggedness. Fortitude may be sour and wrong-headed and cynical, but it is still fortitude. The author of *Schoolboy Into War*, H. E. L. Mellersh, sums it up when he says his generation had come to believe not in the righteousness of Britain's cause, only in the rightness of it. This view was held no doubt even by those deplorable new officers at Blackdown who, according to Ernest Thurtle, on hearing the toast 'The King!' from the mess dining-room, rose in the ante-room saying, 'The Stationmaster at Camberley!' or, 'The Bank Manager at Frimley!' Even in 1917–18 the war did not lack its lighter side. The spirit of skylarking lived on, soldiers continued to fall in love with nurses, gramophones screeched merrily away with ragtime tunes, Buchan's novels were in fierce demand, people queued everywhere to see Charlie Chaplin and the knock on the door was not always the knock of doom: sometimes it brought news of a boy decorated for wiping out a machine-gun nest or shooting down a Gotha. There were fierce family excitements as well as dull family sorrows. In Kent a retired colonel called Borton, who saw his two callow sons join up from school, was saluting them as major-generals by the war's end (see *My Warrior Sons: the Borton Family Diary*).

Certainly the spirit of 1914 was a long way behind. The war poets were sounding their discordant chime (it is fatally easy to exaggerate their influence), the hydros were full of the shell-shocked and the headlines OFFICER FOUND SHOT and INQUEST ON OFFICER were creeping into the News in Brief. The year 1917 had been one of deadening disillusion. All the stirring headlines could not disguise the fact that the Army was still fighting for the same fields and ridges and villages. In December of that year Lloyd George, whose public manner was one of inveterate buoyancy, had been reduced in private to 'black, annihilating despair' by the implications of Russia's withdrawal from the war. To the public at large, the men in the frock coats and the men in the braided caps looked all too like figures of straw. The press, which had inflated their reputations, was distrusted, even by those who repeated its slogans. What people thought of Parliament, the abode of the snappish, the frustrated, the malicious and the information-starved, was probably summed up by a cartoon in which Mr Punch, standing outside Westminster, asks a policeman what is happening, learns that Parliament is reassembling, and then asks 'Why?'

Industry, as we have seen, was a prey to bloody-mindedness largely induced by war exhaustion – and the great munitions plants were organised on the basis that the war would last at least two more years. Soldiers returning to Britain on leave shrank from what they found. Edmund Blunden, after Passchendaele, noted 'the large decay of lively bright love of country, the crystallisation of dull civilian hatred on the basis of "the last drop of blood" '. Charles Edmonds found a general beastliness, pessimism, a preference for fighting with lying propaganda, 'envy, hatred and all uncharitableness'. They were echoing the sentiments of the gallant Siegfried Sassoon who had invited court-martial by protesting publicly at 'the callous complacence with which the majority of those at home regard the continuance of agonies which they have not sufficient imagination to realise', and then, after being 'rested' in a hospital for the shell-shocked, returned to the Front, leaving his Military Cross at the bottom of the Mersey.

There were, as many have said, two worlds: the soldiers who could not fathom the mentality of the civilians ('I'd like to see a tank come down the stalls') and the civilians who, well aware by now that the Front Line was a place of horror, as well as an occasional source of lice, were yet baffled by the soldiers' apparent refusal to hate 'old Fritz'. But it is easy to exaggerate the gulf. 'Dear Old Blighty' was not to be judged by the vicious heartlessness of the West End or by the bloody-mindedness of the engineering shops. The basic constitution of the country – and it is necessary to emphasise it – remained sound, despite the feverish pustules on the surface. Defeatism, real defeatism, existed in pockets only. The anti-war campaign might well have been stronger if its proponents had been less crass, less arrogant and less in love with suspect creeds; even the best of them kept bad company. The would-be revolutionaries had made fools of themselves at Leeds and could be discounted. And there was much still to be entered up on the credit side. First, conscription; admittedly it was a far from perfect system, but at least it was belatedly spreading the sacrifice. Unemployment had vanished and many were enjoying an above-the-borderline existence for the first time in their lives. The belated introduction of rationing was beginning to level out the supply of food; and if it was not the food that people really wanted at least they did not go hungry. Most important of all, as some believed, the Americans were now streaming over in hundreds of thousands (even if their material was curiously slow to arrive). They were to be seen marching in their odd 'Doughboy' fashion, in twinkling white gaiters; shouting 'Rah! Rah! Rah!' for the monarch who watched them playing baseball in London; sitting down to 'Independence Day' spreads laid on by friendly towns; good-naturedly fending off hawks, harpies and tricksters in Piccadilly. They were, as one of their number announced, the first American troops to reach Europe since the United States had helped to exterminate the Barbary pirates.

Oddly, it was the presence of all those American troops in Britain that led Bertrand Russell into his worst indiscretion. Having escaped a gaol sentence in 1916, he now, in the summer of 1918, achieved martyrdom of a sort. In *The Tribunal*, the journal of the No-Conscription Fellowship, he wrote an article which said that, if the war went on much longer, the American troops would be used against strikers, a role for which they are trained in their own country. 'I do not say that these thoughts are in the mind of the Government,' he wrote. 'I think there are no thoughts in their mind at all.' Perhaps it was meant as a joke, like Shaw's notorious advice to soldiers. Whatever it was, it was a comment which, Russell realised, could have been more carefully expressed.

In Bow Street Police Court Russell's friends laughed and cackled at the charges, which were that he had made statements likely to prejudice relations with America. The sentence of six months in the Second Division turned the cackling to ill-stifled fury. All the philosopher's friends could do now was to pull strings to enable him to serve his sentence in the comfort of the First Division, which was intended for offenders of the better sort; and in this endeavour they were encouraged by Russell, who feared that in harsh surroundings his mind would deteriorate. The strings were pulled successfully and the prisoner was able to plan his day on a basis of four hours' philosophical writing, four hours' philosophical reading and four hours' general reading. His cell resembled a library. Lady Ottoline Morrell, forgiving him his trespasses, brought him lavender and scented soap. Very different were the conditions of the broad-arrowed conscientious objectors for whom Russell had been the inspiration. If the war had lasted any longer he himself would have been called up and his sentence, assuming he became an absolutist, would not have been served in the First Division.

The long-feared German offensive, launched in March of 1918, was perhaps the deadliest menace of the whole war. Many of the under-19s were rushed to France before too many questions could be asked. In April a new Conscription Act was passed, roping in men up to fifty and authorising compulsory call-up of the Irish, a feat fortunately never attempted. The German threat was so stark and obvious that the bad spirit in the pits and industry subsided and prodigies of production were achieved. Lloyd George called the miners' leaders to Downing Street to show them the war map; one glance at it and they withdrew their opposition to the recruitment of 50,000 young men from the mines. Soon afterwards the Coal Controller was complaining of reduced output, for not only were his young workers being called up but their mates were clamouring to join them'. But by the summer, when the German advance appeared to have been held, strikes began to break out in every corner of industrial Britain. In Birmingham 100,000 engineers came out and in the Leeds area the dispute threatened to engulf 300,000. It was a far greater industrial challenge than had ever been mounted on the Clyde and it received universal condemnation. In some towns the men began to go back, but 12,000 highly paid Coventry aircraft workers remained obdurate, rejecting Government and union assurances that the method of allocating skilled men – the main point at issue – was in the national interest.

Churchill, as Minister for Munitions, decided to play his strongest card: the threat to call up strikers. First he took the precaution of informing the newspaper proprietors and asking for their support, which was given. Posters were then put up all over Coventry denouncing the engineers' stand. It was wholly wrong, said this proclamation, that a young man given special protection from call-up in order to perform work of national importance should refuse to do the work and still receive protection. Moreover, 'the utmost rigour of the law' would be applied to all persons conspiring to or inciting a stoppage of work. That weekend there were patriotic rallies in Coventry and last-minute appeals to the strikers. Whether moved by self-interest or patriotism, the engineers called off the strike.

The engineers were not the only workers to rebel. Sir George Askwith lists trouble on the railways, in pits, gasworks, the cotton industry, flour mills, soap works, the grocery trade, the Post Office, the prisons, the fire brigades, the 'co-op' and many other areas. In London bus conductresses claimed the male privilege of withdrawing labour. Refuse workers let the rubbish pile up, and when women swept it into heaps they kicked it about the streets again. In Cardiff a soldier who had come home to bury his wife found that he had to dig her grave, since the diggers were on strike; his mates helped him.

Then, incredibly, in the late summer the London Metropolitan and City police struck (or, as some said, mutinied, since they had taken an oath) to enforce a demand for higher wages and union recognition. The Guards at once took over in Whitehall and 'Specials' were called out *en masse*, to be met with cries of 'scab' and 'blackleg'. In Hyde Park two 'Specials' were beset by thirty police who tried to tear off their arm-bands and threatened to throw them in the Serpentine; a lone Australian soldier went to their aid. Outside Scotland Yard angry constables in plain clothes, tricked out with red-and-white union ribbons, barracked their senior officers, occasionally subsiding into shame-faced half-salutes. General Smuts, a member of the War Cabinet, tried to intervene, but was ignored. Lloyd George met the ringleaders in Downing Street and promised them most of what they wanted, but not union recognition. 'We've won!'

they cried outside. Sir Edward Henry, the Commissioner of Police, resigned and was made a baronet. The police were out for only twenty-four hours or so and there were no serious outbreaks of pillage or assault; but men in hospital blue flung bitter words at the men in dark blue and invited them to 'have a go' at the real enemy. To soldiers returning from the Front it must have looked like the ultimate betrayal.

Pestilence, the Fourth Horseman, arrived on the eve of victory. Throughout the world the pandemic of Spanish influenza wiped out more than had fallen on all the battlefields. The time had come for the civilians to die like flies. Mostly they expired in their beds, suffocating slowly, but some dropped in the streets and fields. In the almost forgotten days of cholera men healthy enough to eat a good breakfast had been in their coffins by nightfall; the Spanish disease was not quite so swift a killer, but some of its victims lasted only twenty-four hours. The climax was acute pneumonia, a condition easily resisting the drugs of the day.

In Britain the death-roll was between 150,000 and 200,000. It was easy to say, as many did, that people were debilitated by war strain and low rations, but the influenza accounted for millions in lands unravaged by war; also it carried off the un-worried young as well as the worried old. Harold Owen, a brother of Wilfred Owen, has described the scenes in Cape Town when the plague came: the city and the surrounding districts were littered with dead, boxed inadequately in orange crates and packing-cases, and great stacks of these stood on railway platforms. At the height of the visitation ships pulled out of harbour and anchored in Table Bay.

Britain's sufferings were less spectacular, but soldiers were to be seen knocking coffins together and digging hasty graves, an exercise with which they were all too familiar. The more cynical among them may have found a black relish in helping to bury patriotic non-combatants. Crowds clamoured outside surgeries and druggists. Schools, cinemas and offices were closed and even public-houses lacked customers for their watered beer. As in the Great Plague of 1665 useless nostrums and disinfectants were offered to the gullible. In some workshops smoking was allowed in the belief that the fumes of tobacco were germicidal.

Streets were sprayed with chemicals and people devised their own anti-germ masks. In the *News of the World* recommended anti-flu precautions included: wash inside nose with soap and water each night and morning; force yourself to sneeze night and morning, then breathe deeply; do not wear a muffler; take sharp walks regularly and walk home from work; do not 'dope'; eat plenty of porridge.

In camps, ships, boarding schools and poor-law institutions the flu carried away its victims in half-dozens, dozens and sometimes scores. But private homes suffered cruelly too. Six persons were found lying dead in a house in Camberwell, eight in a house at Stoke Newington. The milkman or baker on his rounds would report lugubriously how many of his customers had died; but the doctor, possibly carrying a bunch of patients' latch-keys, would tactfully keep this information to himself. The saddest deaths were those of servicemen who had survived martial perils only to die from the universal killer. Among them was Captain Leefe Robinson, VC, who shot down the Zeppelin at Cuffley.

The pandemic came in three waves. It struck first in the Spring of 1918 at Scapa Flow and the northern naval ports. A second wave reached its climax at Armistice time and a third wave came early in 1919. It was an infliction which for once could not be blamed on the Hun, though it was possible to see it as a divine punishment for the decay of morality. Many felt a blind bitter resentment. Dr W. R. Matthews thought it 'probably warped the good sense and good will of the nation' in the immediate aftermath of the fighting.

The war ended more quickly than anyone dared to hope. Haig's ominous 'Backs to the Wall' Order was issued on April 11, 1918, but eventually, at a cost of 40,000 British casualties, the great enemy offensive was blunted. The Germans were unable to mount another and the British Army began to roll them back, an operation which, brilliantly conducted though it was, cost 400,000 more casualties. The death telegrams arrived thick and fast in victory year. For the German Army the 'black day' was August 8, when British tanks burst through at Amiens. Soon the Kaiser, faced with increasing unrest at home, knew it was time to sue for peace. Early in October the German Imperial

Chancellor, Prince Max of Baden, asked for an Armistice on the basis of the Fourteen Points earlier propounded by President Wilson of the United States; and Austria and Turkey begged to be included. Even now, it seemed impossible that the war was really ending.

In November the sailors of the German High Seas Fleet mutinied. In some areas soldiers obeyed Shaw's advice and shot their officers, presumably with the sage's approval. The Kaiser, observing that 'God's hand lies heavily upon us', fled to safety in Holland. The news was stirringly set out on the front page of the *News of the World* on November 10, in such headlines as the British public had hardly pictured in their dreams:

THE WAR IS WON – VICTORY IS OURS
GERMAN ARMY CRASHES TO RUIN
FIRES OF REVOLUTION SWEEP THE LAND
BERLIN IN HANDS OF THE REBELS
RED FLAG OVER CROWN PRINCE'S CASTLE
THE LIBERATION OF FRANCE
BRITISH ONCE MORE AT MONS
RETREAT BECOMING A ROUT

Two days later *The Times* announced the end of the war in single-column headlines, just as it had announced the start of the war.

In Britain only the capital went really mad, and on the day it did so a thousand Londoners died of influenza. The maroons which normally heralded an air raid sounded at eleven o'clock; this time it was the signal for all to rush out of doors. Lloyd George accepted a small first round of applause in Downing Street. The Asquiths began the day by attending their first cremation, returning to find the butler had covered their house with flags. Winston Churchill, at his Ministry, was 'conscious of reaction rather than elation'; his wife arrived, in an advanced state of pregnancy, and they drove to congratulate the Premier at No. 10. In the House of Commons Asquith joined in the cheers for Lloyd George, who for once had no heart for oratory, and the Members trooped to St Margaret's for a thanksgiving service. The House of Lords, with chilly self-control or perhaps total lack of imagination, listened to the terms of the Armistice and then went on to deal with a School Teachers (Superannuation) Bill and a Tithe Bill.

All over the capital men and women were climbing on to motor cars and falling off them, commandeering buses and giving the drivers new orders. In the Mall children frolicked over the rows of captured guns. Medical students bore a skull on a pole crying '*Hoch der Kaiser!*' Bonfires were made with the aid of combustible street furniture, including theatre signboards, and a fire at the base of Nelson's Column left scars which still endure. Big Ben, long muzzled, rang the hours again and the light went on in the Clock Tower. When darkness fell, the crowd danced under the newly turned-up lights in Trafalgar Square, which had recently done duty, in the War Loan interest, as a French village, complete with trenches, ruined windmill and well-simulated dead horses. The élite of Bloomsbury celebrated in a flat in Adelphi, trying hard not to experience vulgar emotions. In fashionable restaurants people stood on tables and women who had hair to let down let it down. The music-halls were in a state of anarchy like that of Boat Race Night. Among the liberated women dancing in the streets were bands of yellow maenads from Woolwich, demanding and receiving kisses. The women police lay low that night, suffering Nature to take her course. It is part of legend that strangers copulated all over London, in symbolism of the triumph of life over death, but they had been doing so with less excuse all through the war, especially in Hyde Park. Malcolm Muggeridge, then aged fifteen, watched the crowds embracing, vomiting, 'making off to the parks', and found it eerie and disturbing, rather than joyful. More than disturbing was the sight of his Socialist father attaching a small Union Jack to the porch of his house; Union Jacks were for Tory rallies and this was 'stupefying in its implications'. However, his father formally apologised for the lapse.

Some towns and villages were too tired, or disillusioned, to celebrate. An exception was St Austell, in Cornwall, where an attempt was made to dance the traditional Floral Dance. 'There was something instinctive, pathetic about it, like a gesture remembered from some former existence,' says A. L. Rowse. Few could recall the routine and in any event the streets were too crowded. At Altrincham the Rev. Hewlett Johnson, lacking bell-ringers, rounded up five eleven-year-old girls from the playing fields, led them to the belfry and, instructing them with hand signals, contrived 'an attenuated peal'. Many public schools were given half-holidays. At Wellington there was high-spirited wrecking and burning, but at Marlborough the influenza victims lay in rows on the sanatorium floor and Francis Chichester could not even raise himself on an elbow when he heard cheering outside. ('Only a few died,' he says.)

In a field at Letchworth Herbert Morrison, by his own account, rested on his spade when he heard the bells and observed a two-minute silence. Helena Swanwick was in the village of Douglas Water in Scotland, where Armistice was celebrated by hoisting a red flag. 'They told me that out of the seventeen men "lifted" under the Conscription Act, thirteen were absolutist conscientious objectors,' she writes. Her friend Catherine Marshall, a former suffragist who had aided the objectors, went into the empty cathedral at Edinburgh and, standing on the chancel steps, sang Schubert's litany with the refrain *Alle Seelen ruh'n in Frieden*, which was either very touching or very insensitive. In Shrewsbury the bells had hardly begun to ring when the parents of Wilfred Owen received a yellow envelope with the Army Council's regrets. Even as the lights were going up the blinds were coming down. And there were great wads of telegrams still to be dispatched, in the ensuing days.

Those who had lost sons did their best to smile at the sight of young munition workers rushing out of the factories to burn effigies of the Kaiser. For the industrial new rich the end of the war was thought to hold a special poignancy. As G. K. Chesterton has pointed out, Samuel Taylor Coleridge had foreseen the profiteer's plight in *The Rime of the Ancient Mariner*:

> The many men so beautiful,
>   And they all dead did lie,
> And a thousand thousand slimy things
>   Lived on, and so did I.

The King who waved down on the crowds from his crimson-draped balcony, lit by stage reflectors, had journeyed to France five times, carried out 450 inspections of troops, visited 300 hospitals and personally conferred 50,000 decorations. His

Sources

INTRODUCTION

Kitchener in Cabinet: *Memories*: Asquith.
Nurses' ordeals: *The Rainbow Comes and Goes*: Diana Cooper; *Autobiography*: Christie.
Telpherage: *Autobiography*: Wells.
Asquith's letters: *Asquith*: Jenkins.
Court-martials for editors: *Hansard*, Nov. 12, 1914.
Guildhall birch: *Sunday Pictorial*, Dec. 19, 1915.
Domestic service: *Virginia Woolf*: Bell; *Sporting Times*, March 17, 1917; *The Great Queen Consort*: Bloom; *Nancy*: Sykes.

1. THE GREAT ANGER

P.O. cables: *The Post Office*: Evelyn Murray.
Attitudes to war: *Memories*: Asquith; *Diaries*: Webb; *Dictionary of National Biography* (*DNB*): MacDonald; *Lloyd George*: Rowland; *War Memoirs*: Lloyd George; *A.P.H., His Life and Times*: A. P. Herbert.
Irish recruits: *The Home Front*: Pankhurst.
Governor of Bank: *Another Part of the Wood*: Clark.
Northcliffe's article: *My Northcliffe Diary*: Clarke.
Invasion plans: *Hove and the Great War*: H. M. Wallbrook; *Folkestone During the War*: Carlile.
Army's eighty motors: *DNB*: Sir John Cowans.
Galsworthy's horse: *Life and Letters of Galsworthy*: H. V. Marrot.
Essex farmer: *Journals*: Bennett.
Sir Owen Seaman: *History of Punch*: R. G. G. Price.
Shaw: *Bernard Shaw 1914–18*: Weintraub.
Piccadilly women: *Goodbye, Piccadilly*: W. MacQueen Pope.
Dumfries 'atrocity': *The Times*, Dec. 29, 30, 1914.
Sock-knitting: *Hansard*, Nov. 17, 1914.
'Truculent young men'; *Diaries*: Cynthia Asquith.
Pulling strings: *Wind of Change*: Macmillan.
West End Pals: *The Times*, Sep. 10, 1914; (Aquascutum) *Tatler*, Aug. 26, 1914.

Edward Thomas: *English Review*, Oct. 1914.

Guildford recruits: *Guildford in the Great War*: Oakley.

Under-age soldiers: *Hansard*, Nov. 2, 10, 15, 1915; *Winston Churchill As I Knew Him*: Violet Bonham-Carter.

Welsh soldiers: *Wales: Its Part in the War*: Nicholson; *War Memoirs*: Lloyd George; *The War and Wales*: Morgan; *Kitchener*: Magnus; *Memories*: Asquith; *Annual Register*, 1914.

Scarborough attack: *Mr Britling Sees It Through*: Wells; *Laughter in the Next Room*: Osbert Sitwell; (Churchill's reply) *Annual Register*, 1914.

Hymn of Hate: quoted in *National Review*, Dec. 1914, and elsewhere.

2. NOBLESSE OBLIGE

Death-roll: Debrett's *Peerage*, 1919.

Dr Lyttelton: *Eton*: Christopher Hollis; *Annual Register*, 1915.

Aristocracy's example: *The First World War*: Repington; *All in a Lifetime*: Blumenfeld.

Bad drains: *Tatler*, Sep. 2, Dec. 30, 1914.

Brighton Pavilion: *Life in Brighton*: Musgrave.

Empress Eugénie: *The Empress Eugénie*: Harold Kurtz; *London During the War*: MacDonagh.

Duke and Duchess of Bedford: *DNB*; *National Review*, Feb. 1917.

Cliveden hospital: *Nancy*: Sykes; *Nancy Astor*: Elizabeth Langhorne.

Lipton yacht: *The Lipton Story*: Alec Waugh.

Lord Derby: *Lord Derby*: R. Churchill.

Lord Lonsdale: *The Yellow Earl*: Sutherland; *Lonsdale*: Lionel Dawson; *DNB*.

Lord Nunburnholme: *Kingston-upon-Hull in the Great War*: Thomas Sheppard.

Sportsman's Battalion: *Tatler*, Nov. 4, 1914; *Daily Mail*, Dec. 9, 1914; *Hornchurch During the Great War*: Charles T. Perfect.

Lord Dundonald: *World Crisis*: Churchill; *Soldier*, October 1953.

Duke of Montrose: *My Ditty Box*: Montrose.

Lord Chetwynd: *War Memoirs*: Lloyd George.

Tipperary clubs: *Tatler*, Feb. 3, 1915.

Footgirls: *Sunday Pictorial* (photo), March 14, 1915; *Diary of a Journalist*: Sir Henry Lucy.

3. SOUND OF THE GUNS

Hearing guns: *Autobiography*: Plomer; *Hornchurch During the Great War*: Perfect; *Quarterly Review*, July 1916; *Winston Churchill*: Bonham-Carter; (Messines) *Manchester Guardian*, June 8, 1917; *New Statesman*, June 16, 1917.

Churchill's flights: *World Crisis*: Churchill; *Winston Churchill*: Pelling.

Riviera: *Letters*: A. E. Housman; *Another Part of the Wood*: Clark; *Letters*: Roger Fry.
Battlefield tours: *Tatler*, March 17, 1915; (ladies at GHQ) *Hansard*, *Lords*, Nov. 16, 24, 1915; (Shaw) *At GHQ*: Charteris; *Bernard Shaw*: Weintraub; *Anvil of War*: Oliver.
Visiting wounded: *The Rainbow Comes and Goes*: Diana Cooper; *All Change Here*: Naomi Mitchison.
Boy's visit: *Vision Ahead*: Huskinson.

4. HALLUCINATIONS

'Russians in Britain': *Window On My Heart*: Olave Baden-Powell; *August 1914*: Tuchman; *Annual Register*, 1914; *In London During the War*: MacDonagh; *Evening News*, London, Sep. 15, 1914; *Diary, 1914–18*: Bertie; *World Crisis*: Churchill.
Mons angels: *At GHQ*: Charteris; *The Angels of Mons*: Machen; *Peeps into the Psychic World*: Crawford; *Find the Angels*: Crosland.
'Spies shot': *Anvil of War*: Oliver.
Spy scares: *Maundy Gregory*: Cullen; *In London During the War*: MacDonagh; *Spectator*, Oct. 24, 1914; *Tatler*, Oct. 7, 1914; *Queer People*: Thomson; *How We Lived Then*: Peel.
Factory raid: *The Times*, Oct. 17, 1914.
Ewell lake-bed: *Daily Mail*, April 3, 4, 1917; *Hansard*, July 25, 1916.
Mackensen: *My Life*: Mosley.
Haldane rumours: *Autobiography*: Haldane; *First World War*: Repington.
Hall/Rintelen: *Officer and Temporary Gentleman*: Wheatley.
Lody trial: *The Times*, Nov. 2, 3, 1914; *Queer People*: Thomson.
Falsely reported shot: (Prince Louis) *National Review*, Dec. 1914; *B-P*: E. E. Reynolds; *Grahame-White*: Wallace; *Dark Invader*: Rintelen.

5. CALLING ALL SWEETHEARTS

'My people': *Autobiography*: Wells.
Posters: Imperial War Museum; *Kitchener Memorial Book* (esp. Irish posters): Le Bas.
Orczy and Mothers' Union: *Ephemera*: Rickards.
White feathers: (at Deal) *Daily Mail*, Sep. 2, 1914; *Life and Times, Octave 4*: Mackenzie; *The Duchess of Jermyn Street*: Fielding; *Towards Tomorrow*: Fenner Brockway; *Hansard*, Feb. 27, March 1, 1915; *The Showmen*: Crosland.
Lady Astor: *Home Front*: Pankhurst.
Bottomley: *Bottomley*: Symons; *Secrets of a Showman*: Cochran; (appeal for funds) *Sunday Pictorial*, July 11, 1915.

War poems: *Punch*, Dec. 8, 1915; *Great War and Modern Memory*: Fussell; *Fighting Lines*: Begbie; (US hit song) *National Review*, August 1915.

6. 'DEAR BELGIANS'

Poirot: *Autobiography*: Christie.

Folkestone reception: *Folkestone During the War*: Carlile.

General reception: *Memoirs*: Samuel; First Report of Departmental Committee under Local Government Board, 1914; *Annual Register*, 1914; press of October, November 1914; *Countess of Warwick*: Margaret Blunden; *Aldous Huxley*: Bedford; *Henry James*: Leon Edel; *Women on the Warpath*: Mitchell; *The Tamarisk Tree*: Dora Russell; *Hansard*, Sep. 15, 1914.

Earls Court: *Four Years in a Refugee Camp*: Powell.

Belgian fisherfolk: *Through War to Peace*: R. Richardson.

Virginia Woolf: *Virginia Woolf 1901–16*: Bell.

Birtley: *The Conditions of the Belgian Workmen Now Refugees in England* (anon., Fisher Unwin 1917).

Cooling off: *Links in the Chain of Life*: Orczy; *Knaves, Fools and Heroes*: Wheeler-Bennett.

Princess Clementine: *Guildford in the Great War*: Oakley.

Belgians in affray: *The Times*, April 12, 1915.

Belgians in Wales: *The War and Wales*: Morgan.

7. THE KING'S ERROR

Czar's dram shops: *New Statesman*, May 13, 1916.

King's pledge: *War Memoirs*: Lloyd George; *National Review*, May 1915, (F. E. Smith) *Salvidge of Liverpool*: Salvidge; *King George V*: Nicolson.

Lloyd George's campaign: *War Memoirs*: Lloyd George; *Tempestuous Journey*: Owen; *Lloyd George*: Rowland; *Asquith*: Jenkins; *Annual Register*, 1915; (250,000 letters) *Sunday Pictorial*, April 11, 1915; (lunch to editors) *War Diary*: Riddell; *Hansard*, April 29, 1915; *The First World War*: Taylor.

No Treating: press of Oct.–Dec. 1915; *Spectator*, Nov. 16, 1915.

Women and drink: *The Times*, Feb. 7, 1916.

Carlisle Experiment: *Punch* ('State Beer for Ever') April 13, 1966; *The Times*, August 7, 1917; Fourth Report of the Central Control Board, 1918.

Reduction in drinking: *War Memoirs*: Lloyd George; Control Board report.

8. HUNWIVES AND OTHERS

'English, please': *The Glitter and the Gold*: Balsan.

Acton 'Hunwife': *Sunday Pictorial*, May 23, 1915.

The Lawrences: *The Memoirs*: Frieda Lawrence; *Not I But The Wind*: Frieda Lawrence; *Frieda Lawrence*: Lucas; *Life and Times, Octave 4*: Mackenzie.

Golf clubs: *The Times*, Oct. 30, 1914.

German teachers: *A Cab at the Door*: Pritchett.

Dead March: *Weekly Dispatch*, June 18, 1916.

German music: *A Mingled Chime*: Beecham.

Libels: (Hambourg) *The Times*, Oct. 29, 1914.

Prince Louis: *Louis and Victoria*: Richard Hough; press of Oct. 30, 1914.

Royal banners: *King George V*: Nicolson; *Kitchener*: Magnus; *In London During the War*: MacDonagh.

Enemy dukes: *Hansard*, Nov. 18, 1914; *Hansard, Lords*, March 13, 1917; *Sphere*, Nov. 16, 1918.

Windsor dynasty: (Wells letter) *The Times*, April 21, 1917; *King George V*: Nicolson; press of June 20, July 18, 1917.

Speyer: *National Review*, Oct.–Dec. 1914, June 1915; *DNB*: Speyer.

Schroder: *Annual Register*, 1914.

Duke of Connaught: *Daily Mirror*, March 8, 1917; *Herald*, March 24, 1917.

Trade with Krupps: *The Times*, Nov. 7, 1914; *Annual Register*, 1914; *Asquith*: Jenkins.

Sanatogen: *Hansard*, Nov. 16, 1914; *The Times*, Nov. 7, 8, 9, 1916.

9. BEHIND WIRE

London camps: *Tales My Father Told Me*: Sitwell; *Goodbye to All That*: Graves.

Frith Hill: *Tatler*, Oct. 7, 1914; *Illustrated London News*, Oct. 10, 1914; *The Times*, Oct. 24, 1914.

Donnington Hall: *Illustrated London News*, March 6, 1915; *The Times*, Feb. 5, 1915; (Quorn) *National Review*, May 1915; *Hansard*, April 28, 1915; *Autobiography*: Margot Asquith; *Morning Post*, March 22, 1916.

Knockaloe: *The Times*, Nov. 28, Dec. 30, 1914; *The Home Front*: Pankhurst.

U-boat prisoners: *King George V*: Nicolson.

Alexandra Park Zeppelin: *Alexandra Park and Palace*: Ron Carrington.

Hardy's camp visit: *Life of Hardy*: Florence Hardy.

Galsworthy's visits: *Life of Galsworthy*: H. V. Marrot; *Galsworthy the Man*: Rudolf Sauter.

Prisoners on land: *Hansard, Lords*, March 29, 1917.

Frongoch whisky: *Shell Guide to Wales*: Vaughan-Thomas & Llewellyn.

Frongoch camp: *The Big Fellow*: Frank O'Connor: *Hansard*, June–Nov. 1916.

Ginnell prosecution: *The Times*, July 29, 1916.

10. UNDER THE ZEPPELINS

Looping party: *The Times*, Jan. 15, 1914; *Grahame-White*: Wallace.

Airman and strikers: *The Times*, May 14, 1917.

'Jew palaces': *The Youngest Son*: Montagu.

Planes for BEF: *Dover and the Great War*: Firth.

Loch Doon: *Memoirs*: Samuel.

Netted buildings: *Buckingham Palace*: Peacocke; *In London During the War*: MacDonagh; *Bernard Shaw*: Weintraub.

Zeppelin attacks: *Defence of London*: Rawlinson; *The War in the Air*: Jones; *Zeppelin Adventures*: Rolf Marben; (Mathy interview) *Daily Mirror*, Oct. 5, 1916.

Crashed Zeppelins: *The Times*, Sep. 4, 5, 6, 25, 1916; *Daily Telegraph*, Sep. 25, 1916; *Weekly Dispatch*, Oct. 1, 1916; *Spectator*, Sep. 9, 1916.

Exultation over Zeppelins: *Bernard Shaw*: Weintraub; *Autobiography*: Russell; *E. Nesbit*: Doris Langley Moore; *The Green Stick*: Muggeridge.

Spy baskets: *Defence of London*: Rawlinson; *Zeppelin Adventures*: Marben; *Daily Mail*, Sep. 6, 1916.

Last big Zeppelin raid: *The Times*, Oct. 20–23, 1917.

Gotha raids: *War Memoirs*: Lloyd George; *Guildford in the Great War*: Oakley; *Political Diaries*: Scott; *My Father*: Borys Conrad; (Underground inquest) *The Times*, Feb. 2, 1918.

11. LIVING WITH TELEGRAMS

Casualty lists: Files of *The Times*, *Daily Telegraph*, *Morning Post*; *All in a Lifetime*: Blumenfeld; *Tatler*, July 15, 1915; *Nancy Astor*: Langhorne; *Memory Hold the Door*: Buchan.

Telegrams: *Testament of Youth*: Brittain; *We Danced All Night*: Cartland; *Tell England*: Raymond; *Seventy Years*: Lady Gregory; *Daily Mail*, Jan. 6, 9, 1917.

Shootings: *Home Front*: Pankhurst; *Hansard*, Nov. 13, 26, 1917, April 1, 1925, Feb. 23, 1932.

Soldiers' relics: *Testament of Youth*: Brittain; *Raymond*: Lodge; (swords) *The Times*, Jan. 2, 1915.

Condolences by servants: *Diaries*: Cynthia Asquith; *Cousin Clare*: Leslie.

Somme films: (Henson) *The Times*, Sep. 1–5, 1916; *Lloyd George Diary*: Stevenson; (Aisne films) *Daily Mail*, Jan. 11, 1917.

Medallion: 'Memorial Plaque' in *Coins & Medals*, May 1974: E. J. Cook; *Daily Mail*, Jan. 4, 1917.

Street shrines: *Daily Mirror*, Oct. 9, 1916; *Weekly Dispatch*, Oct. 22, 1916; *Illustrated London News*, Aug. 19, 1916; *In London During the War*: MacDonagh.

Home memorials: *Leverhulme*: W. P. Jolly.

12. WHISKY ON THE OTHER SIDE

'Woodbine Willie': *The Hardest Part*: Studdert-Kennedy.

Church and war: *Memories and Meanings*: Matthews.

Armageddon pamphlets: British Library catalogue.

Amulets: *Occult Review*, Nov. 1916: MacDonagh.

Immune colonel: *Realities of War*: Gibbs.

'Prayer shop': *Daily Mail*, Jan. 6, 8, 9, 10–13, 17, 1917.

Spiritualism: *Rudyard Kipling*: Carrington; *Diaries*: Cynthia Asquith; *Edward Marsh*: Hassall; ('On the Gate') *Debits and Credits*: Kipling; (Empress of Ireland) *Peeps into the Psychic World*: Crawford; *Raymond*: Lodge; *Spectator*, Nov. 18, 1916; *Daily Mail*, Jan 24, 1917; (Master of Temple) *The Times* Oct. 26, 1917; *Rational Belief in Heaven*: Schreck; *Light*, Feb. 10, 24, March 3, 1917; *Journals*: Bennett.

Seers in flight: *Daily Mail*, Jan. 26, March 2, 13, 1917.

H. G. Wells: *The Time Traveller*: MacKenzie; *H. G. Wells*: Lovat Dickson.

13. STRIFE IN THE FACTORIES

Dockers' Battalion: *The Times*, April 1, 9, 1915, Dec. 26, 1916; *Agitator*: Sexton.

Hove workshops: *Hove and the Great War*: H. M. Wallbrook.

Meyer profits: *Annual Register*, 1915.

Ship profits: *C. F. G. Masterman*: Masterman.

Welsh coal strike: *Industrial Disputes*: Askwith.

TUC, 1915: *New Statesman*, Sep. 11, 1915.

Clyde unrest: *I've Lived Through It All*: Lord Shinwell; *Revolt on the Clyde*: Gallacher; *My Life of Revolt*: Kirkwood; *Milestones in Working Class History*: Longmate; Ministry of Munitions Report on Clyde Munition Workers, 1915; (deportees) *Annual Register*, 1916; (*Hansard*, April 12, 1916; *Weekly Dispatch*, April 2, 1916; (Gaolings) *DNB*: Maxton; *James Maxton*: Gilbert McAllister; *The Times*, April 13, 14, 1916.

William Weir: *Architect of Air Power*: W. J. Reader.

Tribunals: (navvies) *The Times*, Jan. 22, 1917.

Women workers: *War Memoirs*: Lloyd George; *The Pretty Lady*: Bennett; (trousers) *How We Lived Then*: Peel; *Bristol and the Great War*: G. F. Stone & C. Wells; *The Hardest Part*: Studdert-Kennedy.

Prosperous workers: *All in a Lifetime*: Blumenfeld; *Weekly Dispatch*, Aug. 6, 1916; *Daily Telegraph*, Sep. 13, 1917.

1917 strikes: *The Times*, May 11–24; Commission of Enquiry into Industrial Unrest (G. N. Barnes) 1917; *World Crisis*: Churchill.

NUR v. ASLEF: *The Times*, Oct. 17–20, Nov. 29, 1917; *New Statesman*, Aug. 25, 1917: *Annual Register*, 1917.

14. 'COMING TO FETCH YOU!'

Recruiting letter: *Hansard*, July 7, 1915.

Calling up single men: *A Woman and War*: Warwick.

Derby Scheme: *Lord Derby*: R. Churchill; *The Times*, April 1, 1916.

Round-ups: *Daily Mirror*, Sep. 11–15, 1916; *Daily Mail*, Sep. 5, 8, 9, 12, 1916; *Journals*: Bennett.

Khaki 'fancy dress': *Disenchantment*: Montague.

Newman on comb-out: *Hansard*, Oct. 11, 1916.

'Shirking' clergy: *Philip Snowden*: Colin Cross; *The Times*, Sep. 8, 1916; *DNB*: Randall Davidson.

15. BEFORE THE TRIBUNAL

Critics of tribunals: *Memoirs*: Clynes; *The First World War*: Repington; *Diaries*: Webb.

Preston tribunal: *For Remembrance*: Cartmell.

Individual cases: (under-priced clerks) *Weekly Dispatch*, Feb. 27, June 11, 1916; (organist) *Daily Mirror*, Aug. 11, 1916; (woodman) *Daily Mirror*, Aug. 10, 1916; (*Comic Cuts*) *The Home Front*: Pankhurst; (milkman) *Daily Mail*, April 5, 1917; (Epstein) *The Times*, June 7, 1917; *Augustus John*: Holroyd; (deaf applicant) *Daily Mirror*, Sep. 28, 1916; (film producer) *Daily Mirror* Oct. 7, 1916; (Huntingdon nurseryman) *John Bull*, May 26, 1917.

Widow's last son: *Croydon and Great War*: H. K. Moore; (Barking) *The Times*, Nov. 4, 1916; (Hull) *Daily Mirror*, Oct. 11, 1916; *Daily Mail*, April 5, 1917.

Jews: (Cohens) *Morning Post*, March 14, 1916; *The Times*, March 15, 1916.

CO's: Commons protests: March 15, 16, 22, 1916.

CO's individual cases: *My Lives*: Meynell; *Autobiography*: Morrison; *Herbert Morrison*: B. Donoughue; *Kingsley*: Rolph.

'Rape' question: (Keighley) *Hansard*, March 22, 1916; (censorship) *Hansard*, March 8, 1916.

Six COs in family: *The Times*, Aug. 15, 1918.

Dislike of COs: *Letters*: Huxley; (Wells) *Autobiography*: Russell; *Diaries*: Webb; *Episodes*: Childs.

Clifford Allen: *Morning Post*, April 10, 1916.

Garsington: *Huxley*: Bedford; *Strachey*: Holroyd; *Ottoline at Garsington*: Gathorne-Hardy; *Ottoline*: Darroch; *Virginia Woolf*: Bell.

COs at Dartmoor: *Hansard*, March, April and *passim* 1917, April 24, May 16, 1918; *Daily Mail*, April 9, 16, 19, 23, 1917; *Objection Overruled*: Boulton.

COs disfranchised: *Hansard*, Nov. 21, 1917.

16. THE NASTIEST RUMOUR

'Woodbine Willie': *The Hardest Part*: Studdert-Kennedy.

Kadaver reports: *North China Herald*, March 3, 21, 1917: *The Times*, April 16–26, May 17, 1917; *Daily Mail*, April 17, 26, 1917; *Hansard*, April 30, 1917, Nov. 24, Dec. 2, 1925; *Kipling*; Birkenhead: *John Bull*, April 28, 1917; *Punch*, April 25, 1917; *Truth*, June 27, 1917; *Nation*, Oct. 31, 1925.

Department of Information: *C. F. G. Masterman*: Lucy Masterman.

Charteris: *The Times*, Oct. 22, Nov. 4, 7, 1925.

17. A WHIFF OF REVOLUTION

'Welcome' rallies: *Herald*, March 31, April 7, 1917; *Lansbury*: Raymond Postgate; *Searching for Truth*: Johnson; *Manchester Guardian*, June 11, 1917.

German peace move: Note Communicated by US Ambassador Dec. 12, 1916, and ditto (from US President) Dec. 20, 1916; *Hansard*, Dec. 19, 1916; Reply to German Peace Note . . . to US Ambassador in Paris, Dec. 30, 1916.

Leeds conference: *Yorkshire Post*, June 2, 4, 1917; *Manchester Guardian*, June 4, 1917; *The Times*, June 2, 4, 5, 1917; *Herald*, June 9, 1917; *Revolt on the Clyde*: Gallacher; *Truth*: June 13, 1917; *War Memoirs*: Lloyd George; *Autobiography*: Morrison; *Autobiography*: Russell; *Queer People*: Thomson; *My Life's Battles*: Thorne.

Sailors and MacDonald: *The Times*, June 9–July 9, 1917; *Herald*, June 16, 1917; *Ramsay MacDonald*: Marquand.

MacDonald and Reichstag: *Hansard*, July 26, 1917.

Church riot: *Herald*, Aug. 4, 1917; *Daily Mirror*, July 30, 1917; *The Times*, July 30, 1917; *Autobiography*: Russell.

Stanley row: *Salvidge of Liverpool*: Salvidge; *Lord Derby*: R. Churchill.

East End Russians: *Hansard*, April 23, July 11, 13, 24; Aug. 1, 16, 22, Oct. 30, 1917; *Daily Mail*, April 4, 1917 and *passim*.

Jewish Regiment: *The Times*, Feb. 2, 1918.

18. MORALITY AT BAY

Precocious flappers: *London in War Time*: Sheridan Jones.

Women at camps: *I Have Been Young*: Swanwick; (Damer Dawson) *Inside the British Isles*: Arthur Gleeson; *Lady in Blue*: Allen.

War babies: *Lloyd George Diary*: Stevenson; *Lloyd George*: Rowland; *A Woman and War*: Warwick.

Cavendish Hotel: *Duchess of Jermyn Street*: Fielding.

Café Royal: *Augustus John*: Holroyd; *Autobiography*; John.

Music-hall promenades: *Contemporary Review*, Nov. 1916: *The Times*, July 24, 1916; *Weekly Dispatch*, April 23, May 28, June 25, 30, 1916.

Lauder's earnings: *Weekly Dispatch*, Nov. 26, 1916.

Smith-Dorrien case: *The Times*, April 5, 1917.

Bishop of London: *Cleansing London*: Winnington-Ingram

Tea-rooms: *Sunday Pictorial*, July 18, 1915.

Tango: *Bystander*, Sep. 9, 1914: *Manchester Guardian*, Aug. 25, 1917.

Cinema Commission: *The Times*, Jan. 5, 9, 30, April 3, 1917; *Hansard*, Jan. 12, 1917.

Venereal Disease: *Glitter and the Gold*: Balsan; *Diaries*: Cynthia Asquith; *Sporting Times*, March 24, 1917; *Journals*: Bennett; *Hansard, Lords*, March 8, 1917.

Potiphar's wife: *The Times*, Dec. 23, 1916, Jan. 4, 1917; *Sporting Times*, Jan. 13, 1917; *John Bull*, Jan. 13, 1917.

Malcolm trial: *Daily Telegraph*, Sep. 11, 1917; *Manchester Guardian*, Sep. 12, 1917.

Bristol murder: *The Times*, Nov. 22, 1917.

Divorce and bigamy: *News of the World*, Jan. 13, 1918; May 26, 1918 and *passim*.

Commons grille: *Annual Register*, 1917.

Flag sellers: *Manchester Guardian*, June 11, 1917.

'Whitsun girl': *The Times*, July 20, 1917.

WAAC prosecution: *News of the World*, Aug. 25, 1918.

Pretty Lady: *Arnold Bennett*: Pound.

Drugs: *London in War Time*: Sheridan Jones; (cocaine restrictions) *The Times*, July 29, 1916; *Weekly Dispatch*, Feb. 20, June 11, 1916; *Lady in Blue*: Allen.

Moral collapse; *While I Remember*: McKenna.

Lesbians: *Great War and Modern Memory*: Fussell.

19. MOST EXCELLENT ORDER

Lists: *The Times*, Aug. 8, Aug. 25, 1917; Jan. 8, 1918; June 8, 1918; *Handbook of the Order of the British Empire*: Burke.

Criticisms of awards: *New Statesman*, Sep. 1, 1917, June 8, 1918; *Herald*, Sep. 1, 1917; *Revolt on the Clyde*: Gallacher; *Hansard*, June 14, 1918.

OBE poem: quoted in *Sphere*, Nov. 16, 1918 and elsewhere, author not known.

Honours unwanted: *Chamberlain*: Montgomery Hyde; *Kipling*: Birkenhead; *Bennett*: Pound; *Clara Butt*: Winifred Ponder; *The Tamarisk Tree*: Dora Russell.

Peers' protest: *The Times*, Aug. 29, 1918.

Honours scandals: *Maundy Gregory*: Cullen; *The Times*, Aug, 8. 1917; *National Review*, February 1917; *Hansard, Lords*, Aug. 7, Oct. 31, 1917.

20. 'EAT SLOWLY'

Deadliest secret: *A Good Innings*: Lee.

Food regulations: *Annual Register*, 1916–18, *passim*.

Romano's menu: *Daily Mail*, March 2, 1917.

King's proclamation: press of May 3, 1917; reproduced in *Ephemera*: Rickards.

How poor live: *First World War*: Repington.

Saving bread: *Journals*: Bennett; ('I am a slice') *How We Lived Then*: Peel; (baker gaoled) *The Times*, Sep. 4, 1917.

Toffee letter: *Spectator*, June 2, 1917.

Sugar or beer: *The Times*, Jan. 3, 1918.

Ploughing up: *A Good Innings*: Lee; *War Memoirs*: Lloyd George.

Allotments: *The Home Fronts*: Williams; *Guildford in the Great War*: Oakley.

National kitchens: *In London During the War*: MacDonagh.

Ritz meal: *Herald*, Nov. 24, 1917; *My Lives*: Meynell.

Rationing: *Memoirs*: Clynes; *The Times*, Jan. 17, 18, 1918.

Hoarding: (Corelli) *The Times*, Jan. 3, 1918; (MP) *News of the World*, Feb. 10, 1918; (Watford) *The Times*, March 20, 1918; (amnesty) *The Times*, Feb. 13, 1918.

Butter from France: *Britain's Post Office*: Howard Robinson.

Daylight saving: *Roads to Ruin*: E. S. Turner.

Gas-bag motoring: *Tatler*, Sep. 26, Oct. 3, Dec. 19, 1917.

Curzon: (*Observer*) *Daily Mail*, March 3, 1917; *Political Diaries*: Scott.

21. THE UNSEEN HAND

Protest meetings: *In London During the War*: MacDonagh.

'It Is For England': *The Times*, Nov. 13, 1916.

Billing's election address: *Swaff*: Tom Driberg.

Wireless spies: *Hansard*, Feb. 12, 1918.

Wheeldon case: *A Good Innings*: Lee; *The Times*, March 7, 8, 12, 1917; *Annual Register*, 1917.

Boloism: *Hansard*, Nov. 15, 22, 26, 29, 1917; *Herald,* Nov. 10, 1917; (Spring-Rice) *Hansard*, Feb. 19, 21, 1918.

Black Book: press of May 30–June 6, 1918; *Spectator*, June 15, 1918; *New Statesman*, June 15, 1918; *While I Remember*: McKenna; *Northcliffe*: Pound; *Daily News*, June 6, 1918.

Lloyd George's German mail: *Hansard*, July 11, 1918.

Kitchener telegram: *News of the World*, Aug. 25, 1918.

22. 'VICTORY IS OURS!'

Disloyal toasts: *Time's Winged Chariot*: Ernest Thurtle.

Lloyd George's despair: *Tempestuous Journey*: Owen.

Cartoon on Parliament: *Punch*, Oct. 17, 1917.

Soldiers' views: *Undertones of War*: Blunden; *A Subaltern's War*: Edmonds.

Russell gaoled: *Life of Russell*: Clark; *Autobiography*: Russell; *Ottoline*: Darroch.

1918 strikes: *World Crisis*: Churchill; *Industrial Disputes*: Askwith; *Spectator*, Sep. 7, 1918; *The Story of Scotland Yard*: Basil Thomson; *The Times*, August 31, 1918; (soldier and wife's grave) *News of the World*, June 23, 1918.

Influenza: *Memoirs of The Owen Family*: Harold Owen; *The Deluge*: Marwick; *News of the World*, Nov. 3, 1918; *Memories and Meanings*: Matthews.

Armistice: *Autobiography*: Margot Asquith; *Winston Churchill*: Pelling; *Hansard, Lords*, Nov. 12, 1918; press of Nov. 12, 1918; *The Green Stick*: Muggeridge; *A Cornish Childhood*: Rowse; *Searching for Light*: Johnson; *The Lonely Sea and the Sky*: Chichester; *Autobiography*: Morrison; *I Have Been Young*: Swanwick.

Ancient Mariner: *Autobiography*: Chesterton.

Royal brandy: *Buckingham Palace*: Peacocke.

Select Bibliography

Allen, Mary S. *Lady in Blue*. Stanley Paul. 1936.

Askwith, Lord. *Industrial Disputes*. Murray. 1920.

Asquith, Cynthia. *Diaries, 1915–18*. Hutchinson. 1968.

Asquith, Herbert (Earl of Oxford and Asquith). *Memories and Reflections*. Cassell. 1928.

Asquith, Margot. *Autobiography*. Eyre and Spottiswoode. 1920.

Balsan, Consuelo. *The Glitter and the Gold*. Heinemann. 1953.

Bedford, Sybille. *Aldous Huxley*. Chatto with Collins. 1973.

Beecham, Sir Thomas. *A Mingled Chime*. Hutchinson. 1974.

Begbie, Harold. *Fighting Lines*. Constable. 1914.

Bell, Quentin. *Virginia Woolf*. Hogarth Press. 1972.

Bennett, Arnold. *Journals, 1911–21*. Cassell. 1932.

Bennett, Arnold, *The Pretty Lady*. Cassell. 1918.

Birkenhead, Lord. *Rudyard Kipling*. Weidenfeld and Nicolson. 1978.

Blumenfeld, R. D. *All in a Lifetime*. Benn. 1931.

Blunden, Edmund. *Undertones of War*. Collins. 1965.

Bonham-Carter, Violet. *Winston Churchill as I Knew Him*. Eyre and Spottiswoode and Collins 1965.

Borton Diary, see Slater G.

Boulton, David. *Objection Overruled*. MacGibbon and Kee. 1967.

Brittain, Vera. *Testament of Youth*. Gollancz. 1933.

Carlile, Dr J. C. *Folkestone During the War*. F. J. Parsons, Folkestone.

Carrington, Charles. *Rudyard Kipling*. Macmillan. 1978.

Cartmell, Harry. *For Remembrance*. George Toulmin (Preston). 1919.

Charteris, Brig-Gen. John. *At GHQ*. Cassell. 1931.

Chesterton, G. K. *Autobiography*. Hutchinson. 1936.

Childs, Maj-Gen. Sir Wyndham. *Episodes and Reflections*. Cassell. 1930.

Christie, Agatha. *An Autobiography*. Collins. 1977.

Churchill, Randolph S. *Lord Derby*. Heinemann. 1959.

Churchill, Winston. *The World Crisis*. Butterworth. 1923.

Clark, Ronald W. *The Life of Bertrand Russell*. Cape and Weidenfeld. 1975.

Clarke, Tom. *My Northcliffe Diary*. Gollancz. 1931.

Clynes, J. R. *Memoirs*. Hutchinson. 1937.

Cooper, Diana. *The Rainbow Comes and Goes*. Hart-Davis. 1958.

Crawford, M. MacDermot. *Peeps into the Psychic World*. Eveleigh Nash. 1916.

Cullen, Tom. *Maundy Gregory*. Bodley Head. 1974.

Darroch, Sandra. *Ottoline*. Chatto and Windus. 1976.

Doyle, A. Conan. *The New Revelation*. Hodder and Stoughton. 1918.

Edmonds, Charles. *A Subaltern's War*. Peter Davies. 1929.

Ferris, Paul. *The House of Northcliffe*. Weidenfeld and Nicolson. 1971.

Fielding, Daphne. *The Duchess of Jermyn Street*. Eyre and Spottiswoode. 1967.

Firth, J. B. *Dover and the Great War*. Alfred Leney, Dover. 1920.

Gallacher, William. *Revolt on the Clyde*. Lawrence and Wishart. 1936.

Gathorne-Hardy, Robert. *Ottoline at Garsington*. Faber. 1974.

Gibbs, Sir Philip. *Realities of War*. Heinemann. 1920.

Graves, Robert. *Goodbye to All That*. Cassell. 1957.

Haldane, R. B. *An Autobiography*. Hodder and Stoughton. 1929.

Hassall, Christopher. *Edward Marsh*. Longmans. 1959.

Holroyd, Michael. *Augustus John*. Heinemann. 1975.

Holroyd, Michael. *Lytton Strachey*. Heinemann. 1973.

Huxley, Aldous. *Letters*. Chatto and Windus. 1969.

Jenkins, Roy. *Asquith*. Collins. 1964.

Johnson, Hewlett. *Searching for Light*. Michael Joseph. 1968.

Jones, C. Sheridan. *London in War Time*. Grafton. 1917.

Jones, H. A. *The War in the Air*. Oxford. 1935.

Kirkwood, David. *My Life of Revolt*. Harrap. 1935.

Koss, Stephen. *Asquith*. Allen Lane. 1976.

Lawrence, Frieda. *Memoirs and Correspondence*. Heinemann. 1961.

Lawrence, Frieda. *Not I But The Wind*. Heinemann. 1935.

le Bas, Sir Hedley. *The Lord Kitchener Memorial Book*. Hodder and Stoughton. 1916.

Lee, Lord, of Fareham. *A Good Innings*. Murray. 1974.

Leslie, Anita. *Cousin Clare*. Hutchinson. 1976.

Linklater, Eric. *Fanfare for a Tin Hat*. Macmillan. 1970.

Lloyd George, David. *War Memoirs*. Ivor Nicholson and Watson. 1936.

Lodge, Sir Oliver. *Raymond, or Life and Death*. Methuen. 1916.

Longmate, Norman. *Milestones in Working Class History*. BBC. 1975.

Lucas, Robert. *Frieda Lawrence*. Secker and Warburg. 1973.

Machen, Arthur. *The Angels of Mons (2nd edn)*. Simpkin Marshall. 1915.

MacDonagh, Michael. *In London During the War*. Eyre and Spottiswoode. 1935.

McKenna, Stephen. *While I Remember*. Butterworth. 1921.

Mackenzie, Norman and Jeanne. *The Time Traveller*. Weidenfeld and Nicolson. 1973.

Macmillan, Harold. *Winds of Change*. Macmillan. 1966.

Magnus, Sir Philip. *Kitchener*. Murray. 1958.

Marquand, David. *Ramsay MacDonald*. Cape. 1977.

Marwick, Arthur. *The Deluge*. Bodley Head. 1965.

Masterman, Lucy. *C. F. G. Masterman*. Nicholson and Watson. 1939.

Matthews, Rev. W. R. *Memories and Meanings*. Hodder and Stoughton. 1969.

Meynell, Sir Francis. *My Lives*. Bodley Head. 1971.

Mitchell, David. *Women on the Warpath*. Cape. 1966.

Montagu, Ivor. *The Youngest Son*. Lawrence and Wishart. 1970.

Montague, C. E. *Disenchantment*. Chatto and Windus. 1922.

Morgan, Rev. J. Vyrnwy. *The War and Wales*. Chapman and Hall. 1916.

Morrison, Herbert. *An Autobiography*. Odhams. 1960.

Muggeridge, Malcolm. *The Green Stick*. Collins. 1972.

Murray, Evelyn. *The Post Office*. Putnam. 1929.

Musgrave, Clifford. *Life in Brighton*. Faber and Faber. 1970.

Nicholson, Ivor and Trevor Lloyd-Jones. *Wales: Its Part in the War*. Hodder and Stoughton. 1919.

Nicolson, Harold. *King George V*. Constable. 1952.

Oakley, W. H. *Guildford in the Great War*. Billing, Guildford. 1934.

Oliver, F. S. *The Anvil of War*. Macmillan. 1936.

Orczy, Baroness. *Links in the Chain of Life*. Hutchinson. 1947.

Owen, Frank. *Tempestuous Journey*. Hutchinson. 1954.

Pankhurst, Sylvia. *The Home Front*. Hutchinson. 1932.

Peacocke, Marguerite D. *The Story of Buckingham Palace*. Odhams. 1951.

Peel, C. S. *How We Lived Then*. John Lane. 1929.

Pelling, Henry. *Winston Churchill*. Macmillan. 1974.

Pound, Reginald. *Arnold Bennett*. Heinemann. 1952.

Pound, Reginald and Geoffrey Harmsworth. *Northcliffe*. Cassell. 1959.

Powell, C. A. *Four Years in a Refugee Camp*. Baynard Press.

Raymond, Ernest. *Tell England*. Cassell. 1922.

Rawlinson, A. T. *The Defence of London*. Andrew Melrose. 1923.

Repington, Lt-Col. C. *The First World War*. Constable. 1920.

Rickards, Maurice and Michael Moody. *The First World War: Ephemera*. Jupiter. 1975.

Rolph, C. H. *Kingsley*. Gollancz. 1973.

Rowland, Peter. *Lloyd George*. Barrie and Jenkins. 1975.

Rowse, A. L. *A Cornish Childhood*. Cape. 1942.

Russell, Bertrand. *Autobiography, 1914–44*. Allen and Unwin. 1968.

Russell, Dora. *The Tamarisk Tree*. Elek. 1975.

Salvidge, Stanley. *Salvidge of Liverpool*. Hodder and Stoughton. 1934.

Samuel, Viscount. *Memoirs*. Cresset Press. 1945.

Scott, C. P. *Political Diaries*. Collins. 1970.

Sexton, James. *Agitator*. Faber and Faber. 1936.

Sitwell, Sir Osbert. *Laughter in the Next Room*. Macmillan. 1949.

Sitwell, Sir Osbert. *Tales My Father Told Me*. Hutchinson. 1962.

Slater, Guy (ed). *My Warrior Sons: The Borton Family Diary*. Peter Davies. 1973.

Stevenson, Frances. *Lloyd George: A Diary*. Hutchinson. 1971.

Studdert-Kennedy, Rev. G. A. *The Hardest Part*. Hodder and Stoughton. 1918.

Sutherland, Douglas. *The Yellow Earl*. Cassell. 1965.

Sykes, Christopher. *Nancy, the Life of Lady Astor*. Collins. 1972.

Symons, Julian. *Horatio Bottomley*. Cresset Press. 1955.

Swanwick, Helena. *I Have Been Young*. Gollancz. 1935.

Taylor, A. J. P. *The First World War*. Hamish Hamilton. 1963.

Thomson, Basil. *Queer People*. Hodder and Stoughton. 1922.

Thorne, Will. *My Life's Battles*. Newnes. 1925.

Tuchman, Barbara W. *August 1914*. Constable. 1962.

Wallace, Graham. *Claude Grahame-White*. Putnam. 1960.

Wallon, Justin. *Une Cité Belge sur la Tamise*. 1917.

Warwick, Countess of. *A Woman and the War*. Chapman and Hall. 1916.

Webb. Beatrice. *Diaries, 1912–24*. Longmans. 1952.

Weintraub, Stanley. *Bernard Shaw, 1914–18*. Routledge. 1973.

Wells, H. G. *An Experiment in Autobiography*. Gollancz. 1934.

Wells, H. G. *Mr Britling Sees It Through*. Cassell. 1916.

Williams, John. *The Home Fronts*. Constable. 1972.

Williamson, Henry. *How Dear Is Life*. Macdonald. 1954.

Winnington-Ingram, Rt Rev. A. F. *Cleansing London*. Pearson. 1916.

Index